Essays on Phenomenology and the Self

Essays on Phenomenology and the Self

Chasing the Self:
The De Sedimentations of Phenomenology

Existential Psychoanalysis:
Sartre's Phenomenological Dialectic between
Self-Deception and Moral Development

Prolegomena to the Possessive Self:
Modernity's Anthropological Mistake

Dr. Kevin Boileau

Zero Point

Vol. 1

EPIS Publishing Co.
323 16th Ave. E, Suite 103
Seattle, WA 98112
epispublishing1@gmail.com

ZeroPoint Series is an imprint of
EPIS Publishing Co.

The ZeroPoint name and logo are
trademarks of EPIS Publishing Co.

Printed in the United States of America

First Edition April 2012

Library of Congress Cataloging-in-Publication Data
1. Psychoanalysis 2. Phenomenology

Cover design: Tia Hopkins
Cover photo: Damon Anderson

ISBN 978-0-9849512-0-8

For
Professor D. A. Boileau

Contents

I. Chasing the Self:
The De Sedimentations of Phenomenology

II. Existential Psychoanalysis:
Sartre's Phenomenological Dialectic between Self-Deception and Moral Development

III. Prolegomena to the Possessive Self:
Modernity's Anthropological Mistake

Preface

These three essays represent a period of intense philosophical research and writing in conjunction with Professor David A. Boileau (now deceased) during the early years of this new millennium. Like so much other intellectual work, I consider them as preliminary and introductory—unfinished in many ways. Before his passing, David Boileau and I were working on various theoretical criticisms of modern humanism, especially how inadequate conceptions of phenomenology resulted in anthropological distortion, in moral theory, social relations, and psychology. It is in these essays that I attempt to begin working out the phenomenological problems in psychology, examining the relation between ego distortions and moral behavior, and finally proposing a line of inquiry into radical subjectivity. This volume is the very first volume in the proposed *"ZeroPoint Series,"* which initiates a line of inquiry into the possibilities for introspective and radical cognitive autonomy, which might have applications for clinical work in psychoanalysis, cultural criticism, social and political philosophy, and moral theory. It is my belief that each essay can be further developed and that together they can lead to new critical perspectives in the accounting of radical subjectivity. I am planning further volumes in this series. I also acknowledge that although I have turned to a number of thinkers for discussion and understanding of this work, it contains a number of mistakes and lacunas, all of which are solely mine.

Dr. Kevin Boileau, Ph.D., J.D., LL.M.
Writing from the Existential Psychoanalytic Institute & Society
Seattle, Washington
USA
January, 2012

Chasing the Self:
The DeSedimentations of Phenomenology

Part One:
Criticism of the Natural Science Model and Its Influence on Freud

Introduction

In this book, I argue that the philosophical origins of the natural science trend in contemporary psychology rest upon too narrow a conception of phenomenology. In my view, contemporary psychology distorts the nature of the self by viewing consciousness as a thing. In so doing, much of contemporary psychology (and the psychology of the twentieth century) precludes an ethical foundation and an adequate phenomenology. I provide an existential account of this theoretical lack and begin a preliminary sketch of what an adequate phenomenology and ethical foundation might include.

I assume that contemporary psychology has the intellectual responsibility to investigate the full range of human experience in a way that will satisfy the demands of science. Therefore, we must scrutinize the adequacy of the kind of science we have been using in psychology for the last hundred years. It is no secret that in its beginnings psychology borrowed the methodology and worldview of the natural sciences, assuming that this worldview represented the best expression of total reality. While it may be true that the procedure of the natural sciences is adequate to natural phenomena, I argue that it does not adequately comprehend the phenomenon of human experience. What is more mysterious and problematic is in what an adequate anthropological and phenomenological account of humans could consist. I locate it in an ethical foundation.

It can be asserted that psychology, as a modern science, began in 1879 when Wundt started his laboratory in Leipzig. At this time, it needed a scientific paradigm within which to work and the only established one was the natural science model of physics. When psychology imitated the methods, viewpoints, and techniques of science, it simply took over the methodology of natural science. I believe that for the most part, contemporary psychology has not strayed from its early, natural science presuppositions. This includes all the schools and programs, including behaviorism, psychoanalysis and, to some extent, the humanistic schools in America. There are two main philosophical presuppositions of the natural sciences. The first is that we can explain the relation of all bodies in space, including human beings, in terms of a sophisticated understanding of causality.[1] The second is that there is a rigid distinction between a subject — the independent observer — and an object, which is the phenomenon to be scrutinized.[2]

While it is true that these assumptions have been seriously challenged in the twentieth century, I also believe that they have led to a limited and inadequate understanding of human psychology, thereby leading to an insufficient anthropology as well. This essay is an exploration of this inadequate phenomenology as well as an inquiry into what a new kind of anthropology and methodology might look like. Before we continue, though, I must point out that I am going to limit my scrutiny to psychoanalysis, given that it is one of the main approaches to psychology, is theoretically rich, and was started by Freud who perhaps still is the most powerful thinker in this domain. We leave for another project similar scrutiny of other approaches to psychology, including behaviorism and American humanism. This limitation, however, does not mean that I will not make passing references to psychologists outside of the psychoanalytic tradition.

Let us discuss the proposition that psychology adopted the paradigm of natural science and that it has continued to operate within this paradigm's deeper philosophical assumptions late into the twentieth century and beyond. It is now common knowledge that psychology broke away from philosophy in the late nineteenth century. Then each of the various schools attempted to provide scientific legitimacy to its own type of psychology. Yet, it was Wundt who initiated psychology's drive toward scientific independence from philosophy, actively lecturing in both experimental physiology and medical physics.[3] Wundt continued his program well into the early twentieth century, never leaving his basic argument that the human psyche ought to be viewed as a natural phenomenon, properly studied through the methods of the natural sciences.

Perhaps the most important point is that psychology's objective became the measurement of mental processes and their quantitative presentation. William James believed that psychology ought to adopt the method of the natural sciences, that it was acceptable to bypass many of the deeper metaphysical assumptions about humans.[4] Ebbinghaus argued that this new discipline ought to treat the thoughts and impulses of man as material bodies.[5] Behaviorists like Watson argued that psychology was a division of natural science.[6] There are countless other examples of psychologists who advocated natural science methods for psychology, but these are best left for an extended volume of history.

Treating psychology as a natural science for psychologists of the twentieth century, especially up to the 1960s, implies that human behavior can be described objectively, manipulated, controlled, and studied just like other natural events.[7] It also connotes controlled observation and measurement, including the quantification, deduction, and explanatory systems of mathematics.[8] Further, the choice of methodology has always been represented as a dilemma in which one could choose between natural science or philosophy. Moreover, psychology was viewed as the domain that could never be quite as rigorous as physics or chemistry, as long as each was subject to the rules of natural science.[9]

Nevertheless, there is a suppressed tradition that has tried to situate psychology as a human science and not as a natural science. Initially, it was Wilhelm Dilthey who argued that there could be a bifurcation in the sciences, and that psychology ought to be studied as a human science.[10] Methodologies for these two domains of science would be different, yet both would be equally rigorous. Hodges summarized Dilthey's idea by saying that, instead of explaining particular events through general laws, we would attempt to understand the complexities of human life by interpreting their meaning in history.[11] Kluback showed that, for Dilthey, the natural sciences would deal with the non-human world, in which phenomena were taken out of context, symbols substituted for them, and through mathematics manipulated these symbols to create laws of phenomenal behavior. In contrast, the human sciences would deal with a human world that was the product of a history that resulted from the exercise of free will. The human sciences, therefore, have studied the structures of knowledge and value that are based on a particular worldview or *weltanschauung*.[12]

For Dilthey, psychology as a natural science gave us inadequate descriptions about the more sublime aspects of humanity such as value (including ethics), understanding, sympathy, and religious devotion. In addition, its methodology led to uncertain results. Instead of using an explanatory methodology, in which we assume general laws beforehand, Dilthey thought we should use a descriptive approach in which we would attempt to find laws through empirical analysis that are given through experience. For him, mental life is a functional unity that cannot be theoretically reduced to non-functional hypotheses. The real unity of mental life is not a sensation or feeling but a reaction of the complete self to any situation confronting it. Each reaction (*Erlebnis*) includes a structural relationship of three types of elements, which are the cognitive, the affective, and the conative. This structural system is not discovered by inference or hypothesis but is actually given in experience and can be described. Here, he contrasts structural relations with causal relations. Whereas causes can be inferred, structural sequences have meaning in themselves. Thus, in the natural sciences, we have explanation and knowledge, but in the human sciences, we have interpretation, understanding, and meaning.

Franz Brentano, who greatly influenced Husserl,[13] was also writing around the time of Wundt and argued that the ultimate data of psychological analysis are the manifestations of consciousness. According to Ryle, these psychic phenomena are direct manifestations of mental functioning rather than inferences or constructions.[14] Brentano thought that explanations of conscious phenomena in terms of physiological substrata or unconscious dynamics did not adequately explain conscious phenomena. He also argued that mental phenomena were irreducible and, most importantly, that they were characterized by intentionality. Implied here is the notion that psychic content is always characterized by direction toward some object. It was Brentano's plan to differentiate psychological phenomena according to their type of intentionality.

Now that we have differentiated the natural science approach from the human science approach, we can go back and recognize that even Wundt recognized both. For example, he argued that to understand some of the higher forms of human thought, we would need to engage in a kind of historical analysis of groups of men.[15] There were other psychologists, as well, in the early twentieth century, whose work contained elements of the developing human science paradigm. This list includes William James, whom we have mentioned, as well as Eduard Spranger, William Stern, and William McDougall.[16] Even Gordon Allport recognized the need for a human science paradigm, although he knew that its methodology would have to be refined.[17]

There were even those psychologists who tried to bifurcate the discipline into two domains or to synthesize them. For example, Fernberger argued that one would be a science of behavior and the other would be a science of consciousness.[18] In like fashion, Fearon thought that both approaches were necessary, but that they ought to be divided into separate disciplines. He argued that the physical psychologist ought to observe facts through the senses aided with instruments but that the metaphysical psychologist would interpret the deeper reasons for human behavior. Most importantly, he thought that both were needed for a full understanding of humans.[19]

Philosophers have been pointing out the conceptual confusion in psychology throughout the twentieth century. Kockelmans shows how Husserl was aware that psychology had developed in the absence of a systematic framework of basic concepts.[20] Sartre writes about the conceptual disorder within its very foundation.[21] Even Wittgenstein was concerned that there was confusion about the very nature or subject matter of psychology.[22] It is clear, however, that psychology wanted to move away from the speculative and deductive methods of philosophy in order to develop a detached approach that utilized inductive reasoning and that was publicly verifiable.

Investigating psychology as a natural science requires both the adoption of a methodology that is empirical, positivistic, reductionistic, quantitative, genetic, deterministic, predictive, and to have an independent observer. In the main, the objective is to reduce all data to quantifiable terms that can be understood mathematically. Yet, these criteria unduly limit the phenomena that are being investigated and also determine the kinds of questions that we ask. By valorizing a so-called "objective" observer, we squeeze out from the very foundation an immanent ethical component, which necessarily distorts the range of phenomena within our purview. In the natural science approach, the leading question always concerns the measuring of phenomena, and that which cannot be measured is suppressed and ignored. For example, it is difficult to measure friendship or love, yet we believe these phenomena are integral aspects of the human condition and important to psychology. It is true that not every psychologist has believed that measurability of phenomena ought to be the sole way of determining relevance.[23] Even so, psychologists such as Taylor argued that they could not do science unless they engaged in some quantitative methodology.[24] What has not been adequately posed in our view is whether we can create a rigorous science that is not quantitative at all.

During the twentieth century, even clinicians have expressed dissatisfaction with traditional explanations, as the various "schools" developed different sorts of techniques.[25] These therapists became less interested in wanting to understand particular neuroses or psychoses as deviations from some theoretical conception of man but rather as variations in the structure of that particular person's existence. Thus, attention shifted away from technique to the dialectic about the underlying assumptions of human nature and whether some common anthropology could be formulated that could underlie all the different approaches of the schools. Again, though, we ran into the anxiety that psychology would again be swept up back into philosophy. Given that phenomenological viewpoints did not already have a firm methodology, clinicians were left to grasp at the only paradigm that did and that was the approach of modern natural science.

Criticism of Psychology's Natural Science Model

As I have stated, it was with Wundt that psychology sprang loose from philosophy. Yet, he was cautious, arguing that "as a coherent science, experimental psychology still awaits its foundations."[26] Even William James was tentative about the efficacy and value of the natural science model, saying that "we must not assume that [the natural science model] means a sort of psychology that stands at last on solid ground." Instead, he strongly urged us to "never forget that the natural science assumptions with which we started are provisional and revisable things."[27] In its desire to break away from the speculative and deductive methods of philosophy, psychology adopted a new style of investigation that included inductive reasoning, public verifiability, and a detached observer. Yet, in making this switch in methodology, psychology never engaged in a fully reflective and critical study of exactly how it ought to proceed.

When psychology accepted the methods of the natural sciences it also accepted their underlying philosophical assumptions. This meant that the phenomena to be investigated were viewed in terms of the previously-established methods. Any conflict that resulted between method and content, i. e., the phenomena, was resolved in favor of the method, which occupied a privileged position. Psychologists made the phenomena fit the method rather than the other way around. So, what psychologists thought was *the* scientific method was actually only the scientific method of the natural sciences. This required psychology to meet the demands and characteristics of the only scientific method that was known at the time.

I submit that the methods and criteria of the natural sciences limit the psychological phenomena that are being investigated as well as condition the types of questions that can be legitimately asked. Within the natural science model, all questions center around measurement rather than the pursuit of meaning. If a phenomenon cannot be measured it is ignored. Thus, a phenomenon *is* only to the extent that it can be measured. This means that the status of a phenomenon is dependent not only on how it appears but also in terms of methodological operations, including measurability. The important question is whether the pursuit of measurement is the only way to rigorously interrogate the phenomena in question.

It is self evident that any explanatory system covers less than the entire universe of knowledge and experience, and that what is allowed to conceptually enter that system is also limited. With regard to the natural sciences, it is only one aspect of phenomena that is given priority. This is the spatio-temporal aspect, and facts of this nature operate as a foundation. Further, the general notion of objective space-time is a derivative of an even deeper presupposition of the natural sciences, and this is the notion of corporeality, which comes from Descartes. So, for example, in physics we have bodies in motion, elementary particles, and forces. In biology we have organisms, genes, and instincts. The important point is that in science we must reduce phenomena to fact, in accordance with the dictate to keep the observer out of the equation.[28]

In the above sense, fact operates as phenomena devoid of human consciousness. This obviously puts psychology — as the study of human consciousness and behavior — in a strained position. Thus, if we view psychology in terms of function, this is like viewing physics in terms of facts. Here, functions are reified into a complex that exists in relation to the brain, which serves as the corporeal existent. A phenomenon, therefore, *is* to the extent that it meets the pre-established criteria of reified function. Whatever phenomenon is observed that does not fit into this concept does not receive psychological consideration. Within this scientific paradigm, we search for signs of an individual's psychological functioning that indicate abnormality, for a dysfunction that indicates disease.

There has been a tendency of most psychology of the twentieth century to reduce human phenomena to causal relationships, as in the case of experimental physiology. The goal was to make psychic phenomena calculable and predictable, as we have said. Thus, there was an all-out effort to discover causal connections between phenomena and especially to discover the first cause in a causal chain. The assumption was that by eliminating the effect of the first cause that we could eliminate the causal chain, thereby dissipating pathological effects.[29] Yet, I am not confident that psychology should continue emulating the methods of the natural sciences. I argue that, in fact, the natural science model of investigating psychological phenomena is inadequate and that we should re-examine our aims and objectives.

It is not at all clear that psychology is unified in its objective. Nor is it clear what the objective of psychology should be. Yet we can argue with some force that the initial adoption of the methods of natural science has put us in a situation whereby we do not investigate psychological phenomena in a meaningful way. It is my position that the chief way we have been doing psychology does not do justice to the phenomena, and that we unduly limit the problems we attempt to investigate by framing them in terms of natural science methodology. Thus, the tension is between adherence to the phenomena at hand and faithfulness to a certain idea of what science is.

Let us be clear that the methods of the natural sciences were not originally intended for the study of psychic processes of human beings. The methods of the natural sciences have always included reduction and analysis that is directed toward isolated stimuli and elemental processes, as well as the dissection of causal connections of material objects in space-time. When applied to psychology, we study man as natural man, but not man as a human or a person. Natural man exists in time and space and has a corporeality that can be measured. This allows us to treat humans as objects. Nevertheless, it is my contention that we could measure a human extensively, and we would never see the richness of his existence that presences itself phenomenologically in a way that is beyond space-time constructions. Indeed, we can reveal certain truths about man and his relation to his environment as well as to biological determinants. However, we will never reveal the full richness of man as a person unless we adopt a completely different conception of science.

We must understand that the limits of natural scientific conceptions of humans concomitantly delimit the kinds of findings about them. The frame of reference projects implicit boundary conditions from the beginning, as in any scientific quest. Thus, the natural science frame is not the only way to do psychological science and we should be clear about that. For the sake of the unity of psychology — and there is currently a very sharp lack here — we ought to consider which conception of science does justice to the largest range of phenomena. We maintain that the natural science approach only opens a sliver of the full range of the phenomena at issue.

I also believe that psychology no longer needs to flee from philosophy. It has been true that psychology has liberally borrowed from the other sciences, for example, from physics, neurology, mathematics, sociology, and so forth. Yet, the irony is that psychology is laden with philosophy from the bottom up. As I have pointed out, psychology is thoroughly imbued with presuppositions it has taken over from both Newton and Descartes, along with influences of British empiricism (in the need for perceptual data) and operationalism.[30] Further, it is precisely from philosophy that any psychology takes its frames of reference and foundations. I am hoping here to suggest important considerations in reframing the psychological enterprise in a way that brings to light more human phenomena instead of keeping them hidden if they cannot be measured or quantified.

At this point it is safe to assert that all the measurement techniques in the world cannot answer questions about meaning, interpretation, understanding, feeling, love, and the like. What's more, we believe that questions about the construction of meaning may be the most important ones for psychology. This is doubly so given our realization that the approach of the researcher is worthy of study, that there is no such thing as an independent observer. Whether or not this is true, I believe that the very nature of psychology ought to be reviewed. We ought to re-scrutinize the essence of the phenomena we are studying, then see if our current methods are up to the task. Further, we ought to understand the underlying motives and philosophical foundations of the type of science we employ. In fact, we ought to spend time perhaps redefining what "science" is in the first place. What I am suggesting is a science of psychology that remains empirical, but one that is true to the full continuum, range, and richness of psychic phenomena.

Before moving on to a discussion of how the natural science model has influenced psychology, it is important to explore this discussion about the nature of science. In order to do this, we want to present some of the ideas of Thomas Kuhn and Michel Foucault. The purpose of this is to help the reader understand that scientific paradigms do change and also to see that the very construction of a scientific paradigm is a political process and involves questions of power and motivation. Moving beyond natural science models in psychology is hampered by the deep belief that science is capable of solving all the riddles of human existence and, as a *praxis*, it is able to guarantee man's unlimited control of nature, including man himself.[31] This position, of course, has always assumed that it was natural science that could discover reality. Further, deep assumptions of this position include the idea that there is a single reality that can be known through a unified science. Because the natural sciences developed first, it has been assumed that they were *the* method that could find that reality and thus their methods were prioritized.[32] Yet, from a phenomenological viewpoint, the goal is not so much the unification of the results of the various sciences, but rather a scrutiny and explication of their common starting point and foundation.

This attitude of the priority of the natural science model, as we have seen, has also emerged in psychology, over all other standpoints. However, we must realize that any scientific stance has its root in common, everyday experience.[33] What we are concerned about is that the success of the natural science approach has overshadowed and hidden its roots in everyday, lived experience, and that we are not looking at some aspects of this phenomena. Keep in mind that Western science has been dominated by empiricism and, in the twentieth century, logical positivism. Within this foundation, we have assumed a correspondence between good theory and the events and processes of the world. Facts are established through objective observation and theories offer different explanations of those facts. Experimentation then determines the correctness or error of the theory and science thereby proceeds through an accumulation of observations and confirmed hypotheses. Scientific understanding changes through the absorption of earlier theories into more inclusive theories.

Nevertheless, in the second half of the twentieth century this earlier view of objective science was confronted by a series of "*weltanschauung*" analyses.[34] In this competing view to the tradition, science is not an unbroken line of closer and closer approximations to the truth. In this new view, there are no purely objective facts and observations that lie outside of theory. Instead, theory itself — that is, one's way of thinking — determines how one observes and therefore, what counts as a fact. We have thus come to realize that observation itself is theory-laden. In this way, science is politicized. It is politicized because it takes place within a community of individuals and from within a conceptual perspective — a *weltanschauung*. What "science" means is open to debate, and a historical review shows us that conceptions of method have transformed from the very beginning of recorded history.[35] Kuhn believed that truth was unknowable and the purpose of science is really to solve problems. For him the history of science is a series of "ways of seeing the world" and solving problems.[36] The more influential

paradigms or ways of seeing do not necessarily incorporate
the preceding ones. They actually represent a series of
alternative solutions that emerge from the data and their
conceptualizations. Each major paradigm forms a framework
for observation and theorizing for a period of time but is
eventually replaced by a new one that may solve different
sorts of problems. Thus the ruling paradigm determines what
data are to be taken as real and meaningful, what methods are
to be considered valid, and where scientists ought to orient
themselves to their object of study.

Kuhn argues that it is difficult to distinguish between the
"scientific" component of past observation and belief based
on errors and superstitions. It can be argued that earlier
scientific views were no less scientific than the ones we have
produced in more modern times. If those out-of-date beliefs
are just myths, then myths can also be produced today by
the same sorts of methods that lead to current scientific
knowledge. In contrast, if those myths are to be called
science, then we must conclude that science has included
bodies of belief incompatible with our current beliefs. Thus,
just because a scientific belief has been discarded does not
make it unscientific. Yet, this makes it difficult to argue that
science progresses in a linear fashion.

Kuhn distinguishes between normal science and scientific
revolution. Normal science is founded on the assumption
that a scientific community already knows generally what
the world is like. Communities of scientists utilize paradigms
that guide their thinking and their methodology in terms of
their basic assumption. There is shared agreement about the
epistemological assumptions, the methodological approaches,
and the observational perimeters. In this mode, normal
science suppresses radically new approaches because they
are subversive of their basic theoretical commitments. After

the peak period of a paradigm has passed, new data emerges
from outside the boundaries of the dominant paradigm, which
causes conflict amongst the participants. Some remain true to
the old paradigm and discount the validity of the new data.
Others try to stretch the paradigm to accommodate the new
data. Finally, others try to shift paradigms altogether. Thus,
when anomalies appear to subvert the existing tradition, then
extraordinary investigations eventually lead the profession
to a new or modified group of commitments. This is scientific
revolution. Science is social practice, and it implies a way
of approaching the relevant phenomena. It is, therefore, a
dialectical process between conservation and progress, and
ultimately each phase is overcome. It is foundationally a
social and political process with chains of hierarchy built into
those practices themselves. Kuhn recognizes that paradigms
gain their status because they are more successful than
their competitors in solving a few problems that a group of
practitioners has recognized as the most important. To be
more successful is not to be either completely successful
with a single problem or successful with any large number
of problems. It does not even mean that its solutions are true
where others are false.

As Greenberg and Mitchell correctly point out, "Kuhn and
other proponents of *weltanschauung* analyses have come
under criticism of various sorts."[37] Amongst other criticisms,
Greenberg and Mitchell rightly assert that "proponents of
weltanschauung analyses in general have been accused of giving
too little weight to the place of rationality in science, . . ."[38] In
response to these sorts of criticisms Kuhn revised his position
in an attempt to steer a middle course between the traditional
view and his early view. In his later work he specifies the
objective criteria that do play a part in theory choice and
has even rejected the use of the vague and ambiguous term,
"paradigm." In his later work Kuhn suggested that the

cognitive commitments of a group of scientists constitute a "disciplinary matrix." Within such a matrix there are different kinds of models that serve as heuristic devices or which provide a framework of orientation, serving as "objects of metaphysical commitment: the heat of a body is the kinetic energy of its constituent particles, or, more obviously metaphysical, all perceptible phenomena are due to the motion and interaction of qualitatively neutral atoms in the void."[39] It is within this sort of model that psychoanalytic theorizing organizes itself. Thus, when we describe, examine, and critique various psychoanalytic models later on in this section, we are focusing on the metaphysical commitments the various theorists have made.

When we apply Kuhn's ideas about theoretical commitments and models to the modern history of psychological thought, we can begin to see how the construction and destruction of theory has a politically useful life. As Greenberg and Mitchell say, "Psychoanalytic theories operate as models reflecting metaphysical commitments because they are based upon untestable premises concerning four fundamental issues."[40] They go on to describe these issues, which include first, the basic unit of analysis; second, motivation; third, development; and fourth, structure. The approaches to these various issues thus act as a framework for the generation of hypotheses and interpretive possibilities. In psychoanalysis, the main tension in the twentieth century was between the drive theorists and the relational theorists, even though both groups agreed on the premise that the self had a reified structure or that one could be developed through therapeutic intervention. We will see later in our discussion of Sartre's ontology of the self that the assumption of self-structure is also a metaphysical commitment which leads to lines of theorizing that are very different from a Sartrean approach. As a part of that later discussion, we will also take a look at the work of Sullivan, who himself was hesitant to reify the self into structure and who substituted in the idea of "dynamism."

Traditional psychology has solved a great number of problems well, but it is our charge that this paradigm is becoming increasingly deficient for solving important contemporary problems in this domain of human existence. Think about 20th-Century developments in psychoanalysis. Some analysts stayed true to classical Freudian theory. Others stretched and modified the old paradigm to accommodate new data (and we can see how difficult a time Klein had with this). Finally, others such as the object relations theorists have broken completely from drive theory, replacing it with relational concepts.

As the reader progresses through this text, I invite him to consider whether existing paradigms of psychological science adequately speak to the phenomena at hand. I also invite the reader to consider that different approaches in psychology have already demonstrated what happens when normal science does not satisfy us. For example, it can be argued that psychoanalysis was in part a reaction against inadequacies of psychiatry, or that American humanistic psychology has been in large part a reaction against both behaviorism and psychoanalysis. We invite the reader to ask about the nature of questions that psychology ought to answer and whether current forms of psychology meet that burden. Perhaps it is even true that we do not know all the questions to ask because our current paradigms hide them from us.

By now we all more or less accept the role of the scientist as human being, and that science is a political process, as well. For example, in studies of the perception of incongruity, anomalous features were consistently fitted into already-existing conceptual categories without any trouble.[41] Scientists constantly use concepts of which they are not explicitly aware. For instance, in 20th-Century psychology, scientists used Cartesian and Newtonian concepts as a part of their daily work, but for the most part these assumptions were more or less implicit; they were part of the overall worldview and not questioned. Unfortunately, our conclusions have been based on the natural sciences and not on the broader, underlying life-world. It seems that psychology ought to address the behavior of the scientists that engage in psychological science about the psychology of humans. This project would have a different stance than explaining humans in terms of natural science, for it would involve a different starting point and a different methodology, one that we believe opens untapped realms of phenomena.

Another problem that bolsters the limiting effects of the natural science perspective is objectivism. This is the belief that there is one true reality that exists independently of any observer. This position is Cartesian in that it creates the subject-object bifurcation. It also presupposes that there is only one way of knowing this one, true reality, which is through the methods of the natural sciences. According to this way of thinking, any knowing that involves the subjectivity of the knower is downgraded. More problematic is that in this natural science approach we study man *as an object*, but not man *as a person*. In this case, knowledge cannot be merely personal; rather, it becomes a search for the thing-in-itself and therefore knowledge becomes interpersonal — and thus a political process. We must realize, however, that the stance of objectivism is just one attitude one can take toward phenomena. For example, we see with Heidegger the alternative attitude of care or concern. The point is that different scientific attitudes reveal different aspects, so we should realize that one attitude cannot capture all of a phenomenon.

We will next take a look at some of the work of Michel
Foucault because it will help us understand how a community
of scientists can get locked into certain discourses of "truth."
This will shed some light on Kuhn's argument that science
is a political process. It will also shed some light on the
objectivist position. Then we will make some comments
about the nature of phenomenology and how its method can
start opening up new perspectives about the future direction
of psychology. While we treat Foucault at some length in a
previous work, it is important to make some notations here.[42]
For Foucault, "truth" is a function of some discourse and is
underwritten by relations of power within that discourse,
both conscious and unconscious.[43] The idea that there is one
objective truth allows power to operate within the discourses
surrounding that claim to truth. This means that there is a
hierarchy of voices or positions within that discourse; each
has its own relation to the truths that operate within it.
When applied to our present discussion about contemporary
psychology, Foucault would argue that a discourse of truth
has been operative ever since Wundt opened his experimental
laboratory. Natural science was taken as the deep paradigm
of truth, and all succeeding discourses have been weighed in
terms of it. But it is power relations that keep this discourse
dynamic and operative; we here present a position that
is in dialectical opposition with this major paradigm and
understand that it will be judged in accordance with the
standards of truth already cycling within the discourse.

According to Foucault, there is a disciplining form of power
in contemporary culture that is marked by techniques of
surveillance. These techniques appropriate the bodies of
individuals and subject them to control and regulation based
on normalizing standards. Along these lines, he argues that the
actual physical bodies of humans are fractured into various
objective truths; this includes medicine and also psychology.[44]

Thus, aspects of human bodies are appropriated by the various
scientific disciplines and claims of truth are made about them.
In psychology, as we have seen, the dominant discourse has
involved an objectification of humans through techniques of
measurement, prediction, and control. Thus, the dominant
claims to truth within the discourse have operated in terms
of the deep logic and assumptions we have been exploring
above, stemming from Newton and Descartes. We hope
that this discussion of Kuhn and Foucault may give insight
about how a discourse like psychology can become entrapped
in its own limitations and about how difficult it can be to
overcome them. We will re-address Foucault later, in extensive
discussion of Sartre and Lacan. What we want to explore next
is phenomenology itself. Then we will turn to Freud.

Recall that my basic argument is that the philosophical
origins of contemporary psychology rest on too narrow a
conception of phenomenology. For a fuller treatment of some
of the history of Continental phenomenology, please refer to
my earlier work.[45] For the purposes of this study, we turn to
Ernesto Spinelli, who said: "As odd as it may seem to non-
psychologists, the study of consciousness has held little appeal
for twentieth-century psychology," having been devalued
by both behaviorism and psychoanalysis.[46] Originally,
Husserl and others explored our subjective experience in
order to discover how consciousness obscures pure reality.
By bracketing conscious experience we might come to
understand reality better. Husserl's goal was to arrive at pure
essences or forms of reality, and this type of phenomenology
is transcendental. Other phenomenologists came to believe
that this goal could not be met and instead focus on the very
meaning of existence, which is existential phenomenology.

The phenomenological method both clarifies and exposes
the hidden assumptions and biases of the major systems of

psychology, such as psychoanalysis or behaviorism, and may lead the way toward a more unified psychology. Most importantly, phenomenology analyzes the premise that we all arrive at unique interpretations of our existence, even though these are mediated by invariant limitations of environment and biology. We have to start first with the ordinary view that there is an objective reality that exists independently of our conscious awareness and that we have direct access to it through our senses. Under this view, objective reality is actually separate and apart from us conscious knowers. Phenomenology questions this viewpoint, arguing that whatever true reality there is will remain forever unknown to us. What we call reality under this view is linked to our perceptions and mental processes, as well as to our ability to construct meaning. Objects that we perceive exist for us only through the meaning that each of us gives them. Further, the meaning we give them has more to do with the perceiver than the thing itself.

Under this view, we must acknowledge the interpretational process that occurs whenever we construct meaning. It is actually this process that is the reality being perceived. That is, our conclusions are relative to our culture, as well as to our personal history and to biological factors, and thus our phenomenal reality remains open to a multitude of interpretations. Phenomenology denies the possibility of correct interpretations because that would presuppose that we had knowledge of ultimate reality. Further, what most of us term a correct interpretation of reality is not based on objective truths that have been universally determined; instead, these judgments are influenced by consensus viewpoints that are agreed upon by a community of individuals. This view does not deny that, more or less, many of us share similar interpretations of reality. Even so, they remain interpretations. The important point is that the creation of meaning is implicit in our experience of reality, but this does not imply that any particular meaning is the truth about reality.

In attempting to resolve the conflict surrounding the distinction between external reality and our perception of it, thinkers have either argued that nothing exists except what is in the mind or that objects do exist independently from the mind. Phenomenologists, instead of falling into either of these two positions, are concerned with the difference between the appearance of things and those things as they actually are. Recall that the aim of transcendental phenomenology was to expose such differences and discover ultimate reality. After the Husserlian project failed, however, phenomenologists admitted that we could not ever discover ultimate reality. Nevertheless, their attempts to clarify phenomenal reality provided a solution to the debate between objectivist and subjectivist accounts.

Phenomenology proposes that our experience of the world is always the product of an interaction between the raw matter of the world and our mental faculties. We never perceive only raw matter nor do we perceive only mental phenomena. Instead, we always experience the interaction between the two. Even though, as members of the same species, we share the same biological limitations that give a common structure to the development of our mental frameworks, each of us adds a number of variables from our individual life experiences. Each of us develops increasingly complex schemata through various maturational processes and social experience that determines how we interpret raw matter. Through the combination of common processes and individual variables, each person develops unique interpretations of the world. Moreover, it is also the case that perceptual variation exists even for one individual. This means that we perceive the very same raw matter differently through time.

Our current beliefs about the raw matter of the world come from theories of the physicists. Yet it is true that even they understand that the conclusions of all sciences are subject to the mental faculties of the individuals generating the theories. This means that we must constantly revise our theories about the physical reality of the world because we can never get to a final interpretation. So even if there is some objective reality, for humans it is unknowable in principle.[47] This led to Husserl's argument that all constructions of meaning by humans could be understood in terms of intentionality.[48] What he means is that we humans constantly translate raw stimuli of the world into meaningful constructions of reality. Consciousness is always directed toward the world, and it is always consciousness of something. Thus, we always experience the world in terms of objects or things about which we are concerned. Objects do not appear except in terms of our interpretations of stimuli.

What is important for our discussion about psychology is Husserl's distinction between *noema* and *noesis*, which are the two experiential and correlational poles of every act of intentionality.[49] For Husserl, *noema* is what we experience; *noesis* is the mode of experiencing. *Noema* is the directional element of experience. It is the object that we direct our attention toward, or the whatness, which is made up from the content of what we experience. In contrast, *noesis* is the referential element of experience. It is the mode or howness through which we define objects. It contains referential elements dealing with each individual's unique cognitive and affective biases that add further elements to the construction of meaning. Together, the *noematic* and *noetic* foci cause a person to interpret raw experience in a particular way.

I believe that in contemporary psychology there is a tendency
to minimize this correlation by focusing either solely on
the *noematic* focus or by minimizing the unique experiential
variables that add to an individual's *noetic* focus. This is not
to say that phenomenology is not interested in understanding
the shared features of humans' experience. Rather, what it
purports to help clarify and understand is just those features
of experience an individual shares with others, based on
factors associated with the environment, biology, and culture,
but more importantly, those factors that lead to individual
interpretations.

We will now focus our discussion on the effects that the
natural scientific paradigm has had on the psychoanalytic
movement. We will focus our inquiry on Freud because of
his vast and profound influence. We will also comment on
the reformulations of Freud attempted by the later drive
theorists, the relational theorists, and Jacques Lacan. Our
questions will ultimately revolve around the adequacy and
accuracy of Freud's anthropology, and we will argue, as
Binswanger did, that Freud's view of the nature of man was
unduly limited.[50] By utilizing Sartre's phenomenology, we aim
to expose the limitations inherent in Freud's project, subject
to a later criticism of phenomenology itself.

(Introduction to) Psychoanalysis: Freud

Husserl originally proposed that all sciences should be
constructed along phenomenological lines. The main point
involves the criticism that traditional natural science is
exclusively *noematic* in its orientation and therefore only
able to arrive at limited conclusions. Phenomenology urges
us to also take into account *noetic* considerations. What we
must understand is that even though we value the traditional

findings of psychology, we want to reassess and reconstruct its assumptions and methodologies along phenomenological lines so as to develop a broader, deeper, and richer view of humans, especially by adding an account of conscious experience.

Classical Freudian psychoanalysis reduces consciousness to an epiphenomenon of unconscious psychic forces guided by scientific laws of cause and effect. In this move, Freudian metatheory looks behind conscious experience for explanations that lie outside that experience. Freud himself defines metapsychology as a scientific endeavor to redress the constructions of metaphysics, which he views as superstitious beliefs, by transforming metaphysics into metapsychology.[51] It is questionable, however, whether Freud has merely replaced metaphysics with a metapsychology that is cloaked as scientific positivism.

According to Freud, our basic motivation is the pursuit of pleasure and the avoidance of pain, which involves the organismic return from excitation to equilibrium. The return to zero energy charge is perceived as pleasure, and this is known as the "principle of constancy," which is the bedrock of his theory. Thus, there is not much of a difference between the pleasure principle and his later formulation of the death instinct, given that both involve the absence of excitation. His unified system includes four hypotheses, which are the economic, the topographic, the dynamic, and the structural. The economic hypothesis includes concepts of energy flow, inhibition, and displacement. The topographic hypothesis includes the conscious, unconscious, and preconscious areas of the psyche. The dynamic hypothesis explains the psyche in terms of opposing forces (the Hegelian aspect). Finally, the structural hypothesis includes the Ego, Superego, and Id.

In his economic hypothesis (which he never abandons),

Freud uses the metaphors of charge and discharge from
modern physics to explain psychical processes in terms
of neurophysiology. It explains the connection between
the psyche and its objects (*cathexis*) and the formation of
neurotic symptoms through displacement, condensation, and
conversion. Freud assumes that libidinal energy is the main
motivational force of each human and uses this idea to explain
normal development and pathology in terms of conscious and
unconscious energetic displacements and permutations. For
him, the meaning of normal and pathological development
is located in the neurons and not in personal choice and
self-creation of meaning.[52] He firmly believed that the most
fundamental explanations of psychological disturbances
would eventually be understood in terms of neurophysiology.
Yet, the idea of the hydraulic metaphor, that the psyche
attempts to relieve itself of tension, that the mind is a machine
driven by energy flow, has fallen out of favor.[53]

I must point out that Freud's theory of the connection
between consciousness and its objects is a mechanical
paradigm and not a paradigm based on the construction of
meaning and value. His term *cathexis* refers to the amount of
psychical energy that one attaches to an object of some kind,
and he believed that this amount could be measured. Further,
he thinks he can explain various types of psychopathology,
such as hysteria or narcissism, in terms of the displacements
and condensations of this cathected energy, thus reducing
explanation to neurophysiology. I cannot stress enough
Freud's abiding belief that the primary motivating force for
humans is libido and that its effects can lead to both neurotic
symptoms as well as to normal growth and development.
For example, when immediate gratification is thwarted, the
ego develops as a reality-based structure that uses effective
judgment in postponing discharge. Yet, neurotic symptoms
can result from the repression or displacement of this energy.

According to Freud's theory of equivalence, whatever is repressed in consciousness is activated in the unconscious. Energy displaced from one activity to a substitute activity retains its original intensity while transferring its content. For example, one washes one's hands with the same intensity that one wishes to engage in "dirty" activities and the unconscious takes pleasure in the substitute activity as an equivalent for the repressed wish.[54] This is known as reaction formation. Another example is the case of Dora, whose hysterical cough was a substitute gratification for an unconscious wish for oral sex.[55] This is known as conversion.

Freud conceptualizes instincts in terms of biology, which is the bridge between his neurophysiological theory and his evolutionary theory. At first Freud viewed the sexual instinct in opposition to the ego instincts,[56] but later as the life instincts in opposition to the death instincts.[57] For Freud, an instinct or drive has an aim, a source, and an object. According to his theory, the real meaning of symptoms and behavior in general lies in the aim of the instinct and not the aim of the conscious subject. Freud believed that in all kinds of sexuality it is the sexual instinct that acts as the primary motivator in human action. Instincts lie in the region between the somatic and the psychic and give rise to primary process thinking, which seeks immediate gratification through real or hallucinated objects. This mode is under the authority of the Id, which is the source of unconscious fantasy and dreams. Then there is secondary process thinking which, under the authority of the ego instincts, adheres to the reality principle in order to survive. He later argues that even the ego instincts originate in the Id and derive from libidinal *cathexis* to the Ego.

Freud was highly influenced by Darwinian and Lamarckian theory, whose paradigms interpreted human behavior in terms of biological survival and preservation of the species.

This means that for Freud, the return to a zero energy charge was one of the aims of sexual discharge. The other was the preservation of the species. To view instinctual behavior in terms of biological function is obviously incongruent with the view that consciousness is actually at the root of behavior. Basing his assertions on Darwinian principles, Freud explains psychopathology as a regression to more primitive stages of sexual development that have not developed into a genital arrangement that would continue the species.[58] For example, he explains the Oedipus complex and guilt in terms of Lamarckian inheritance of acquired characteristics.[59] He thinks that the incest taboo gains part of its power from a phylogenetic memory. He speculates that the primal brothers murdered their father because of his monopoly over sexual relations with women, which gave rise to guilt. Thus, we can see in Freud's work a continuing theme of categorizing and treating "primitive" states of mind in terms of the natural scientific paradigm.

Freud's theory of the death instinct, as well, emerges from his use of a biological paradigm. In this system, the forces of evolution are in dialectical opposition to the forces of involution. In this line of thinking, his paradigm of mental illness requires an opposing force capable of reversing biogenetic achievements through regression to earlier stages of development. The return to death is a cessation of all charge; it is also an impulse to return to earlier forms preserved in the psycho-Lamarckian phylogenetic memory of the race. This memory must include the emergence of life from inorganic matter. Here we can see an isomorphism between his evolutionary theory and his neurobiological theory, both based on natural science paradigms of the day. We can see how his evolutionary theory supports various aspects of his metabiological theories, including aggression, the pursuit of pain, the repetition compulsion, and other regressive psychical tendencies.

We know that drive theory — the economic hypothesis — is at the heart of his metatheory, and he considers the existence of the unconscious to be a proven fact, basing his argument on the phenomena of self-deception, memory lapses, *parapraxes*, dreams, and symptoms.[60] For Freud, the unconscious includes the deep unconscious, which is the source of instincts that can never be brought into consciousness, as well as the dynamic unconscious, which is comprised of repressed wishes and memories. There is also the preconscious, which can always be brought into consciousness. The only way Freud can explain both parts of the unconscious is in terms of the economic hypothesis, which is at the root of the dynamic hypothesis. This dynamic hypothesis and the closely related topographical hypothesis postulate conflicts between psychic systems in terms of repression and displacement of instinctual energy and conflicts between opposing sets of instincts.[61] The drive theory is also at the root of the structural hypothesis, the explication of which ought to shed some light on the basic thesis we are advancing in this work.[62]

For Freud, psychic structures develop as a means to manage the drives. For example, the Id, which is present at birth, is the origin of the drives, and has no basis in human social reality. In contrast, the Ego is the location at which conscious life adjusts itself to the demands of the outer world.[63] He later reformulates the idea of the Ego as a structure that mediates between the demands of the Superego, the Id, and the outer worlds, and as having both conscious and unconscious elements.[64] The Ego develops from the frustration of immediate drive gratification. The Superego results from a resolution of the Oedipus complex as a result of the internalization of various parental prohibitions against drive satisfaction. What is salient is that Freud's conceptualization

of psychic structure implies a system of interpersonal
relationships that is solely based on instinct. According to
this line of thinking the drives create their objects through
repeated satisfaction. Thus, Freud says that the object "is not
originally connected with [the instinct] but becomes assigned
to it only in consequence of being peculiarly fitted to make
satisfaction possible."[65]

Love, for Freud, is nothing but the instincts cathecting to
various objects. Friendships and social relationships are not
fundamental but are derivations of instinctual tendencies
resulting from drive frustrations and permutations. We
can see here how Freud interprets all human phenomena
in terms of his mechanical and biological metatheory. This
especially highlights how profoundly he was influenced by the
methodologies of natural science, especially those of physics
and biology. Keep in mind that we want to illuminate how his
metatheoretical paradigm unduly limits our understanding of
the human phenomena at hand. For example, it is arguable
that humans do not always seek to reduce their tension, in
contradiction to the principle of constancy. It is also arguable
that this metatheory — including the Oedipal conflict,
sublimation, symptom formation and the like — does not
satisfactorily explain why some people do not pursue pleasure.

Further, one can argue that the complex array of human
emotional states involves something more than the lack of
immediate discharge of a drive. Perhaps it is true that human
emotion is not reducible to the tension between pleasure and
pain, and that human relations are more complicated than
mere sublimations of instinctual energy. Further, we will
see in a later section on object relations theory that to see
the Other as just a libidinal object creates a confusing and
inadequate meta-foundation for this analytical development
in contemporary psychoanalysis. I hope to show that a

broader phenomenological view of humans would allow the development of a far richer and more accurate meta-theory than drive theory. Most importantly, let us acknowledge that Freud's mechanical explanations of human experience were drawn from other sciences. Let us be clear that his treatment of a human being's reality as if it were only an object subject to the laws of cause and effect unduly limits the nature of the exploration into that reality.

Now that we have delineated some of the basic elements in Freud's metapsychology, let us explore more deeply some of the consequences. It was Ludwig Binswanger himself who made the first major attempt, through phenomenology, to correct what he thought were the shortcomings in Freud's view of man and human experience.[66] Jacob Needleman asserts that Binswanger's criticism "suggest[s] the possibility that the history of psychology and psychiatry during the last hundred years is the history of an illusion," that "phenomenology's role in revealing that illusion is to suggest that our perception and description of the self is conditioned by our conception of nature (or 'reality'), and that this conception, in turn, cannot be justified by the scientific method which is based on it since all the objects which the scientist attends to will be perceived and described in its light."[67] Further, Needleman asserts that the various trends in psychology must reevaluate "not only their mode of explanation, but of their very perception of the phenomena they seek to explain."[68] Both Needleman and Binswanger urge psychology to review and reconsider its starting point.

Needleman's discussion of the distinction between understanding (*verstehen*) and explanation (*erklärung*) is helpful.[69] Explanation attempts to reduce phenomena of some conceptual system with which we are already familiar to something that we already consider a basic reality. In contrast,

in order to understand a phenomenon or experience, we must
"approach the object to be understood on its terms, to see in
it structures that emerge from *its* side, and not from ours."[70]
In order to do this, we must not reduce the phenomena
to what we believe are ultimate laws or reality. When we
explain, we transform phenomena by subsuming them into
laws that relate them to other phenomena, or we break them
down into parts that are taken to be more real than the whole
phenomena. If one argues that explanation really does result
in understanding we can reply that, at best, the level of
understanding is limited to the previously accepted categories.
In the light of Kuhn's and Foucault's trenchant accounts of the
politics of knowledge, it is questionable whether explanation
provides understanding at all, for it is in these reductive
strategies that we lose sight of the phenomena in question.

Let us be clear that natural science is an explanatory system,
one amongst many in history, and includes such disciplines as
physics, chemistry, and biology. What is most salient is that
in this system we abstract parameters of space and time and
attempt to relate them causally. Here, we pull out just one
aspect of phenomena — or, rather, we reduce the phenomena
to their space-time aspect, prioritizing corporeality, and
overlooking all other aspects as irrelevant. We can see the
obvious influences of both Newton and Descartes operative
in this reductionism. For biology we rename these things
as organisms, and in medicine, human patients. Most
importantly, this scientific attitude attempts to isolate pure
corporeality away from consciousness and to quantify it
mathematically. Within this methodological attitude, natural
science makes every attempt to keep the consciousness of
the observer out of the facts drawn from the phenomena.
Derivatively, this allows other, independent observers to
verify and confirm the conclusions.

Psychology, which is a science both of consciousness, unconsciousness, and human behavior, has a dialectical tension operative within its very foundation. In order to be objective like its sister sciences, it must keep consciousness out of the phenomena described; in contrast, its mission is to study consciousness, which Descartes rules out of the equation. The problem is that the psychologist investigates the same processes as those by which he conducts that very same investigation. The psychologist, as Binswanger correctly noticed, attempts to bring into the investigation exactly what Descartes excluded. For the objective world of the *res extensa* is just the world without consciousness. As Needleman explains, "scientific method cannot reduce that which is doing the reducing, consciousness, thought, perception — self."[71] Further, he correctly states that "psychology cannot explain those processes that are of the same order as that by which it conducts its investigation without dictating at the outset what those processes are like; without dictating to the data in advance."[72]

One strategy to cope with this problem is behaviorism, the exploration of which we leave for a later project. In this line of inquiry, consciousness is completely excluded from the exploration, whereby the perceiver is eliminated and the focus is solely on corporeality. Yet, it is questionable whether with the elimination of the self from the inquiry we are still doing psychology. This problem is instructive though, for we can see that in the attempt to emulate the methodology of physics we necessarily reduce the parameters of our investigation too much. By restricting our attitude and our approach in such a way to prevent any subjectivity, i.e. consciousness, from creeping in, we end up with verifiable conclusions that do not satisfy the appeal of the phenomena. Another helpful contrast Needleman makes is that in any of the hard sciences, data only gains meaning through its connection with a pre-established conceptual scheme. In contrast, "in psychology each datum, a human perception, thought, emotion, etc., itself has its own meaning to the perceiver, thinker, feeler — to the human being."[73] Thus, the very virtues of the natural science method, especially the total reduction of consciousness, squeeze out the very phenomena that we wish to explore in psychology — consciousness and its intentional structure. Under this methodology, psychology destroys the meaning to a particular self of the phenomena of consciousness that it seeks to explain, in the very act of explaining.

Psychology as a natural science faces the task of investigating consciousness as a part of the realm of pure corporeality, as the *res extensa* that Descartes clearly demarcated. Yet, this is self-contradictory because the *res extensa* is independent of consciousness, by definition. This means, as stated by Needleman, that "psychology must strip consciousness of consciousness in order scientifically to investigate consciousness."[74] But this is exactly what Freud does, for his concept of the unconscious is an attempt to view consciousness as being in the realm of the res extensa. It is a shifting of the Archimedean point in such a way to de-center consciousness, so that consciousness itself is only a function of the psychic processes and certainly not their essence or most general characteristic. The consequence is that as soon as the major part of the psychic processes are placed outside of consciousness and into the realm of pure corporeality, they become susceptible of mathematical quantification and observation by scientific method. Freud himself extols the possibility of using mathematics as methodology in the study of unconscious processes.[75]

Furthermore, in contrast to behaviorism's annihilation of consciousness, in his system Freud keeps all the important constituents of consciousness, including feelings, thoughts, and perceptions, in terms of their meaning to a particular self. Yet, he recognizes that even at the stage of the description of phenomena we implicitly apply certain concepts to our naming of phenomena. The idea of the unconscious connects facts about dreams, hypnosis, slips of the tongue, and so forth. Yet, underneath this process are the more foundational assumptions that help us determine what counts as a fact. In Freud's system, which follows the natural science model, this includes the ideas of objectivity and Cartesian corporeality. One of the fundamental assumptions Freud makes is that "observed phenomena must take second place to forces that are merely hypothesized."[76] For Freud, these hypothesized forces are "the drives, the instincts . . . whose elemental nature is the same in all men and which directs him to the satisfaction of certain primal needs."[77] Psychoanalysis thereby explains psychic phenomena by reducing them to their instinctual component; this reduction transforms phenomena into their function relative to drives.

While Freud reduces phenomena of consciousness to unconscious instincts, he keeps intact the underlying assumption of their intentionality. This allows him objectivity because these human phenomena can be studied by detached and disinterested observers, yet he maintains the essence of consciousness — intentionality — and thus seems to avoid being overly reductive. We can see how this differs from a science such as physics where all remnants of intentionality ought to be avoided, even though more of us now can perhaps accept that even this science cannot be completely objective. For Freud, the instincts must have their source in the unconscious in order to allow them to be explained by his conceptual system, the drives, and the laws that govern them. This move allows Freud to preserve the data in terms of meaning to a self, something that behaviorism cannot do. Thus, we make the distinction between conscious and unconscious intentionality. Conscious intentionality has necessary reference to an agent or a self; in contrast, unconscious intentionality does not. We can see here how intentionality in general is preserved, in terms of similarities between people, but since we lose the intentionality of a particular conscious agent, we lose the uniqueness of an individual self.

Before making a few comments about Freud's anthropology, I want to say a bit about his notion of the unconscious. There has been much criticism written about the unconscious, for example, Sartre's, so we won't spend much space doing that here.[78] The unconscious, for Freud, is a theoretical construct that unifies and explains psychic phenomena. For him, the assumption that all mental acts are conscious fails to explain adequately psychological processes. Yet, when we add the unconscious, beyond direct experience, we are able to gain meaning and connection. Here, Freud obviously borrows the concept of instinct from biology, and interprets emotion, thoughts, and behavior as transformations of instinct. We can again see the natural science influence in this conceptual move because he thinks the unconscious provides a way to determine causal relations amongst phenomena that, when viewed directly, do not manifest this causality. Further, whether or not the unconscious is viewed as an entity or as a process, the problem of proving its existence as real or merely theoretical still remains. What we can agree on, though, is that it still finds a foundation in its biological nature, as instinct. We can see here how Freud's positivist approach assumes exactly what it is that he tries to prove, thereby limiting humans to a conception of *homo natura*.

Freud is intrigued by an individual human's relation to culture, and attempts to develop a system of psychic laws that explain the psychic determinism of individuals. Thus, in line with Locke's psychological empiricism, he follows the principle of "*nihil est in homine cultura, quod non fuerit in homine natura.*" Further, he believes that for each individual, at birth there is a biological blueprint — the instincts — upon which individual and cultural potential operates. He postulates the Id as the most fundamental psychic reality. It has no organization and no unified will, only an impulse to satisfy primitive needs in accord with the pleasure principle. Contradictory impulses co-exist and compromise in order to discharge their energy. Given the nature of the Id, *homo natura* is amoral, unfree, irrational, and unhistorical.[79] It is motivated by instinct in order to gain pleasure, is inhibited by society, and has a developmental history. This is the result of removing consciousness from the zone of investigation. Meaning is reduced to (unconscious) wish fulfillment, given that the goal of instinct is pleasure.

Freud's view of man as *homo natura* strips man of all aspects that flow from the conscious construction of meaning within a culture, *homo existentialis*. He believes that the deepest essence of who we are is instinctual, with the same elemental nature in all humans. He believes that observed phenomena must be interpreted in terms of his conceptual apparatus, including the unconscious, instead of describing them in their own terms or, for that matter, in terms of any other conceptualization. Thus, phenomena are subjugated to theory. His ideas follow from the influence of the Cartesian-Newtonian notion of mechanism. The entire mechanism of the psychic apparatus starts from the Id, in terms of a wish, and flows out of the combination of our natural organization, as well as supervening environmental factors. Humans do not strive for pleasure as such, but for things that bring pleasure. Thus, we are directed in terms of the meanings that things have for us. More importantly, Freud's scientific construct can only exist by destroying humans' experiential knowledge of themselves.

The methodological paradigm of natural science in psychology allows us to organize our knowledge of humans into discrete areas that can be controlled and manipulated by economic forces.[80] The consequences are that humans are now ruled by these discourses of truth about them. This politico-scientific machinery subsumes all the phenomena of humans, both individual and social, into various theoretical constructs, except for that critical space that allows us to evaluate the kind of science we are doing. Meaning exists with singularity for each one of us, but when we develop the kind of psychology that transforms unique individuals into objects, we lose all the richness of the personal and the subjective dimension.

As Binswanger says, natural science "ignores the most basic anthropological fact that *Dasein* is always *mine, yours,* or *ours* . . . [that] it ignores the entire structure of ontological problems that surrounds the question as to the genuine *who* that so relates itself, the question as to the human self."[81] Further, Binswanger asserts that psychology can go in two directions. First, psychology can lead "away from ourselves toward theoretical determinations, [or it can lead to] anthropology, which concerns itself with . . . the possible modes of our existence."[82] Binswanger's astute concern is that the natural-scientific view has prioritized itself over all other ways of apprehending being and, in so doing, has leveled our conception of man to but a small part of who we are. He worries about the consequences of conceptualizing humans in terms of only particular ideas, i.e., the pleasure principle for Freud, because of the loss of consideration of all other ways of revealing our being. Further, note that pleasure is viewed in terms of accumulation and quantity, and not in terms of meaning. He (Binswanger), like Foucault, is very concerned with our need to proclaim scientific truth, and correctly understands that it involves the deeper imperative to act. We harness scientific truths in our quest to predict and control our world. In doing so, however, we stand alienated in our understanding from all other aspects of our being.

I believe that Binswanger's early concerns are justified and that with Freudian analysis, there is a tendency to focus solely on objects — the *noematic* pole — as well as to minimize the unique experiential variables that add to an individual's *noetic* focus, i.e., how a person constructs conscious meaning. Later, I will delineate and explore Lacan's review and reconstruction of Freud, pulling out Lacan's metapsychology, and evaluating it in accord with the phenomenological premises we have been advancing so far. Before I do that, however, I must discuss the legacy with which Freud left psychoanalysis. It is important to note that Freud's failure to develop beyond the paradigm of 19th-Century materialist science contributed to the failure of contemporary psychoanalytic theorists to move beyond the illusion of substance as they attempted to describe the development of the ego or self.

Notes

1. Isaac Newton, *The Principia*, trans. I. Bernard Cohen and Anne Whitman (Berkeley: University of California Press, 1999).

2. René Descartes, *Discourse on Method*, trans. Desmond M. Clarke (London: Penguin, 1999).

3. E. G. Boring, *A History of Experimental Psychology*, 2nd. (New York: Appleton-Century-Crofts, 1950).

4. William James, *Principles of Psychology* (New York: Holland Co., 1890).

5. H. Ebbinghaus, *Readings in General Psychology* (Chicago: The University of Chicago Press, 1923).

6. J.B. Watson, "Psychology as a Natural Science," in Skinner, C. E. (Ed.), *Readings in Psychology* (New York: Holt, Rinehart and Winston, 1935), 810.

7. G. A. Kimble and N. Garmezy, *Principles of General Psychology*, 2d. (New York: Ronald, 1963).

8. D. J. Lewis, *Scientific Principles of Psychology* (Englewood Cliffs, N.J.: Prentice-Hall, 1963).

9. R. J. McCall, *A Preface to Scientific Psychology* (Milwaukee: Bruce, 1959).

10. Wilhelm Dilthey, *Selected Works, Volume I: Introduction to the Human Sciences*, eds. Rudolf Makkreel and Frithjof Rodi (Princeton, N.J.: Princeton University Press, 1989).

11. H. A. Hodges, *The Philosophy of Wilhelm Dilthey* (London: Routledge, 1944).

12. W. Kluback, *Wilhelm Dilthey's Philosophy of History* (New

York: Columbia, 1956).

13.   See my previous work in, *The Algebra of History* (New Orleans: Loyola University Press, 2004), for discussion about Husserl's influence.

14.   G. Ryle, "Phenomenology I," *Proceedings of the Aristotelian Society*, Supplementary Vol. XI, 1932, 68-83.

15.   W. Wundt, *Elements of Folk Psychology*, trans. E.L. Schaub (New York: Macmillan, 1916).

16.   E. Spranger, *Types of Men*, trans. P.J.W. Pigoors (Halle: Niemeyer Publishing, 1928); also see W. McDougall, *Body and Mind* (London: Methuen, 7th ed., 1928).

17.   G.W. Allport, "Scientific Models and Human Morals," *Psychol. Rev.*, 1947, 54, 182-192; also see, *Becoming* (New Haven: Yale, 1955).

18.   S.W. Fernberger, "Behaviorism versus introspective psychology," in Skinner, C.E. (Ed.), *Readings in Psychology* (New York: Holt, Rinehart and Winston, 1935), 36-38.

19.   A.D. Fearon, *The Two Sciences of Psychology* (Englewood Cliffs, N.J. : Prentice-Hall, 1937).

20.   J. Kockelmans, *Phenomenology and Physical Science* (Pittsburgh: Duquesne University Press, 1966).

21.   Jean-Paul Sartre, *Sketch for A Theory of Emotions*, trans. P. Mairet (London: Methuen, 1962); also see my section on Sartre in my previous work, *The Algebra of History*.

22.   See reference to Wittgenstein in D.F. Gustafson, (Ed.), *Essays in Philosophical Psychology* (Garden City: Doubleday, 1964), xiv.

23.   See K. Koffka, *Principles of Gestalt Psychology* (New York:

Harcourt, Brace & World, 1935).

24. R. G. Taylor, Jr., "Qualitative vs. Quantitative Methods in Scientific Research," *Human Potential,* 1968, 1, 85-87.

25. See Rollo May, E. Angel and H.F. Ellenberger (Eds.), *Existence: A New Dimension in Psychiatry and Psychology* (New York: Basic Books, 1958).

26. W. Wundt, "Contributions to the Theory of Sensory Perception," in T. Shipley, (Ed.), *Classics in Psychology* (New York: Philosophical Library, 1961), 51-78.

27. William James, *Psychology* (New York: New World Publishing, 1892 and 1948).

28. But see theoretical changes brought about by principles of 20th-Century quantum physics.

29. See M. Boss, "Anxiety, Guilt, and Psychotherapeutic Liberation," *Review of Existential Psychology and Psychiatry,* 1962, 2, 173-195.

30. See E.G. Boring, *A History of Experimental Psychology,* 2nd ed. (New York: Appleton-Century-Crofts, 1950).

31. S. Strasser, *Phenomenology and the Human Sciences* (Pittsburgh: Duquesne University Press, 1963).

32. We will see in our discussion of Foucault, later in this section, how this prioritization can occur politically. Also see: Kevin Boileau, *Genuine Reciprocity and Group Authenticity* (Lanham, Maryland: University Press of America, 2000, Chapters 2 & 3, for an extensive discussion of this issue.

33. Dilthey called this the "Lebenswelt," or lifeworld; in this regard see, *Dilthey, Introduction to the Human Sciences, Volume I: Selected Works,* trans. Michael Neville, eds. Rudolf A. Makkreel and Frithjof Rodi (Princeton, N.J.:

Princeton University Press, 1989).

34.   F. Suppe, *The Structure of Scientific Theories*, 2nd ed. (Chicago: University of Illinois Press, 1977).

35.   Thomas Kuhn, *The Structure of Scientific Revolutions* (Chicago: The University of Chicago Press, 1962).

36.   *Ibid.*, 4.

37.   Jay Greenberg and Stephen Mitchell, *Object Relations in Psychoanalytic Theory* (Cambridge, Mass., Harvard University Press, 1983), 18.

38.   *Loc. cit.*

39.   T. Kuhn, *The Essential Tension* (Chicago: University of Chicago Press, 1977), 298.

40.   Jay Greenberg and Stephen Mitchell, *Object Relations in Psychoanalytic Theory*, 19.

41.   See L. Postman and J. P. Egan, *Experimental Psychology: An Introduction* (New York: Harper & Row, 1949).

42.   See Kevin C. Boileau, *Genuine Reciprocity and Group Authenticity*.

43.   *Ibid.*, Chapters 2 & 3.

44.   *Ibid.*, Chapter 3.

45.   See *The Algebra of History*.

46.   Ernesto Spinelli, *An Introduction to Phenomenological Psychology* (London: Sage Publications, 1989).

47.   See Kant's distinction between phenomena and noumena.

48.   This is a concept he borrowed from Brentano. See, *The Algebra of History*.

49. See Don Ihde, *Experimental Phenomenology: An Introduction* (Albany: State University of New York, 1986) for a nice discussion of this point.

50. H. Bonner, *On Being Mindful of Man* (Boston: Houghton Mifflin, 1965).

51. Sigmund Freud, "Project for a Scientific Psychology," [1895], in *The Standard Edition of the Complete Psychological Works of Sigmund Freud*, (hereinafter *SE*), J. Strachey, (Ed.) (London: Hogarth Press, 1966), 1, 281- 343. Arguably, this article was Freud's first significant attempt at constructing a metapsychology, which he later develops into additional hypotheses about the nature of mind.

52. *Loc. cit.*

53. We will discuss this in our sections on Lacan and the relational theorists.

54. Freud, *SE*, Vol. 10 and 12.

55. Freud, *SE*, Vol. 7.

56. Freud, *SE*, Vol. 7 and 14.

57. Freud, *SE*, Vol. 18, 21, and 23.

58. Freud, *SE*, Vol. 7, which discuses the oral, anal, phallic, and genital stages of psychosexual development.

59. Freud, *SE*, Vol. 13.

60. See Sartre's critique of the idea of the unconscious, in *Being and Nothingness* (New York: Washington Square Press, 1966); also see: Sartre, *Existential Psychoanalysis* (Washington, D.C.: Regnery Gateway, 1988).

61. Freud, *SE*, Vol. 11 and 12.

62. Freud, *SE*, Vol. 19.

63. Freud, *SE*, Vol. 2.

64. Freud, *SE*, Vol. 19.

65. Freud, *SE*, Vol. 14, p. 122.

66. See *Being-In-The-World: Selected Papers of Ludwig Binswanger*, trans. and with a Critical Introduction by Jacob Needleman (New York: Harper Torchbooks, Harper & Row, 1968).

67. *Ibid.*, xiv.

68. *Ibid.* xvii.

69. *Ibid.*, p. 32.

70. *Ibid.*, p. 38.

71. *Ibid.*, p. 43.

72. *Loc. cit.*

73. *Ibid.*, p. 44.

74. *Ibid.* p, 48.

75. Freud, "Repression," [1915] in *SE*, Vol. 14, 141.

76. Quoted by Binswanger in *Being-in-the-World*, 156.

77. *Loc. cit.*

78. See, for example, A. C. MacIntyre, *The Unconscious* (London: Routledge & Kegan Paul, 1958).

79. There are moral considerations that flow from this structure, but this exploration goes beyond the parameters of this study. We will also find ourselves in the ethical domain in our later discussion of Levinas.

80. See the work of Michel Foucault in this regard, as well as the work of the Frankfurt School, including that of Habermas, for extensive discussion of these issues.

81. Ludwig Binswanger, "Freud's Conception of Man in the Light of Anthropology," in *Being-in-the-World*, 171.

82. *Loc. cit.*

Part Two:
Phenomenological Criticism of Post-Freudian Drive Theory, Object Relations Theory, and Lacan

Introduction

Now that we have seen the influence of natural science methodology on Freud, we must explore his own influence on the drive theorists who followed him and the later relational theorists who broke from some of his basic premises. What we are trying to discern is the effect that Freud's theories have had on the long line of psychoanalytic theory in the twentieth century up to the present. While we are not going to address every important analytic thinker, we hope to discuss enough in order to develop a picture of Freud's materialist influence upon contemporary psychoanalysis.

Recall that for Freud, others are valued not first for their human qualities but rather for their abilities as objects for gratifying instinctual desires. For him, the mechanistic origin of interpersonal relations is the discovery that other people can help in the reduction of physical tension. Nevertheless, theorists who came after Freud did not have a consistent system within which to place their ideas about the relation of selves to others. They could only ground these phenomena within drive theory. As Betty Cannon says, "the most significant issues for post-Freudian theory are the problem of accounting for relational needs which indicate a desire for something other than instinctual satisfaction and the concomitant problem of accounting for the structuralization of the self or ego which results from the satisfaction/frustration of these noninstinctual needs."[1] Even mainstream theorists such as Jay Greenberg and Stephen Mitchell recognize the problem of reconciling drive theory with relational needs as the main problem in post-Freudian psychoanalytic theory.[2]

As we will see, many post-Freudian theorists accepted Freud's structural theory, which eventually crystallized in *The Ego and the Id*, Standard Edition, Vol. 19, with the full division of the psyche into Ego, Id, and Superego.[3] This gave impetus to explore ideas about how the Ego emerges out of its undifferentiated matrix, ideas about ego defenses, and ideas about the development of the ego in relations with others. Yet these theorists saddled themselves with the problem of explaining how infants have relational needs for self-esteem, mirroring, positive regard, and affection. This brought them to a theoretical impasse for explaining an infant's use of significant others to attain a sense of self. Drive theorists found it difficult to link the need to use others as a source of self-definition to the need to use others as a source of instinctual gratification.

Let us discuss object relations theory so we can better grasp the theoretical impasse that occurred in post-Freudian drive theory. According to object relations theory, humans always act and react to actual others as well as to internal others which are psychic representations of real others that came before in a person's life. Most significantly, these psychic representations have the power to influence a person's cognitive and affective states, as well as behavioral patterns. That is, one's interpretation of one's experience is always shaped by these internal others that one carries around as memory. They operate as social assumptions or starting points in one's interpretation of any new social experience and often involve issues of personal identity or anticipations of how one will be treated. In a person's history there are crucial interactions with significant others, some of which are internalized as memory, and they act to shape perception and attitude toward the world.

Object relations theory tries to answer questions that relate to the functionality, causal power of, and types of these internal objects. At the most basic level they try to understand the relation between internal and external objects, between the imagined and the real. As Greenberg and Mitchell acknowledge, "the concept of object relations originated as an inherent part of Freud's drive theory."[4] For Freud, though, the object is the libidinal object. It is the target of a drive. In more contemporary accounts, Freud's concept of drive is dropped as an inherent element of object relations. In this new theoretical setting, object relations involves at its most basic level an individual's interactions with real and imagined others and to the relation between these internal and external worlds.[5] We will see that in place of the idea that at the most basic level humans pursue pleasure, more recent views about object relations hold the view that at bottom humans pursue the development of a self.

Please focus on the fact that there has been a theoretical impasse in the transformation from pure drive theory to an object relations approach that discounts the metaphysical assumptions of the drives altogether. As 20th-Century analytic theorists proceeded, they became increasingly aware that what infants needed was relatedness to significant others, not only for nurturing and support, but also for the development of a self. Here, we offer a short summary of the conclusions of a few of these thinkers, starting with Melanie Klein, who was caught in the wave of Freud's drive theory.

Klein struggled with the tension she discovered between her commitment to drive theory and to the relational insights she discovered in her work. As Cannon says, "she [Klein] rejects Freud's concept of primary narcissism, and she proposes the existence of developed affects in infancy which can hardly be attributable to transmutations of drives."[6] According to Klein, humans are object-related from the beginning of life through *a priori* images of the penis, breasts, and so forth. Her idea of *a priori* images results from her attempt to develop Freud's notion of phylogenetic memories, but thereby calls into question Freud's concept of primary narcissism as well as his subordination of objects to the drives. Klein explains that infants have an urge to repair the mother they had previously attacked (at least in fantasy) as a bad partial object. The infant entering into Klein's idea of the depressive position, where the bad/frustrating and good/gratifying images of the mother come together as one person, does not simply seek gratification from the mother. The infant actually loves the mother and grieves her fantasized destruction not merely as a libidinal object but as a person. As others have pointed out, Klein's theoretical positions are much more cogently explained in terms of relational stages rather than in terms of psychosexual drives.[7]

Margaret Mahler was also interested in the structural formation of the ego during infancy and childhood. Although she used the language of drive theory it is apparent that she discovered the importance of the relational needs of all humans at the earliest stages of life. For Mahler, it is crucial that a child develop a strong sense of self in a context of being related to others in loving ways. She is most noted for her careful construction of what she calls the "separation-individuation" process, which lasts from five months to three years in age, and which includes the active participation of the child in negotiating human relatedness. Even though Mahler attempted to relate the various subphases of this process to the psychosexual stages of Freud, what really emerges are the nondrive-oriented relational needs of the process. Thus, even though Mahler used Freud's terminology, it is apparent that she demonstrated the existence of early relational needs in humans that have little to do with drive satisfaction. These relational needs cluster around the development of self-esteem and a firm sense of self through touching, mirroring, and other types of physical and emotional responsiveness from primary caregivers. She claimed that such responsiveness would lead to the development of a conflict-free ego sphere. In fact, her work illuminates the negative and severe consequences of ignoring a child's early relational needs. All this contributes to the conclusion that it is the mirroring object, not the libidinal object, that is essential for normal development, that it is not drives but affective attachments and needs for self-esteem that are truly at work here.[8]

A few remarks about the work of Otto Kernberg are also instructive. Kernberg took issue with Freud's belief that instinctual needs rather than affects are primary, arguing that pathology results not from libidinal overinvestment of the ego but rather from thwarted needs for self esteem. Freud believed that primary narcissism is an objectless state in which an infant is totally invested with himself and does not even recognize an external world. Kernberg argued against this, asserting that one's relationship with oneself is always mediated by one's relations with others and vice versa. He wrote that "when there is an increase of narcissistic investment [self-love], there is a parallel increase in the capacity to love and to give, to experience and express gratitude, to have concern for others, and for an increase in sexual love, sublimation, and creativity."[9] Further, he argued that the maintenance of conflicting ego states by borderline and narcissistic patients which result from the failure of a child to integrate the good and bad partial images of the mother is caused by fear that the bad partial image will completely engulf the good partial image; it is the good image that is needed in order to maintain self-esteem and a positive sense of self. He also believed that the lack of ego integration in borderline and narcissistic patients resulted from a failure to resolve Mahler's rapprochement phase, thus involving the separation-individuation process. In sum, Kernberg argued that the shaping of the drives out of the undifferentiated matrix of primal energy comes from interactions with real others. We can see here how he has redefined the drives as emotions and that he thinks that affects, not drives, are the primary organizers of early experience. If anything, drives result from affective cathexes and not the other way around. Again, we see the problem of retaining the drive language, but also the valuation of the development of ego structure in humans.

These and other early drive theorists discovered that important others are fundamentally related to children, not as instinctual gratifying objects, but as other consciousnesses like their own. It is not the other as a mirroring object that figures so importantly in a child's developing self. Instead, this importance is given to the other as a subject for whom one is oneself an object. Thus, relational needs can be understood as part of an attempt to create a reflective view of the self from the reactions one gets from earliest relations with others.[10] Recall one of the main problems that we are exploring in this section: that of accounting for the structuralization of the self or ego which results from the satisfaction/frustration of noninstinctual relational needs. We are trying to trace Freud's legacy to 20th-Century analysis and psychology, and it is our belief that his commitment to materialism has pervaded the field in a way that unfairly distorts the phenomena of the human being. By exploring the relational theorists who came after the drive theorists we just discussed, we can see how this assumption and need to build structure came right from Freud.

In recent developments of psychoanalytic theory, we see the introduction of the phenomenological term "self" in place of the (Freudian) structural term "ego."[11] This is due to the transformation from drive theory to relational theory, even though the Freudian influence continues. Analogous to Freud's reification of the ego, as part of a material structure of the psyche, newer theorists reify the self as a thing. We must explore the nature of the self and attempt to determine whether it is a thing of substance at all or something else. Furthermore, we must examine the discovery by these theorists of each human's need to create a substantial self, as well as arguments, for example by Sartre, that we must overcome the idea that we can actually have such a substantial self. Let us take a step back and recall why this is important. Remember, we are arguing that the Cartesian-Newtonian methodology of natural science was borrowed by psychology from physics. Remember that we are asking whether this attempt to quantify our materialist data is true to the nature of psychical phenomena. As we have shown, Freudian metapsychology neatly falls into the causal determinist models of natural science, even though there is some movement away from this model. If we can show that contemporary psychology carries within it some of these deep materialist assumptions, then we can make similar criticisms toward our present methodologies as we can toward their parent.

We can now take a look at how some of the relational theorists view the nature of the self, especially in infancy, in stark contrast to typical drive theorists and Freud himself.

For example, it was Harry Guntrip who argued that it was time to discard drive theory and replace it with a "consistently psychodynamic theory of the unique individual in his personal relations."[12] Other theorists are less direct in their transformation of Freudian terms and concepts. For example, Harry Stack Sullivan's "tenderness theorem" indicates relational needs for giving and receiving love.[13] Fairbairn asserts that "libido is not primarily pleasure-seeking but object seeking."[14] Michael Balint replaces primary narcissism with "primary object love," which he defines as the desire to be loved.[15] The meaning of these relational needs is different from the pleasure- seeking/tension-reducing aim of Freudian drive theory. As Cannon says, "their aim is the creation of a self rather than the pursuit of pleasure."[16] Even Kohut renames them "selfobject" needs to distinguish them from the "libidinal object" needs of Freud.[17] Yet it may be that these needs do not actually involve the other as object but rather the object as subject for whom we are the object.

Further, there seems to be confusion about just what the self is in the first place. Although relational theorists opt for speaking of a personal self rather than an impersonal ego, they are still influenced by Freud's idea that the psyche is a thing that has substance and structure, that it is a reified *thing* that can be objectified. For example, Kohut's idea of the "structuralization of the self" replaces discussions about the "structuralization of the ego" or, for Winnicott, we must replace the "false self" with a "true self," by engaging in authentic living, and both of these selves he regards as entities. Further, there is confusion about the nature of the self as subject and as object, which James Masterson illustrates in his work.[18] Here, Masterson gives a summary of various psychoanalytic perspectives on the self, mixing drive terms with relational terms, and attempting to differentiate self from ego. Yet, let us again take stock about what is at stake here. We have been arguing all along that 20th-Century psychology has unduly restricted the phenomena of the self, that by objectifying it as a thing, we capture it, study it, and describe its nature. Yet, by unduly restricting the data we also unduly restrict our view. We saw with Freud the theoretical — and perhaps clinical — problems that result from restricting the phenomena in this fashion. Here, we are arguing that Freud's influence still lingers, which means that we constrain a deeper and richer understanding of ourselves, as well as a more fruitful clinical methodology.

Sullivan

Next, we want to explore Harry Stack Sullivan's struggle with the articulation of the nature of the self that goes beyond simple objectivization. Recall, in our phenomenological investigations, I am trying to suggest new avenues for psychological and psychoanalytic methodology that transcend the limiting features we have delineated earlier. We see that Sullivan wrestled with this, even though his life's work occurred in the twentieth century, and even though he never completely shook the objectivizing influence of Freud. This discussion is important because it leads us straight to Sartre's conceptualization of the self that avoids structure and therefore the Cartesian substantial self.

Sullivan was a relational theorist. As such, he abandoned Freud's drive theory, emphasizing the importance of one's earliest relations with others in the construction of a self, and prioritizing the substantial impact of culture on interpersonal relations, even in the biological family unit. As Greenberg and Mitchell say, [for Sullivan] "language . . . is very dangerous; it is possible to speak of all sorts of places and processes, objects, structures, and drives, presumably inside the patient's head or mind. The sharpest differences between Sullivan's version of the relational model and those developed with the British school of object relations concerns precisely the use of language suggesting 'internal' objects, structures, and processes with presumed phenomenological referents."[19] To some extent, Sullivan's thinking resembled existentialism insofar as he was cautious about the use of objectivizing theory, and respectful of the uniqueness of each individual's experience. For example, he asserted that "there is an essential inaccessibility about any personality other than one's own . . . There is always an ample residuum that escapes analysis and communication. . . ."[20] He emphasizes that one ought not take theory too seriously, that the actuality of the living person always outstrips theory or diagnostic formulations.[21] Thus, we see in Sullivan a strong caution about concluding that we can ever capture a complete knowledge of someone by objectifying them through theoretical construction.

According to Sullivan, human "personality can never be isolated from the complex of interpersonal relations in which the person lives and has his being."[22] For him, knowledge about another person is mediated through interaction. We come to know another by what he does and by observing ourselves in interaction with that other person. Yet, when we gather data about another, we are never a simple objective reporter but always a participant observer. Thus, "personality is made manifest in interpersonal situations, and not otherwise"[23] Sullivan argues that personality is not an entity or a concrete structure that can be perceived, known, or measured. In contrast, it is a temporal phenomenon, a patterning of interaction over time. He suggests that the "ultimate reality in the universe is energy."[24] This assumption is at the foundation of his objection to the language of structure in psychoanalytic theory, which generates psychic entities such as the ego and superego. For him, there are no structures, just the transformation of energy.

Greenberg and Mitchell believe that Sullivan's ideas about energy are as different from Freud's as 20th-Century physics differs from Newtonian physics.[25] Recall that Newton thought the world was constituted by matter and force. Energy acts upon matter, causing movement. Analogously, in Freud, the psychic apparatus is propelled by the drives. In contrast, for contemporary physics, matter is energy — the two are interchangeable. Just as this change in the theorizing about physics is a paradigm shift,[26] Sullivan substitutes in his idea of patterns in energy transformation for concrete and substantial mechanism, which avoids the idea of structure.[27] Thus, for him, psychopathology does not include disease entities but rather patterns of integrating relations with others. It is the relation between an infant and its mother that begins this mediating process. It is through Sullivan's idea of the "tenderness theorem" that we begin to understand that a child needs others for the development of a self, which is very different from the function of Freud's drive theory.

More importantly, we want to delve into Sullivan's vision of what the self is. For him, personality refers to the entire functioning of a person, especially to his patterns of behavior. In contrast, the self refers to how a person experiences himself. One's personality is what one is, and one's self is what one takes oneself to be. In his early work, Sullivan argued that the self is made up of reflected appraisals of significant others.[28] Experiences consistent with appraisals of significant others are organized into the self; experiences incongruent with the appraisals of significant others remain functional within the personality, but since they are outside of awareness, they are not part of the self. Thus the self protects itself through rationalization and self-deception. In his later work, Sullivan holds that the self is no longer just a collection of reflected appraisals. Instead, the self is now a complex organization of experience, derived from but not lifted out of the child's interactions with significant others, and is motivated by the avoidance of anxiety.[29]

It is the self-system for Sullivan that initially regulates access to awareness. As a child ages, this process becomes more complex, leading to what Sullivan calls "security operations." These operations, he says, include "an extravagant, superior formulation of the self" that aids in overcoming anxiety.[30] Through these operations the self-system perpetuates the shape that the self took during early childhood, which perpetuates its isolation within the personality. New kinds of experiences that arouse anxiety are thereby avoided. Further, these operations also evoke the use of old, illusory patterns of interaction with fictitious others in order to avoid anxiety. Yet, this strategy, by borrowing from past integrations, either distorts or obscures actual relatedness in the present. Thus, in Sullivan's system, anxiety about anxiety is the core of all psychopathology; it is the basic organizational principle of the self.[31]

Sullivan distinguishes between needs for security and needs for satisfaction. Needs for satisfaction are selfless and do not require self-reflexivity. Yet, anxiety interrupts this flow, arousing the need for security, which is responded to by the self. For Sullivan, the self moves away from anxiety that emerges in the flow of life by creating an illusory sense of power and control. All security operations are derived from a (false) sense of "I" and have as their mission the protection of the self. This creates a tension between needs for satisfaction and needs for security. The pursuit of satisfactions leads toward constructive integrations with others; in contrast, the pursuit of security leads toward disintegration and non-constructive integrations, as well as to fantasy and illusion.

In contrast with Freud's idea of drives operating within an individual psyche, wherein current relations with others are understood as the transference of internal processes, for Sullivan the basic units are the interpersonal field and the types of relations that emerge from it. The individual psyche is always viewed as a part of this larger whole, within a social context. Sullivan thought that we could not study the human psyche in isolation, that we could only understand it in terms of past and present social relations. Personality, he thought, which is one's habitual patterns of interaction with others, can only illuminate itself in the context of others. We can see from Sullivan's position how much he was at variance with Freud's doctrine of the instincts. For Sullivan, needs for satisfaction necessarily draw humans into relation with others, thus implying the need for an object from infancy. For Freud, the body's erogenous zones are the sources for drive components. For Sullivan, the body's "zones of interaction" are the vehicles for interactional needs. In addition, needs for security, which comprise the need to be free from anxiety, are also relational.

For Sullivan, the content of conflictual areas of the personality are determined not by universal factors but by the character of parental figures and their relationships with their child. Although he views the organization of personality as the product of early relations with significant others, he objects to terms such as "introjection" or "incorporation" which describe these residues in concrete, structural language.[32] As I mentioned earlier, Sullivan thought the reification of psychic processes into structure was problematic. Even so, all psychoanalytic theory rests on *a priori* philosophical principles that it brings to the data. All psychoanalytic theory presumes invisible, hypothetical processes that we cannot directly observe or consciously experience. Nevertheless, even Sullivan could not avoid giving names to hypothetical intervening variables linking an individual's past with his present. Sullivan hints at, and then backs away from, formulating internal structures while still arguing that past residues of interactions with significant others shape our future assumptions.[33]

We want to highlight Sullivan's struggle with psychic structure as well as his determinism. For example, Erich Fromm is very critical of what he thinks is Sullivan's denial of the possibility for the authentic uniqueness of each individual.[34] Greenberg and Mitchell point his "failure to provide a framework for viewing nonpathological, authentic functioning" and his "deterministic approach to the issue of the will."[35] We can see here how Freud's influence has pervaded Sullivan's thought, especially through a review of Sullivan's hesitations surrounding the formation of structure, but also with his determinism. Fromm's criticism, while well-taken and well-meant, does not solve Sullivan's struggle, but it does stimulate us to move in a direction away from the quantification and normalization tendencies of objectivizing thought. Our next step is to take a long look at Sartre's construction of the self, for it opens up phenomenological lines of investigation that counter the Newtonian-Cartesian influence, and which creates new paths for psychological and psychoanalytic exploration. Recall, we are trying to move away from psychology's use of Descartes's materialist construction of the self that makes its exploration fall prey to the unsatisfactory (and borrowed) methodology of contemporary physics.

Sartre

For Sartre, we humans pursue the ideal notion of a substantial self through strategies of self-deception.[36] Add to that the analysts' assumptions that there is self structure or ego structure and that therapeutic process must necessarily

involve re-structuring or new structuring. In contrast
to Freud's reduction of meaning to psychophysiological
drives, Sartre asserts that the primary human aim is to
create value. For Sartre, it is not psychobiological aims
but one's sense of becoming that is the basic human reality.
We attempt to use the world to get a sense of self, which
he calls the "circuit of selfness." This is the perception by
consciousness of its possibilities. Instead of reducing meaning
to neurophysiological forces and evolutionary aims, Sartre
believes that we choose meaning in every act, referring
ourselves to the future rather than to the past, although the
past enters into our future teleology. Thus, my choice of
myself in the world and the world itself are identical. That is,
the self and the world need each other to be what they are.

Without denying the physiological givens of the human
condition, we cannot say that there is first an instinct that
strives for satisfaction through external objects. Rather,
consciousness is desire or lack of a future fullness, but this
desire discovers itself outside in the world rather than in the
recesses of the self.[37] This is not, for Sartre, primarily sexual in
nature, although sexuality is a mode of expression. It is a desire
of Being rather than a desire for pleasure or the cessation
of tension. As an ontological desire, it is not a desire that
consciousness has but a desire or lack which consciousness
is. For Sartre, given that self discovery and creation goes
beyond the satisfaction of elemental physical needs, he does
not require a reductionist system in which the higher activities
of human beings are explained by lower level drives. That is,
consciousness can find fulfillment in any number of activities
that are not necessarily traceable to sexuality.

Consciousness is a lack and, as such, creates its own
fundamental project that varies among individuals. But for
all of us this desire is a desire for a future fullness, which

is the desire to be a substantial self and yet to remain a free consciousness. It is a desire to be an object among objects while remaining free, which is an impossible project according to Sartre. Recall that for him, in contrast to consciousness, which is a lack, being-in-itself is solid and includes a coincidence with itself. Consciousness exists as the negation of being in itself as it moves forward into the future. Because we are consciousness, Sartre thinks that human reality is a perpetual surpassing toward that which it lacks, toward a coincidence with itself that is never given.[38] A synthesis between consciousness and being in itself (the given) is impossible for Sartre, because they can never quite coincide — consciousness is always projecting itself forward. Sartre believes we have hypostatized this impossible synthesis as a transcendence beyond the world, which we call God (who is defined as self-identical, self-conscious, and a full plenitude of being). God is a necessary being, the necessary foundation of himself.[39] Most importantly, because it lacks and desires this self-identical and necessary being, the being of human reality is suffering.[40]

"God" is the *ens causa sui* of the Aristotelian and Thomist project, precisely the combination of a substantial being with a transcending consciousness, the substantiality of an object with human freedom. No matter what I do I am always faced with new freedom and a new possibility for decision. In contrast, I can never be an object like an object is. For instance, I can never be a table like a table is. Thus, I can never establish myself once and for all as a certain kind of person for I can always make a new choice. According to Sartre, we all try to create a self every day. Our fundamental problem, therefore, is how to create a self in a world where one can never quite coincide with the self that one has just created. Thus, we have personality and other psychological tests that try to help me figure out who I am in the substantive sense. The serious man identifies with his role by hiding from himself that he has a free consciousness in order to attain a substantial self. This, for Sartre, is the attempt to create oneself as an object, and is essentially the Freudian position, self as object. Nevertheless, the strategy of believing that my ego is my nature or character is in bad faith, an illusion, because it hides the fact that we have a spontaneous facet to ourselves that can always make a new choice.[41] For Sartre, Freud's position of "seriousness" is false because it denies one's presence to the world as conscious choice.

If we analyze Sartre's construction of the self, perhaps we can understand how it is that the self is not an object, that it is always beyond the sort of quantification and measurement psychology has been subjecting it to from the beginning of Wundt's experimental laboratories. As Hazel Barnes carefully points out, Sartre uses the term "self" in three different ways, even though he does not formally make these distinctions.[42] First, there is the spontaneous self of pre-reflective consciousness, which is the center of action; this is the self as agent. Second, there is the self of reflective awareness, which Sartre calls the "ego," and which is an object rather than a subject. Third, there is the self as aim or value; this is the self which is the future goal and meaning of human activity, one's project of being. This is the self as a pursuit and not as an actual entity. Although it can be reflected upon it is frequently misconceived. According to Sartre, this self is frequently conceived in terms of the aim of substantive freedom, which we have been discussing above.

Such a pursuit of self or meaning is never isolated and always occurs through the interfacing of the body with the world. According to this view, the enclosed psyche of Freudian theory is not a possibility, for it is only the reflective glance backward or forward that gives one a sense of having a

self in the substantive sense, which we are arguing is false
and illusory. The post-Freudian relational theorists create a
theoretical problematic when they confuse the self as agent
with the self as object.[43] Thus, psychotherapists who follow
the relational views — and the concomitant confusion about
the self — only serve to perpetuate the illusion and pursuit of
the self as substance, falling into bad faith themselves.

It is true that most of contemporary psychoanalysis is
operating within an Aristotelian framework. According to
Aristotle, everything is composed of form and substance.
Each thing or entity also is imbued with a potential that it
might realize. When applied to the human realm we end
up with a psychology that pursues a true self or something
like it. In this system the goal is to free oneself from a
false construction of that self in order to realize one's true
potential. In contrast, Sartre would argue that the pre-
reflective self lacks structure and substance. In this line of
thought, pre-reflective choice, but not the realization of some
a priori potentiality, is at the center of human experience.
Recall Sartre's famous line that "existence precedes essence."
What this means is that the self as ego, the reflected upon
self, is given form and substance only by the pre-reflective
self. In this mode, the self becomes a pseudo object; it is
no longer a living consciousness, but rather only an image
or representation of that consciousness. Thus, there is a
confusion in treating the self as object as a real experiencing
self rather than as a mere construct of consciousness.

The pre-reflective self is the wellspring for the other two
modes of selfness, for Sartre. It is not a potentiality of an
inner essence to be realized but rather carries with it a field
of possibilities as it interfaces with the world. Possibility
for one's life is not an inner potency waiting to be realized.
Instead, it emerges from one's awareness and interpretation

of one's future within the world. Recall that according to Sartre, human reality is a lack. Consciousness is aware of a gap between itself and its objects of desire, which it lacks. This awareness of distance between self and the world is "nothingness," and even mere awareness is a nihilating act, he thinks. Thus, nihilation is the kind of distantiation that allows the world to be for me. It is through an awareness of the distinction between myself and the objects I desire that I am an intentional being, that I become conscious of things. In contrast, a consciousness that was completely full of being (the impossible synthesis) could not encounter the world. As Cannon correctly points out, "the Freudian psyche so often appears to be a closed intrapsychic system: Its substantiality leaves no room for the world."[44] Pre-reflective consciousness, for Sartre, has none of the attributes normally associated with the personality, and it is only personal in the sense of being present to itself. Since pre-reflective consciousness is translucid it contains none of the structural properties normally associated with the human subject.

The pre-reflective self is only an awareness of the gap between the self and the world, but not yet an awareness of the self as object. In this mode the self is aware of not being the material world or coinciding with any particular interpretation of the world. It is an openness to being, an awareness of temporal continuity. Since it is pre-reflective we cannot even talk about it as an "I" or a "me." For Sartre, both "I" and "me" are objects, not subjects, in ordinary discourse because they come after reflection and the consciousness that characterizes them is beyond the object being characterized. The self of pre-reflective consciousness is never equivalent to the self of reflective consciousness. Reflective judgments about the self crystallize into the ego; this is not one of the elements of the Freudian tripartite structure but is rather the whole psyche. In distinction to the pre-reflective self, which is translucid, the ego is opaque. According to Sartre, the ego "is neither formally nor materially *in* consciousness: it is outside, *in the world*."[45] The act of regarding oneself as an object is similar to the apprehending of other objects in the world and thus also open to error.

Given Sartre's premise that the ego is an object for consciousness, personality traits are not a source but a product of one's reflective view of the self. The ego is "the transcendent unity of states and actions," which is an ideal whole that is created out of past states and actions.[46] In positing the "I" aspect of the ego, consciousness sees itself as the transcendent unity of these past actions. I can also make my past feelings and actions into the "me" aspect of the ego. For instance, one's hatreds and loves can come to define oneself. Yet hatred and love are states that can only appear to reflective consciousness. Pre-reflectively, one may feel repugnance or anger in someone's presence, but hatred and love imply a permanence that momentary emotions do not have. Thus, when I claim a hatred for someone I have made my hatred an object in consciousness, which it can never really be, or a motive for behavior, which it is not. Thus, Sartre says, the "faults, virtues, tastes, talents, tendencies, instincts, etc." which we attribute to ourselves and others are only hypothetical qualities.[47] We view them as potentialities or forces within ourselves, but they are really reifications of repeated feelings or actions. They, just as the ego, only exist *a posteriori*, even though they are commonly thought of as the source of the characteristics that define them.

The ego even seems to have claims on the future as well as the past. Thus, if I have been a certain sort of person in the past, I can say that I will be this in the future.[48] The purpose of constructing an ego may be to give the impression of substantiality or security regarding the future. It may be that the flux of the pre-reflective consciousness is just too terrifying to maintain especially because a future self may betray my present self by making a radically different choice in the world. Accordingly, Sartre maintains that "perhaps the essential role of the ego is to mask from consciousness its very spontaneity."[49] By creating the ego one attempts to substantialize consciousness, and this process always results in a distorted view of oneself given that it always involves a strategy to hide one's radical freedom. A further danger that we will take up in our later discussion of Lacan is present when one substitutes in one's own judgments about oneself with judgments from significant others.[50]

The third aspect of the self for Sartre involves the self as a value-making enterprise as it heads into its future possibilities. It is the self as value because it is that which consciousness lacks and therefore desires. This lack is a lack of self and the ultimate pursuit is substantial freedom, as we have been saying. As we are aware that we are not various objects we see and imagine, we also are aware of ourselves as a general lack. Thus, the self as value is a self-making process but not an actual entity. Although pursuit of the future is not necessarily reflective it can be. Yet, much of life is lived unreflectively. In contrast, when we reflect we enter into a value making process as we characterize ourselves as this or that. If we understand that the self we are trying to make will never be finished, that it is just a lifetime pursuit, then we are acting in good faith. But there is always a temptation toward bad faith. This is an inclination toward believing either that one is not the self one has been because one has no connection with those previous choices, or that one is or will become the self that one is pursuing. Recall that for Sartre it is not the ego that is the source of one's character, actions, and states; instead, this is just a product of free choice and we can always make another choice.

When we apply these concepts to the practice of
psychotherapy, we must recognize that one has the
responsibility of creating value, not finding it. We must
attempt to overcome the serious belief that we are a product
of external forces, for all time, and realize that we have the
freedom to take new positions and make new interpretations
of our current situation. We must attempt to release
ourselves from the illusion of substance and transform this
into a commitment of responsibility for a life that we are
always making but that never completes itself. This requires
us to repudiate or transcend the ego. Recall that for the
contemporary relational psychoanalysts, the primary human
motivation is to pursue a self, not pleasure. Some think the
self has structure and substance, and some such as Sullivan
are not sure and perhaps view the self less as an entity and
more as a process. Thus, instead of fostering the belief in
a substantial self, therapists and analysts can embark on a
different project that would transcend the need to create such
a self. For the most part, the establishment of a firm identity,
self, or ego has been the goal of psychoanalytic theory
from the ego psychologists to the self psychologists. Even
Sullivan falls short as he stumbles with his own formulation
of the nature of the self and its healthy development. Even
though Sullivan does not regard the experiencing subject
as a thing, he does advocate the ultimate human aim to be
the maximization of security and lack of dissonance. Sartre,
however, would argue that this search for a secure self is in
bad faith and illusory.

In Sartre's world, the self is never self-identical. That is,
consciousness can never coincide with itself because it is
always at a distance with itself, and this is because of its
temporalizing nature. We are never just what we have
chosen for the present, because of future possibilities,
and this works in the reverse as well. On the reflective

level, the consciousness reflecting is never equivalent to
the consciousness reflected on. The moment I look at my
spontaneous actions I am no longer the spontaneous choice
of myself which I previously was. Instead of pursuing a
substantial self, which is what both the drive theorists and
the relational theorists attempt to do, the nature of the self in
all of its modes suggests that we view the self not as a thing
but more as an unfinished process. Pursuing a *what* gives way
to pursuing a *way* of being. In this transformation, we must
realize that the pre-reflective self is mere translucidity and
temporality. It is no thing at all, which may have significant
consequences for psychotherapy. Thus, instead of shoring up
the structure of a client's ego or self, which ironically may be
part of the pursuit of a substantial self by the therapist, the
new goal would be to recognize that there is no substantial
self at all, just the process of time moving forward.

The Sartrean approach to psychology can help individuals
see the futility in trying to create a substantial self,
especially by using others to do it. This wards off any
kind of psychotherapeutic practice that attempts to build
structure, but moreover, would encourage us toward a kind
of pure reflection.[51] Pure reflection, as opposed to impure
reflection, is the presence of the consciousness reflecting
to the consciousness reflected on. It is a realization of and
confrontation with our spontaneous capacity for freedom.[52]
For Sartre, pure reflection "keeps to the given without setting
up claims for the future."[53] The essence of pure reflection
is that it lacks a motivation for making choices that falsely
pursue a substantial self, for the self is not a static object. It is
the realization of oneself as pre-reflective spontaneity without
any further goal.

Sartre's views about the self offer quite a challenge to all
the schools of contemporary psychology, but let us continue

to focus on psychoanalysis, as a therapeutic application
of psychological theory. Sartre provides us with a clear
conception of the self that can be used to further develop
the valuable insights of the relational theorists. If we do not
understand the nature of the self as Sartre presents it then
we may fall back into the trap of objectifying the humans
we are trying to treat. It is our contention that this strategy
misses a fuller, richer, and more comprehensive view of who
we are as humans. By focusing on the pre-reflective aspect
of consciousness, psychotherapists can help clients and
patients validate the spontaneity of their free choice. This
moves away from an objectivizing practice and encourages
the valorization of individuals. Since the pre-reflective
aspect of the self is translucid and not opaque, all therapeutic
attempts to build structure must be abandoned. Instead of
re-poisoning the client, therapists can focus a client's efforts
on re-conceptualizing a faulty relation between pre-reflective
and reflective consciousness. Instead of incorporating new
value from the therapist (and therefore new structure), the
client attains a new way of being with his pre-reflective self.

Recall that according to Sartre, we are faced with the desire
for a substantial self. This desire, in my view, is a product
of our historical era, including the Cartesian-Newtonian
influence. The danger is that clients and patients come
looking for new selves, carrying anxiety about the new self
they obtain in the therapeutic process. But this is all a red
herring at best and, at worst, a perpetuation of bad faith.
Instead of investigating so-called unconscious phenomena,
therapists would look for reflective distortions of spontaneous
experience and strategies used to construct a reified self.
What we will find in a later section on Michel Foucault is the
danger that occurs through the objectification of patients by
psychotherapists. With Sartre's plan, a therapist does not fix
the meaning of symbols beforehand and, instead, allows them

to emerge within the context of one's history. This would
encourage individuals to convert to an approach of radical,
ontological freedom, instead of believing in the possibility of a
fixed self. Now that we have taken a look at a Sartrean-styled
criticism of both drive theory and object relations theory, let
us also see how this phenomenological criticism works in the
case of Jacques Lacan.

Psychoanalysis: Lacan

Lacan bases his theory of the unconscious on language and
transforms Freud's pronouncements about the family and the
body into assertions about culture. For him, psychoanalytic
theory becomes a study of the construction of the subject in
language.[54] Repressed unconscious desire becomes the search
for meaning in language. The symbolic father of the Oedipal
struggle becomes the power relations imbedded within
language. Finally, sexual difference noticed through the penis
becomes the basis for all difference in meaning. Lacan, like
Heidegger, is a complex thinker, and it is not our purpose
here to present a full-length analysis or criticism of his work.
We do, however, wish to focus on his metapsychology and
to take a look at some of his basic assumptions so as to
understand his own scientific positivism, especially relative to
that of Freud's.

Lacan believes that the unconscious can only be accessed
though speech and writing. He is interested in Freud's dream
analysis and techniques of free association, and he argued that
the unconscious was structured like a language. In his quest,
Lacan appropriates Saussure's linguistic theories in order to
conceptualize the unconscious as part of an endless chain of
unconscious meanings that we can find only in language in the
spaces between conscious meanings. He modifies Saussure's
structural model of meaning by arguing that there is an

endless signifying chain from the conscious construction of meaning down to the unconscious, which constantly reveals itself in language. A sign is a physical object that has meaning just like a word, and it has two parts. The first part is the signifier, which is the physical, tangible part of the sign, such as characters on paper or an object of some sort. The signified is the meaning that is attached to the signifier.

For Lacan, it is the interdependence of both the words and the gaps, such as hesitations, blunders, and sighs, that endow the whole system with meaning. No signifier can signify independently of other signifiers; it is the differences between them that give the meaning. For example, "love" has a different meaning from "live." Standing at the limit of the differentiations of meaning is material plenitude or totality, including psychosis and death. This is the realm of the "Real," which we will discuss. Recall that Freud uses two concepts to interpret dreams, including displacement and condensation. Lacan transforms these Freudian terms into his own linguistic paradigm, labeling them as metaphor, which is the identification of one known with another known, and as metonymy, where a part stands in for a whole. He argues that these two concepts explain the connections between signifying chains of conscious meaning.

According to Lacan, subjectivity emerges from these strings of interconnecting meanings and structures in language. Personal identity arises from the way personal narratives are created within these meanings. This Lacanian subject is always inhabited by the "Other," which is comprised of all others and other significations within the overall linguistic structure. The subject, or self, always carries around the Other with it and has no inherent substance, personality, or traits of its own; it is dependent upon the intersubjectivity of language for its very existence. In contrast to the object relations theorists which we discuss in the next section, the subject is not an empty container that gets filled up with objects, i.e., its relations with others. In fact, signifying processes are seen as a series of events, and the construction of personal identity takes place through these events. Further, our view of the world is always constrained by the pre-determined meanings that exist. The complete linguistic structure in which one lives is the universe from which one's self can emerge; the danger is that we can never step outside these pre-determined meanings. They act as Kantian filters and mediate our experience of the world, others, and ourselves from our very foundation in being. Thus, we can only interpret reality in terms of the language that we use, the language that speaks us. Further, it is through our use of language in our search for knowledge that we live our repressed desires.

In Lacan's universe, sexuality is the not the mere pursuit of bodily pleasure. In his structural theory, he eroticizes language by linking meaning with underlying bodily desires. Intersubjectivity is made possible by the emergence of repressed desire in language, which propels us from one meaning to another. In fact, we achieve repression through language by driving our unconscious desires downward into the space between words, in our speech acts. A child's discovery of the phallus based on sexual difference is the initial experience for understanding all forms of difference in meaning. Further, identity and language are created in order to attain mastery of the emotional loss of the mother. Language represents symbolic castration of the father, a castration and loss of total fulfillment each of us must recognize before one can become a human self. Yet, language at both the conscious and unconscious levels operates as the possibility of freedom, personal identity, and the attainment of truth because it offers an infinite range of interpretations of our experience.

Lacan rejects the object relations idea that our identity can ever be authentic or coherent. He asserts that our identifications only lead to a sense of identity, not an actual identity, but that it is always based on a misrecognition. In addition to the Real, Lacan divides his structural theory into two other parts, including the Imaginary and the Symbolic. It is within the Imaginary and the Symbolic realms that we create ourselves. Using Freud's idea of primary narcissism, Lacan asserts that when we are infants we initially exist in an undifferentiated ego mass with the mother. Eventually, within this morass of emotion, sensations, and drives, we begin to sense that we have a distinct self with definable boundaries. This is the realm of the Imaginary. Yet this identity is always based on an image of oneself that is reflected back from someone else, much like the reflection from a mirror. He calls this the mirror stage.[55] The person we usually identify with at first is our mother, but although this sense of identity appears real to us it is not because it depends on something external. This early sense of identity comes when we feel, unconsciously, a coherent sense of self through the eyes of the other, even though otherwise our self is dissipated and dispersed. In this state, our self or ego is never our own because it depends solely on our identifications, including people, things, and ideas.

Lacan also argues that we establish another kind of identity, what he calls subjectivity (in translation). We acquire this new kind of identity in the Symbolic realm as we acquire language. Here, we think that the apparently fixed meanings in language give us a much more stable sense of identity, and we look for the truth of who we are in language. By believing that these relatively stable meanings can give us some coherence to our identity, we attach ourselves to the way we define ourselves linguistically. Yet, even in the realm of the Symbolic we do not gain the stable sense of identity that we want. The unconscious reappears in the spaces between words. There is always a gap between our unfulfilled wishes and the language we use to convey identity and desire. This means that for Lacan, phonetic relationships between words are more salient than semantic ones. They may reveal unconscious meanings that are different from the conscious ones.

Our belief that there are stabilized meanings always runs the risk of being de-stabilized by unconscious desire and early loss. There is always a gap between the conscious "I" that we construct and a deeper, unconscious sense of who we are. Lacan seizes upon this assumption and argues that our conscious identity, which we formulate through the use of the regular and conventional categories of language, is always false. The identity we create through language, in the Symbolic realm of consciousness and culture, is only another reflected identity without substance. For him, it is no different than the imaginary one we created in the mirror stage, in the Imaginary realm. So, there are two identities. There is the pre-verbal, bodily one that gets constructed in the mirror stage in the Imaginary realm; there is also the one that gets constructed in the social, cultural Symbolic realm.[56]

Lacan's argument is that we psychologically invest in false images of ourselves in both the Imaginary and Symbolic realms. He believes that there is a fictional element in the construction of our identities from the ground up, and utilizes Freud's theory of narcissism and stress on language as a form of the mastery of early loss. Yet, a major distinction between the two concerns how they view the status of the ego. For Freud, the ego really is a substantial self that can develop from a primitive state of narcissism. In contrast, for Lacan the ego is always false because it is based on reflections in the Imaginary realm.

Lacan replaces Freud's structural model of identity that includes the Id, the Ego, and the Superego with his own system that represents, not parts of one self-identity, but rather various intersubjective, structural orders. We can use these structural orders to analyze the construction of identity. Lacan replaces Freud's concept of biological drive (instinct) with the process of searching for meaning and identity through language, a constant appeal to the Other through language in the hopes of locating the final truth about ourselves. We lose access to the mother's body during the Oedipal crisis, which propels us into a constant search for this lost unity and self-completion in the Imaginary realm. We use linguistic substitutes in the Symbolic realm in the attempt to fill the emptiness caused by this lost unity, but it is an impossible search. Both Freud and Lacan believe that the fulfillment of our desires is an impossible task. For Lacan, symbolic castration by the father, which is represented by the constraints language puts on reality, sets limits to our desires that are created in the Imaginary by coercing us into culturally acceptable meanings and behavior.

In language we find our subjectivity, but we will never find the ultimate meaning about who we are because language cuts us off from the object of our desire, which is the mother from which we lost unity. This object of our desire, the lost mother, exists in the realm of the Real, which is everything that lies beyond the symbolic process. This realm exists in both the mental and physical worlds and includes the ineffable, pre-Imaginary plenitude that we seek out with futility. This plenitude, the all, the lost unity, always lies out of reach of the Imaginary realm and the kind of subjectivity language seems to offer us in the Symbolic realm. The Real includes not only this impossible plenitude, but the materiality of objects, psychosis (where all of the symbolic order is rejected), and death, which is where the real triumphs over subjectivity and meaning. Yet, even though language cuts us off from the objects of our desire (mother and mother substitutes) it returns desire to us. It provides us with a new sense of identity as we move from one meaning to the next in a constant pursuit of correspondence between our constructed subjectivity and the lost plenitude. Language becomes the transformative site for the Oedipal crisis, standing in for the actual father. In fact, language becomes the Other and places itself between us and the objects of our desire, constantly de-stabilizing and moving these objects so that we never reach them. Desire for Lacan is futile. So, even though it is language that hollows the being of the Imaginary realm, it is also through language, through the pursuit of meaning, that we can articulate the fullness of the imaginary and the imagined plenitude.

Lacan makes a distinction between the imagined father (the actual father) and the symbolic father (paternal metaphor). According to Lacan, even in the absence of the father, the child experiences the paternal metaphor, the place of the father, as well as the Oedipal conflict, through language. The child is severed from its object of desire, the mother, through the intrusiveness of the representations of language. The loss of the mother is a hole that gets filled up through grammatical rules and laws of the construction of meaning. The rational categories of language represent the cutting off from or castration of the child from the imaginary realm. They also represent the transformation of the child's need to be the phallus for the mother into an insatiable desire for knowledge and the truth about who one is. The difference between what we are and what we want to be is the foundation of the construction of knowledge and identity, in his system.

At the same time a child is subjected to the laws of language it also recognizes its gender, through sexual difference, by

noticing the phallus.[57] The symbolic father signifies this
sexual difference through his association with the phallus,
which is a sign of power and not the actual physical penis.
This symbolizes sexual difference (the recognition of which
blooms during the Oedipal phase) as well as the underlying
difference between those that have and those that do not. The
unconscious becomes a container for the loss of the mother,
and the associated desire is incited by the recognition that
the child (of either sex) cannot have the phallus the mother
wants. The girl lacks the penis; the boy fears castration.
Thus, the phallus symbolizes both desire and loss. Further, it
signals to the child that having a viable identity can only come
at the price of the loss of the mother and that being human
can only come about as the consequence of the division into
consciousness and the unconscious.

Thus, the child recognizes that identities that are not fused
with the mother in the Imaginary realm come into being
through language, the Symbolic realm, as a result of the
perception of sexual difference, which is represented by the
phallus. The metaphor of the father, which is symbolized by
the phallus, mandates that the child must take its place within
a family that is defined by sexual difference. This allows the
child to understand the concepts of same and difference.
This difference that is represented by the phallus also teaches
the child the concept of exclusion, because it cannot be its
parents' lover, as well as the concept of absence, because of
the loss of the mother. The child thereby forms its identity
based on an unconscious recognition of difference, exclusion,
and absence. Lacan links the sexual world symbolized by the
phallus with the symbolic world of language. As the child
discovers sexual difference it also starts to acquire language.
In its discovery of language the child unconsciously learns
that the units of language only have meaning because they are
different from other units and that signifiers, like the phallus,

can represent things that are absent. Words stand in for objects and operate as metaphors. As the child unconsciously learns about the meaning of sexuality in the discovery of exclusion and difference it also learns about meanings based on difference and exclusion in language. Thus, it moves isomorphically from the bodily, pre-verbal realm into the cultural, linguistic realm of culture. Recognition of the metaphor of the father in the sexual realm prefigures the recognition of the linguistic and symbolic law.

When the metaphor of the father — the phallus — invades the child's Imaginary relation with the mother, it creates the underlying logic and law of how we perceive the world within language and culture. This third term, i.e., the father, alienates the child from the mother simultaneously as it plants itself as pre-established meaning and law. As we have said, this process operates through the concept of difference, and sets limits to our search for meaning through the rules of logic and grammar. These limits create symbolic castration by cutting us off from what we desire while allowing us to enter into culture and to become subjects. Here, we can see Lacan's linking of the psychosexual dimension with the dimension of culture. We unconsciously recognize the phallus as a sign that is a precursor to all signs in language. Language is comprised of empty chains of meanings that have arbitrary assignments so that we can live together in community. By entering into language from the foundation of the phallus, we become members of society with particular subjectivities.

Yet, Lacan recognizes that the power of the phallus is arbitrary and that there is always a misrecognition of its perceived power (where females always signify a lack and boys have the chance to achieve the paternal metaphor). The meaning of the phallus is, therefore, spurious. Given that it is the first signifier on which all other symbolic meanings are based, what follows also involves misrecognition of the identity within language that we create in order to cover up our pain because of the loss of the mother. As a boy begins to recognize his sexual difference he also realizes, unconsciously, castration by the father. He experiences powerlessness. Likewise, as a girl recognizes her sexual identity, she must also accept that she, too, lacks what her mother wants, which includes cultural power and social identity. She constitutes herself negatively, as a lack, because she does not possess the phallus, and this is in addition to her losing the union with her mother's body. Effects for both genders are repressed into their unconscious, according to Lacan.

Lacan asserts that at an unconscious level we understand the illusory nature of the construction of identity that is based on the spuriousness of the phallus. He bases this on Freud's belief that the unconscious constantly subverts the intended meanings of language. Language forces us to abandon the Imaginary realm, but it is also the best source of identification that we have. Through the entry into language we achieve some kind of mastery over our original desire and loss of the loved object. We do this within the rational, objective, and coherent construction of meaning through that language even though this domain never quite satisfies our deep craving for unity. The seduction comes from the apparent stability of meaning within language. For Lacan, the strategy of attempting to ground the meaning of who we are through language, through the foundational metaphor of the phallus is futile, and engages us in an endless search for the meaning of who we are, for our completion. This metaphor functions as a pivotal structural concept that ostensibly regulates all other meanings. Yet, for Lacan, the phallus has no status in reality and our unconscious is aware of this more or less.

In Lacan's conception of the unconscious, there is a constant concealment and distortion of meaning. In free association there is a constant dissolving and evaporation of meaning, as he says, "an incessant sliding of the signified under the signifier."[58] That is, veiled unconscious meanings may be different from the conscious meanings lying at the surface. In terms of our identifications with various discourses of truth about who we are, we think that we achieve a coherent and unified identity. For Lacan, recall that this occurs at the level of the Imaginary ego. Thus, when we believe in any stability and truth in language and knowledge, in actuality we make an imaginary identification with an image of ourselves that is reflected back to us from words whose meanings are as illusory as the identities we build on the basis of them.[59] There is, therefore, a split in our identity between what we are and what we take ourselves to be. For example, when we make an assertion of the kind "I am going to do x," the "I" that is the subject of the sentence is different from the "I" that is doing the enunciating. The "I" of the sentence covers up the "I" that is doing the speaking. We think that both are unified into one self, but they are not, for this conclusion is only in the Imaginary realm. There is no sign that can sum up my entire being and therefore it is impossible to represent. In fact, most of what I am can never be represented through language. For him, the subject is always constructed through the transforming of the Imaginary into the Symbolic, in which we transfer the experience of our senses into the world of the signifer, the world of which we speak.

Now let us explore Lacan's metapsychology of the subject more carefully. Lacan attacks the idea of an essentialist subject that is transparent to itself and fully representable in theoretical discourse. It is this Cartesian subject which is also the subject of the humanist tradition that Lacan calls into question, just as Freud did. For Lacan, "it is nonetheless true that the philosophical *cogito* is at the centre of the mirage that renders modern man so sure of himself even in his uncertainties about himself."[60] Yet, this essentialist illusion, which reduces subjectivity to the conscious ego, reveals itself as a "myth of the unity of the personality, the myth of synthesis . . . all these types of organisation of the objective field constantly reveal cracks, tears and rents, negation of the facts and misrecognition of the most immediate experience."[61] As Lacan says it in the "Freudian Thing," as a result of Freud's discovery of the unconscious, the "very centre of the human being is no longer to be found at the place assigned to it by the humanist tradition."[62] Further, Lacan also opposes any project that asserts the autonomy of the essentialist subject, saying that "the discourse of freedom . . . [is] fundamentally biased and incomplete, inexpressible, fragmentary, differentiated, and profoundly delusional."[63] In fact, it is the very subversion of the subject as *cogito* that makes psychoanalysis possible.[64]

For Lacan, the essence of man is not to be found in his conscious representation of himself.[65] In fact, the subject is not a psychological substratum that can be reduced to its own representation. If, indeed, there is an essence in the Lacanian subject it is as a lack of essence.[66] Nevertheless, his subject is different from the traditional metaphysical notion of the subject that is at the heart of the *cogito*. He takes Freud's idea of *Spaltung*, or splitting, in reference to fetishism and psychosis and generalizes it as constitutive of all humans. Thus, the self is radically ex-centric to itself, heteronomous rather than autonomous, and more attached to the other than to itself.[67] For Lacan, the ego is different from the subject. The ego is a sedimentation of idealized images that are internalized during the mirror stage, which we explained above. Yet, there is always a gap between the imaginary ego and the lived experience of one's body, beginning in infancy. This gap implies that the ego is always an alien alter ego, "whereby the desiring human subject is constructed around a center that is the other insofar as he gives the subject his unity."[68]

Any imaginary unity based on the mirror stage is founded on an irreducible gap: "the human being has a special relation with its own image – a relation of gap, of alienating tension."[69] Unity in the Imaginary is a result of captivation, of a power relation between the infant and its image. This captivation, which anticipates unity and synthesis, does not eliminate the alienating character of its own foundation. Thus, we attempt to identify with anything outside ourselves in order to recover the lost unity. Yet, what seems to be ours always contains an element of difference and alienation. As Yannis Stavrakakis says, "this alienating dimension of the ego, the constitutive dependence of every imaginary identity on the alienating exteriority of a never fully internalised mirror image, subverts the whole idea of a stable reconciled subjectivity based on a conception of an autonomous ego."[70]

It is because the imaginary image of ourselves does not give us a stable identity that we seek it out in the symbolic register, through language. We are not speaking chronologically here, but logically, in that the symbolic always presupposed the imaginary and even pre-exists as a network of anticipated meanings even before birth. Thus, Lacan says that "while the image equally plays a capital role in our domain . . . this role is completely taken up and caught up within, remoulded and reanimated by, the symbolic order. The image is always more or less integrated into this order."[71] Whereas the ego is formed in the Imaginary, the subject emerges in the Symbolic. In fact, the subject takes its very structure from the signifier, which is constitutive for it. The subject of the signifier is the subject of lack, which carries power with it at its very foundation, i.e., the loss of certain possibilities, as well as its acceptance of the Symbolic realm. As it enters into the Symbolic it is constituted through power, and it is, therefore, subordinated to those to which it is attached.

The signifier is the very epicenter of the power that forms the subject and is based on the recognition of difference as well as a certain order. It is psychoanalysis that is the science of the signifier, as applied to the formation of subjectivity. Lacan argues that the symbolic function of psychoanalysis situates it in the "heart of the movement that is now establishing a new order of the sciences, with a new putting in question of anthropology."[72] Further, he claims that "this new order signifies nothing more than a return to a conception of true science whose claims have been inscribed in a tradition beginning with Plato's *Theaetetus*. This conception has become degraded, as we know, in the positivist reversal which, by making the human sciences the crowning glory of the experimental sciences, in actual fact made them subordinate to experimental sciences."[73] Lacan continues his criticism of our modern conception of science by saying that "our physics is simply a mental fabrication whose instrument is the mathematical symbol [and that] experimental science is not so much defined by the quantity to which it is in fact applied, as by the measurement it introduces into the real."[74] Lacan, indeed, was wrestling with scientific methodology, and believed that linguistics could be the foundation for a new scientific order.

Lacan's advice was to "read Saussure."[75] Furthermore, it was Freud himself who saw language as the foundation for his discourse of the unconscious. Lacan recognized this when he asserted that Freud's goal had always been to explore an elaboration of the linguistic structure of dreams, that Freud had already recognized the primary status of language.[76] Thus, Lacan's goal was to reconstruct Freud in

terms of modern linguistics. Even so, we must keep firmly
in mind that Freud's failure to develop beyond the paradigm
of nineteenth century materialist science contributed to
the failure of contemporary psychoanalytic theorists to get
beyond the illusion of substance as they attempted to describe
the development of the ego or self. What remains to be seen is
whether Lacan overcomes the influence of the natural science
model on psychology. In order to explore this, we will take a
look at Lacan, from a Sartrean perspective.

Lacan and Sartre

Lacan agrees with Sartre that the ego is an object, not a
subject, of experience, and that therapeutic attempts to
develop ego structure are misguided. In contrast to Sartre's
belief that humans can transform their behavior and
attitudes into more authentic experience, Lacan believes
the best we can do is accept that we are determined by the
linguistic unconscious. For Sartre, we discover ourselves as
objects of others, but because of the pre-reflective aspect of
consciousness we can overcome this. In contrast, for Lacan
we literally take the other for ourselves and we can never
overcome this fundamental alienation. Further, Lacan is a
structuralist and believes that language speaks the person.
Thus, he is also a reductionist who is searching for a scientific
explanation for psychic phenomena that is experience
distant and not experience near. In contrast to Freud, who
discovers this in our biology, Lacan finds this in structural
linguistics. Sartre, of course, objects to Lacan's determinism
because it prevents the possibility of free and authentic action
of individuals. Here we can see Sartre's prioritization of
consciousness over Lacan's idea of the structural unconscious.

Yet there is some agreement between the two. Sartre would
agree with Lacan's belief that the ego is an object that is more

often an object of misunderstanding than of understanding. Lacan echoes Sartre when he compares the subject to a paralytic who has been hypnotized by his image in a mirror — the ego. Sartre had similarly described the ego as a false representation of itself with which consciousness has hypnotized itself.[77] Sartre's subject is stultified by the image of a substantial self whereas Lacan's subject is hypnotized by the substitution for a self of its own mirror image, and both agree that the rigidity of the ego must be questioned. Derivatively, both thinkers criticize psychoanalytic attempts to build ego structure, given that the ego is illusory for them.

Even so, for Sartre, the therapeutic enterprise would involve building a new reflective relationship with the ego; for Lacan, the ego is a fundamental alienation that can be acknowledged but not overcome. According to Lacan, even though human conflicts may appear on the horizon of the experience of the gaze, their actual origin is not the desire to co-opt the Other as a mirror for me as an object. Instead, their origin comes from the desire to mimic the other and gain a self. Thus, Lacan rejects Sartre's fundamental ontology.[78] For Lacan, both the self and the other are objects, never subjects, which prevents the kind of positive social transformation that is possible within Sartre's ontology, in terms of viewing both the self and others as subjects that are deserving of respect. In Lacan's metapsychology, we all are objects merely trying to capture an image of wholeness by means of which the Other originally captured what might have been a self. In fact, the Lacanian ego is otherness absolutely and completely, and this means that there is no transcendent consciousness that can reflectively alter or develop the ego. In contrast, for Sartre, we can purify the ego by understanding that we are never trapped or determined by it. Here, we give up the false hope of attaining a substantialization of the self by understanding that the ego is only an effect and not a cause. In this process, we would understand that the ego is just a story that we and others tell about ourselves and that this story can be changed as we re-interpret our memories of the past. There are two parts to the ego for Sartre. There are the judgments of others and a reflective *ipseity* that allows us to accept or reject those judgments of others. This reflective capacity could allow for a radical conversion to a philosophy of freedom that promotes authentic relations with others.

As a structuralist, Lacan tries to reduce psychic phenomena to unconscious linguistic structures by removing human intentionality and meaning. By reducing the conscious subject to an "effect of the signifier," Lacan precludes meaningful transformation.[79] His structuralism, as a new positivism, has moved from a determinism based on historical causation to a determinism based on unconscious structural causation. Both forms of determinism are manifestations of an analytical reductionism that misses out on the power of Sartre's idea of intentional *praxis*. For Lacan, we are just playthings of the linguistic unconscious, which prevents us from using language as *praxis*. On this point, see Ragland-Sullivan, who notes that Lacan was "generally pessimistic about the possibilities of altering the Symbolic order."[80] This is consonant with his position that there is no transcendent subject who could possibly effect such change.

Even though Sartre also believes that language inscribes the other into the heart of each person's being, he thinks that we have freedom in how we live that otherness. Such otherness is unconscious in the sense that it is not usually examined, but it is not unconscious in the sense of being beyond consciousness. There is a continuum of sorts between living ourselves in language as *hexis* or as *praxis*. Lacan's position — what Sartre would call *hexis* — is that language speaks us; as such, we are inert objects that are pure otherness and there is no chance for transcendence. As an inert repository of past *praxes*, language is always an invitation to *hexis*. Using language inserts us into a cultural order and, as a result, otherness inscribes itself into our own intentional projects. Sartre's position, on the other hand, is that we can live language as *praxis*, which means to use it creatively and intentionally. It is the creative aspect of language that Lacan avoids. By neglecting intentionality and denigrating consciousness, Lacan's position becomes very close to the one Sartre ascribes to Flaubert.[81] By placing the source of otherness inside the linguistic unconsciousness, Lacan considers normal the kind of alienation Sartre describes in his concept of *hexis*. Lacanian alienation is unsurpassable because it is solely this Otherness that has created me as a speaking subject. For Lacan we always enter into a world that is filled with symbols, and we can never return to a place that is outside the cultural-linguistic order. Thus, as Ragland-Sullivan asserts, Lacan does not include an intentional element in his idea of consciousness. "Instead, consciousness has become a mode of perception which negotiates Desire via substitutions."[82] It is in the dimension of the Other, the unconsciousness, that "the recognition of desire is bound up with the desire for recognition."[83] Thus, it is there in the repressed primal relationship with the mother and in the linguistic laws which have been placed there after the encounter with the primal signifier that the various substitutions one uses make sense. For Lacan, the most one can do is to understand that we are the playthings of the linguistic unconscious, that one is a signified rather than a signifer, an object pretending to be a subject. In contrast, Sartre thinks that we can use language in a way that transcends the Lacanian position. In the next chapter we will entertain some of the ideas of Michel Foucault as we further develop our position that we can move beyond the kind of objectification we have traditionally engaged in, especially in the practical and clinical applications of psychoanalysis.

In the next chapter, we will explore the possibilities for reconciling Lacan's structuralist position with Sartre's phenomenological approach by utilizing some of Foucault's ideas about the nature of the subject. Again, we are trying to uncover some aspect of the self that can escape from the objectifying categories of contemporary psychology. This is, perhaps, not an equivalence to Sartre's idea of transcendence, but it may enjoy similar consequences. Lacanian analysis is not ego analysis, but is discourse analysis, in which we try to understand how conscious discourse emerges from its unconscious source. Recall that Lacan absolutely rejects the attempt by ego psychologists and object relations theorists to reconstruct the development of the ego. For him, these approaches are an unproductive rendering of Freud in that they are directed by the false ideal of "normal" development, a concept that we will see Foucault attack. Lacanian analysis focuses on understanding the illusory nature of the ego in the interest of a fuller experience of subjectivity that subsists beyond the phallic signifier. Thus, Lacan argues that attempts to shore up or reconstruct the ego result in a "reinforced alienation,"[84] primarily because these theorists do not understand that the ego is an illusion.[85] Instead of being a force for reality organization, the ego "represents the center of all the resistances to the treatment of symptoms."[86] This occurs because the ego is organized around the specular images that give the individual a sense of imaginary coherence based on identification. Therefore, ego analysis takes place in the Imaginary register and, in opposition, Lacan believes that effective analysis occurs "on the frontier between the symbolic and the imaginary."[87]

Instead of restructuring the ego, Lacan advocates the reconstruction of the signifying chain by which a person has been constructed. The goal is "full" or "true" speech that occurs without the disrupting intervention of ego identifications. Full speech differs from "empty speech" in that it "realizes the truth of the subject," that subjectivity is an illusion. In empty speech the subject "loses himself in the machinations of the system of language," implying that this loss entails entanglement in "the labyrinth of referential systems made available to him by the state of cultural affairs to which he is a more or less interested party."[88] Thus, for Lacan, movement toward the unconscious is theoretically preferable to movement toward the social order. In order to understand oneself as a product of the "discourse of the Other," one must understand that one is integrated into its circuit. Thus, when we identify ourselves in language, we lose ourselves in it like objects where our future is already determined by the chain of signifiers into which we are inserted. Thus, the best we can do is to understand that "subjectivity" is merely an illusion and to understand our destiny within discourse.

Lacan is advocating a kind of synchronic determinism in which humans are caught in signifying chains. Since we always exist within a linguistic system, we can never step outside of it. We can never transcend it so as to gain subjective perspective. The best one can do is to understand that one is decentered, that one is caught within the "gears" of language and therefore "isn't master in his own house."[89] The problem for him, though, is that no genuine *praxis* is possible in a system where the conscious subject is merely an effect of the unconscious signifiers. As Antoine Vergote says, for Lacan, "the subject is but the locus of the combinative production of autonomized signifiers. The clinician might even wonder if this is not the nonsubject of schizophrenia, the one who is the stake of the word but who is no longer playing the game of language."[90] Yet it is clear that the truth of the human "subject," for Lacan, is in the inhuman interrelation among signifiers, and he inverts Descartes's dictum, saying that "I think where I am not, therefore I am where I do not think."[91]

In contrast with Lacan, for Sartre, therapy would involve not movement toward the linguistic unconscious, but rather a transformation of *hexis* into *praxis* in which one would develop an intersubjective world of intentionality. This does not mean that Sartre believes we have absolute control over the meaning of one's words, for this would be a distortion opposite to Lacan's belief that we are products of the symbolic order. For Sartre, we can actually use the symbolic order to change the phenomenal and intentional order. This is possible because of prereflective consciousness, which can always purify the ego. In this light, Sartre asserts that the "necessary attitude for comprehending a person is empathy."[92] This means that we must go beyond an analytical evaluation which leaves out an understanding of future directed intentionality and its meaning. Further, even though we can attempt to reduce human action to its component parts, including determinist chains of causation, we will never understand humans if we do not attempt to understand our creative abilities to make new meaning out of old structure.[93] That is, even though our facticity suggests lines of *praxis*, this does not mean that it creates subjects out of whole cloth, for Sartre. Language for him includes both possibilities for *praxis* as well as *hexis*. Further, in contrast to Lacan, an individual is both constituted and constituting, and we have the freedom to reconstitute ourselves in such a way that we transcend the objectifying elements of the gaze of others. We will see how, in the very next chapter, Foucault's analysis of the constituted self can shed further light on the relation between Lacan's structuralism and Sartre's phenomenology. This will help us further understand the limits that the phenomenological approach has in its criticism of the influence of the natural science model on contemporary psychology.

Recall that for Sartre, it is the extent to which an individual's ego is other-directed that is the false ego; the aim of therapy would be to purge the ego of alienating otherness. Even so, for Sartre, we can never completely rid the ego of the other, because we can never step outside of our culture, our history, and our concrete situation. Yet, we can reflect on our identifications to the extent that they are based on unreflected appraisals of others. This means to use language proactively and creatively in order to transcend one's way of living as *hexis*. Psychological practice for Sartre would always include the clarification of the relation between one's freedom and the established world of necessity. More importantly, it would promote the transformation of passivity into authentic action, thereby increasing free choice. We have discussed how the drive theorists, the object relations theorists, and Lacan fall prey to the remnants of the methodology of nineteenth century natural science. Now, let us take a look at the work of both Michel Foucault and Gabriel Marcel to see if we can come to some additional clarity and resolution of the phenomenological criticism of the natural science model in psychology.

Notes

1. Betty Cannon, *Sartre & Psychoanalysis* (Lawrence: University Press of Kansas, 1991), 62.

2. Jay Greenberg and Stephen Mitchell, *Object Relations in Psychoanalytic Theory* (Cambridge, Mass., and London: Harvard University Press, 1983), 379.

3. Betty Cannon, *Sartre & Psychoanalysis*, 65.

4. Greenberg and Mitchell, *Object Relations in Psychoanalytic Theory*, 13.

5. See A. Modell, *Object Love and Reality* (New York: International Universities Press, 1968); also see: H. Stierlin, "The Functions of Inner Objects," *International Journal of Psychoanalysis*, 51: 321-329.

6. Betty Cannon, *Sartre & Psychoanalysis*, 68.

7. See Harry Guntrip, *Psychoanalytic Theory, Therapy, and the Self* (New York: Basic Books, 1973), 64; also see: Greenberg and Mitchell, *Object Relations in Psychoanalytic Theory*, 146.

8. See Greenberg and Mitchell, *Object Relations*, 417, for an excellent bibliography of articles by Mahler.

9. Otto Kernberg, *Borderline Conditions and Pathological Narcissism* (New York: Jason Aronson, 1975), 320.

10. See Betty Cannon, *Sartre & Psychoanalysis*, Chapter 3, who argues that Sartre's ontology provides a better foundation for these relational needs than does Freud's drive theory.

11. See theorists such as Sullivan, Fromm, Winnicott, and Hartmann in Greenberg and Mitchell, *Object Relations*.

12. Harry Guntrip, *Schizoid Phenomena, Object-Relations and the Self* (New York: International Universities Press, 1969), 382.

13. Harry Stack Sullivan, *Conceptions of Modern Psychiatry* (New York: W.W. Norton and Company, 1940); also see, Sullivan, *The Interpersonal Theory of Psychiatry* (New York and London: W.W. Norton and Company, 1953).

14. W. R. D. Fairbairn, *Psychoanalytic Studies of the Personality* (London, Henley, England, and Boston: Routledge & Kegan Paul, 1952), 137.

15. Michael Balint, *Primary Love and Psycho-analytic Techniques* (New York: Basic Books) 1969.

16. Betty Cannon, *Sartre & Psychoanalysis*, 120.

17. Heinz Kohut, *The Restoration of Self* (New York: International Universities Press, 1977).

18. James Masterson, *The Real Self: A Developmental, Self, and Object Relations Approach* (New York: Brunner/Mazel, 1985).

19. Greenberg and Mitchell, *Object Relations*, 89.

20. H. S. Sullivan, *Personal Psychopathology* (New York: Norton), 5.

21. *Ibid.*, 306.

22. H. S. Sullivan, *Conceptions of Modern Psychiatry* (New York: Norton, 1940), 10.

23. H.S. Sullivan, "The Data of Psychiatry," [1938] in *The Fusion of Psychiatry and Social Science* (New York: Norton, 1964), 32.

24. H.S. Sullivan, *The Interpersonal Theory of Psychiatry* (New York: Norton, 1953), 102.

25. Greenberg and Mitchell, Object Relations, 91.

26. Discussions of these theoretical changes are monumental in importance but are beyond the scope of this present book.

27. H. S. Sullivan, *The Interpersonal Theory of Psychiatry*, 103; also see: "The Illusion of Personal Individuality," [1950], in *The Fusion of Psychiatry and Social Science* (New York: Norton, 1964), 324.

28. H. S. Sullivan, *Conceptions of Modern Psychiatry*, 22.

29. H. S. Sullivan, *The Interpersonal Theory of Psychiatry*, 166.

30. H. S. Sullivan, *Conceptions of Modern Psychiatry*, 121.

31. See Kierkegaard's work on anxiety; also, see, Rollo May: *The Meaning of Anxiety* (New York: Norton, 1977).

32. H. S. Sullivan, *The Interpersonal Theory of Psychiatry*, 166.

33. H. S. Sullivan, *Clinical Studies in Psychiatry* (New York: Norton, 1956), 232; also see: *The Interpersonal Theory of Psychiatry*, 233.

34. Erich Fromm, *The Sane Society* (Greenwich, Conn.: Fawcett, 1955), 130; also see, Erich Fromm, *The Crisis of Psychoanalysis* (Greenwich, Conn.: Fawcett, 1970), 31.

35. Greenberg and Mitchell, *Object Relations*, 115.

36. See Jean-Paul Sartre, *Being and Nothingness* (New York: Washington Square Press, 1966), also see: the section on bad faith, which is explored in Kevin Boileau, *Genuine Reciprocity and Group Authenticity*, Chapter 1, as well as in Kevin C. Boileau and David A. Boileau, *The Algebra of History*.

37. Perhaps this is the unconscious?

38. Jean-Paul Sartre, *Being and Nothingness*, 139.

39. *Ibid.*, 140.

40. *Loc. cit.*

41. See K. Boileau, *Genuine Reciprocity*, Chapter 1, for a complete description and analysis of Sartre's notion of bad faith.

42. Hazel Barnes, "Sartre's Concept of the Self," in *Review of Existential Psychology and Psychiatry* 27: 41 – 65.

43. See Betty Cannon, *Sartre & Psychoanalysis*, 122 – 139, for an excellent look at how some of the relational theorists attempt to reify the self.

44. *Ibid*, 141.

45. Jean-Paul Sartre, *The Transcendence of the Ego* (New York: Farrar, Straus and Giroux, 1957), 31.

46. *Ibid.*, 70.

47. *Ibid.*, 71.

48. Again, see my earlier work, *Genuine Reciprocity*, Chapter 1, in which I explore Sartre's theory of bad faith, which in part describes this process of falsely constructing a determined future based on how things were in the past.

49. Jean-Paul Sartre, *Transcendence of the Ego*, 100.

50. I will also discuss Foucault in this regard, who argues that we are always pinned from the very beginning by established hierarchies of truth.

51. Hazel Barnes, "Sartre's Concept of the Self," *Review of Existential Psychology and Psychiatry* 27: 44 – 46.

52. *Ibid.* Hazel Barnes points out the conceptual problem

Sartre has in explaining how pure reflection can actually work.

53. Jean-Paul Sartre, *Transcendence of the Ego*, 64.

54. Jacques Lacan, *Ecrits: A Selection* (New York: Norton & Company, 1977); *The Four Fundamental Concepts of Psycho-Analysis* (New York: Norton & Company, 1981); the work of Michel Foucault is especially instructive here.

55. Jacques Lacan, *The Four Fundamental Concepts*, 227, 257, 279; also see, *Ecrits*, Chapter 1.

56. Our very concept of authenticity emerges from the symbolic realm, but Lacan argues that it is illusory.

57. Jacques Lacan, *Ecrits*, "The Signification of the Phallus," Chapter 8.

58. *Ibid.*, 154.

59. *Ibid.*, p. 70.

60. *Ibid.*, 165.

61. Jacques Lacan, *The Seminar of Jacques Lacan, Book III, The Psychoses, 1955-6*, Jacques-Alain Miller (Ed.), trans. Russell Grigg (New York: Norton, 1997).

62. Jacques Lacan, *Ecrits*, "The Freudian Thing," Chapter 4, 114.

63. Jacques Lacan, *Seminar, Book III*, 145.

64. Jacques Lacan, *Ecrits* "The Subversion of the Subject," Chapter 9.

65. Jacques Lacan, *The Seminar of Jacques Lacan, Book I, Freud's Papers on Technique, 1953-1954*, Jacques-Alain Miller (Ed.), trans. Russell Grigg (New York: Norton, 1991), 68.

66. G. Chaitlin, *Rhetoric and Culture in Lacan* (Cambridge: Cambridge University Press, 1996).

67. Jacques Lacan, *Ecrits*, "Agency of the Letter in the Unconscious," Chapter 5, 171.

68. Jacques Lacan, *Seminar, Book III*, 39.

69. Jacques Lacan, *The Seminar of Jacques Lacan, Book II, The Ego in Freud's Theory and in the Technique of Psychoanalysis, 1954-1955*, Jacques-Alain Miller (Ed.), trans. Sylvana Tomaselli (New York: Norton, 191), 323.

70. Yannis Stavrakakis, *Lacan & the Political* (New York: Routledge, 1999), 18.

71. Jacques Lacan, *Seminar, Book III*, 9.

72. Jacques Lacan, *Ecrits*, 72.

73. *Loc. cit.*

74. *Ibid.*, 74.

75. *Ibid.*, 125.

76. *Ibid.*, 259.

77. Jacques Lacan, *Seminar, Book II*, 50; Sartre, *Transcendence of the Ego*, 101.

78. See Sartre: *Being and Nothingness and Transcendence of the Ego*, or K. Boileau, *Genuine Reciprocity and Group Authenticity*, for a detailed examination.

79. Jacques Lacan, *The Four Fundamental Concepts*, 207.

80. Ellie Ragland-Sullivan, *Jacques Lacan and the Philosophy of Psychoanalysis* (Urbana and Chicago: University of Illinois Press, 1986), 303.

81. Jean-Paul Sartre, *The Family Idiot*, Volume 1, trans. Carol Cosman (Chicago: University of Chicago Press,

1981).

82. Ellie Ragland-Sullivan, *Jacques Lacan and the Philosophy of Psychoanalysis*, 91.

83. Jacques Lacan, *Ecrits*, 172.

84. Jacques Lacan, *Ecrits*, 274.

85. Jacques Lacan, *Seminar, Book I*, 53.

86. Jacques Lacan, *Ecrits*, 23.

87. Jacques Lacan, *Seminar, Book II*, 254 – 55.

88. Jacques Lacan, *Seminar Book I*, 50.

89. Jacques Lacan, *Seminar Book II*, 307.

90. Joseph Smith and William Kerrigan, (Eds.) *Interpreting Lacan* (New Haven, Conn. and London: Yale University Press, 1983), 202.

91. Jacques Lacan, *Ecrits*, 166.

92. Quoted by Hazel Barnes, *Sartre and Flaubert* (Chicago: University of Chicago, 1981), 9.

93. For an examination of Sartre's ideas about structuralism, see: *The Critique of Dialectical Reason* (London: NLB, 1976).

Part Three:
Foucault, Marcel,
and Final Remarks

Foucault

In the previous two parts, I have tried to show the deep influence of the natural science model on contemporary psychology. We have focused on psychoanalysis even though we could do a similar study on other strands of psychology such as behaviorism or various forms of cognitivism. My objective is to illuminate the narrowing effect that the natural science model has on the human phenomena available for investigation and treatment. In my view, this narrowing leads to a loss of the moral from its very foundation. We have proceeded by way of a phenomenological criticism, using Sartre's conceptual machinery. Now we want to take a look at this criticism from the postmodern perspective of Michel Foucault, especially with regard to Sartre's idea of the pre-reflective consciousness. Recall that for Lacan, we cannot escape our objectifications, which is a view directly in conflict with Sartre's belief that we can transcend them. Foucault's work is interesting because, while he believes that the self is mostly constituted discursively through relations of power/knowledge, he also believes there is a realm of freedom that is resistant to this tendency toward the kind of objectifications in which our culture engages. Foucault is not a structuralist nor is he a phenomenologist. Yet, he is deeply influenced by these conceptual approaches and finds a creative synthesis of them that can further explain the reliance psychology has placed on the natural science model.

After I sketch a Foucauldian-styled response to the
phenomenological and structural approaches, I will
then turn to the work of Gabriel Marcel, who I treat at
length in a previous work.[1] Marcel was a Catholic and a
phenomenologist, but he found Sartre distasteful, so much
so that he thought their work was not even comparable.[2]
Most likely their theoretical differences stemmed from their
divergent beliefs about whether the fundamental social unit
was the individual or the community. While Sartre believed
that the individual was primary, Marcel believed that it was
the community that was our foundation. This led each to
different ontological conclusions and radically different social
theories. Nothwithstanding these differences, we do believe
that Marcel's notions of availability and presencing do come
to similar social consequences as Sartre's concepts of the pre-
reflective self and genuine reciprocity between individuals.[3]
What is most important here is that we seriously question the
viability of the natural science model in psychology and its
objectifying tendencies. Foucault's work helps us understand
some of the underlying political reasons for this, but also
the limits of both the structuralist and phenomenological
approaches. Marcel's work helps us understand the social
dangers of the natural science model, as well as its limits to
the understanding of ourselves. After our short sketches of
Foucault and Marcel, we will take another look at some of
the ground we have traversed and make some final remarks
about the continued viability of the natural science model in
psychology with an eye toward future investigation.

In an early interview, Foucault argues that he does not
"think we should try to define psychology as a science but
perhaps as a cultural form."[4] In this essay he acknowledges
the deep historical entanglement between philosophy and
psychology, and prefigures much of his later theorizing about
the relation between power and knowledge, as he shows how

psychology colonized other domains in the human sciences. Especially with Freud's discovery of the unconscious, Foucault acknowledges that psychology is now more than a science of consciousness, and that the "individual can no longer stand."[5] Further, he believes that "psychology will be the knowledge of structures," because "there may be among several individuals a certain number of identical processes. . . ."[6] This is not to say that he is advocating structuralism, because, in his own words, he is "not a structuralist."[7] Most importantly, and this claim sets the stage for what follows here in our essay, is that Foucault argues that he doesn't "think psychology can ever dissociate itself from a certain normative program."[8] He understands Dilthey, "who had the strong feeling that the epistemological model of the natural sciences was going to be imposed as a norm of rationality on the human sciences."[9] Moreover, and this is what we will explore next, he believes that in every culture there exist underlying standards of normativity for all domains of human conduct; these standards emerge from formations of power and knowledge, which we explored in our earlier chapter on Freud and Kuhn.[10] This meant that Dilthey knew that hermeneutics had to compete with the natural sciences as a methodology for psychology. We can see how Foucault's insights about the politicization of science and Kuhn's pronouncements about paradigm shifts explain the historical progression in various scientific domains.

In his essay, "Psychiatric Power," Foucault argues that psychoanalysis was one of the great forms of antipsychiatrization in the Western world.[11] He goes on to delineate how the institutional power games that occur in psychiatry give rise to the "absolute right of nonmadness over madness."[12] Further, he argues that in the nineteenth century's demedicalization of madness there is also a concomitant questioning of power by antipsychiatric practice, including psychoanalysis. This is a nice example of how alternative knowledges and practices compete to be the governing paradigm in a particular scientific domain. Coupled with an underlying tendency toward the objectification of human subjects, strategies of scientific normalization determine the "truth" of who we individuals are. In the balance of this section we render a further account of Foucault's project to explain how different modes of subjectivity emerge from the intersection of power and knowledge in various historical conditions.[13]

In his later work, Foucault concerns himself with the processes within which humans are made into subjects. He replaces Sartre's notion of a transcendent, constituting subject with a version of the self that is constituted by relations of power. In Foucault's conception there is a docile aspect of the self that is created by the effects of power. There is also a resistant aspect that can resist power by avoiding the will to truth and, instead, create new forms of subjectivity. In *Discipline and Punish*, Foucault offers a genealogy of the modern individual as a docile and mute body by presenting the interplay of disciplinary technology and social sciences with their standards of normativity.[14] Here, he argues that individuals are socially constructed, based on categories produced by the relations of power in the human sciences. In *Discipline*, he gives an account of the modern history of power from the seventeenth century to the present, showing how power has evolved from being primarily repressive to the current condition where it is mostly productive. By the nineteenth century, power emanates from all levels of society, producing various effects along with the repressing of behavior, a structure that he calls "bio-power."[15]

As modern states promote the growth of their populations, interest in human sexuality and economic production grows.

Scientific knowledge of the processes of the human body explodes as the state forms a disciplinary technology of these bodies for the purpose of manipulating them as objects. By the nineteenth century, the exercise of power had shifted from imprinting itself on bodies through torture to processes of self-surveillance in which subjects are formed through the repressive effects of language. In *Discipline*, Foucault traces this historical development of the modern individual as a docile and mute body by showing the evolution of disciplinary technology within the penal system, but keep in mind that he is also concerned about the docile body in other domains. Most importantly, it is through techniques of self-surveillance and normativity that individuals are constituted as subjects. In *Birth of the Clinic*,[16] Foucault gives us his history of the body, showing how the clinical gaze focuses on the bodies of the dead through autopsy, creates categories of disease, and thereby reveals truth. In this way, the body is fractured into a complex of diseased organs that are responsible for death. Moreover, in *Madness and Civilization*, Foucault demonstrates that madness is also constituted in the domination of individual bodies.[17] Here, the category of madness arises from the practice of separating those with sane minds and productive bodies from those with sane minds and unproductive bodies, confining the insane and unproductive to asylums. Madness, laziness, and poverty are thereby associated in a complex of moral perception that results in the judgment that madness must be isolated and treated by medical experts.

In these historical studies Foucault shows the isomorphism between power exerted on a person's body and the power relations of the society in which he lives. In this schema, the body politic is "a set of material elements and techniques that serve as weapons, relays, communication routes and supports for the power and knowledge relations that invest human bodies and subjugate them by turning them into objects of knowledge."[18] As we have alluded to, the two main strategies used in the new disciplinary technology are surveillance and normalizing judgment.[19] Normalizing judgment places each individual into an objective category and evaluates him by how far he deviates from the norm in any particular way. These strategies force individuals into certain roles in society and account for each person's place in the disciplinary grid. Deviations from the norm are punished so as to correct for improper behavior. Most individuals accept these roles and live by them, although others engage in strategies of resistance.[20] For example, Foucault argues that in the nineteenth century (and this could be applied to the twentieth and twenty-first centuries) the bourgeoisie became concerned with the promotion of healthy and productive bodies in their eugenics projects, in order to prevent the degeneration of their class. The working class was forced to maximize productivity, which meant that forms of sexual behavior always had to be evaluated by their relation to capitalism and the underlying interests of the aristocracy. Behavior that promoted production was considered normal; behavior that was pleasurable for its own sake and which did not add to economic productivity was branded abnormal and subject to correction.

Foucault believes that in our current era of bio-power, influenced by Newton and Descartes, we primarily view the human body as a resource or a machine. Knowledge of the body causes its dispersion into a complex myriad of political strategies and techniques. In contrast to Aristotelian man who was self-grounded, Foucault sees modern man as "as animal whose politics places his existence as a living being in question," as social creations who are not their own ground.[21] As Foucault develops in his work on sexuality and subjectivity, bio-power, in part, views bodies as sexual and operates on them through strategies of law, biology, and psychoanalysis. Sex is driven by knowledge of sexuality that uses various scientific discourses to normalize sexual behavior of the body. Each body is evaluated against the norm, thereby creating a tension within each person. Spontaneity is necessarily opposed to the norm created by a science that is driven by capitalism. Thus, the body becomes divided against itself as it is fractured into various discourses of truth. In order to understand this production of truth, we must discuss Foucault's notion about power.

Foucault was influenced by the phenomenologists and the structuralists but was neither one himself. It is his beliefs about power that tie these influences together and synthesize competing claims about explanation in the social sciences, thus we need to say a bit about what he means. For most of the twentieth century, the debate in the social sciences has been between those who see power as exercised by individuals and those who see power as the result of structural factors within systems. Voluntarist theories view power as being exercised by individuals. Structuralist theories view power as the result of the structures within systems.[22] Foucault attempts to synthesize these contrasting positions by showing that there are two levels or perspectives of power, and that both agency and structural factors have an explanatory role. He presents us with the intriguing statement that "power relations are both intentional and nonsubjective."[23] Foucault's objective is to study the effects of power, and he does this by focusing on how power is exercised rather than how it is possessed and by whom. In contrast to Marxist theories of power, which hold that power is a substance that can be held, Foucault adopts the Nietzschean position and is nominalistic about it. Power, for Foucault, is not a thing and cannot be possessed.[24] Instead, it is the name we attribute to a complex strategic situation in a particular society.[25]

At any point in time a society is structured by a set of rituals of power that create asymmetrical relationships between humans. Foucault analyzes this web of unequal relationships by focusing on how people relate to each other on the most local and interpersonal of levels. Relations of power are thus immanent in all kinds of relationships. Further, power does not come from the top and trickle downward; instead, it emanates from all directions and, as we have said, is productive.[26] Because he believes that power relations are intentional and non-subjective means that they can be explained from two perspectives. He believes that these relations are always imbued with calculation, aims, and objectives.[27] Yet, this does not mean that power is necessarily exercised through the choice of an individual subject.[28] At the local and tactical level of political activity there is conscious decision-making; intentionality is present. Here, individuals are aware of what they do and every act is planned and deliberated. In contrast, at the structural level, which is the underlying matrix of power relations, there is no subject. Exercises of power are not the result of anyone's direct, conscious planning. Thus, relations are non-subjective. This means that even though agents are aware of their decisions, the broader consequences of local actions are not planned or coordinated.[29] There are results that are beyond the intentions of any one agent. Yet, these patterns, which emerge historically, have a logic. They are the result of the underlying strategic interplay of all the unequal relations of domination. The direction of these local practices is provided by the underlying technologies of power that instantiate a particular society at a particular time. Foucault's intention is to analyze these tactical practices.

Foucault argues that there is a government of power relations that limits individual actions in various relationships. It is, as he says, "a total structure of actions brought to bear upon possible actions."[30] This structure provides a context within which possible actions can occur and "consists in guiding the possibility of conduct and putting in order the possible outcome."[31] That is, the underlying structural level governs a field of possible actions at the tactical level in any kind of relationship of power.[32] Rational agents have a range of choices delimited and made possible by the underlying power structure. This structure changes through history, sometimes as a result of successful resistance or by the transgression of previously established limits. Foucault links power relationships and their inherent potential for reversal by arguing that they are unstable states and can easily rupture into the other. These relationships of power are reciprocally relationships of struggle. They limit each other and each is always the possibility for the other. It is the region of struggle that can be explained by the purposeful actions of a subject. When struggle reaches its limit, though, and becomes a relationship of power, actions are better explained by structure, not by subjects. In a power relationship, the nature of that particular relationship determines the limits of behavioral choices each individual has. These individuals are not, according to Foucault, traditional subjects who are their own ground of choice. Instead, the structure of the relationship determines the choices. Thus, even though the behavior of the individuals involved is intentional within the power relationship, this intentionality is grounded within the matrix of power operating within society at that time, and further refined by the specific relation of power involved.

According to Foucault, in the eighteenth century, the modern state reorganized the pastoral power that individualizes humans.[33] He believes that the individualizing power of the modern state was, and is, concerned with the health and welfare of both individuals and the populations as a whole instead of the healing of souls. State power forms a type of individuality with which individuals identify. This power questions the status of and governs individuals by forcing them to scrutinize themselves and see where they fit within patterns of normalization.[34] It forces individuals to seek the truth about themselves and, for Foucault, these phenomena emerge most clearly in the domain of sexuality.[35] Foucault saw the practice of a politically effective ethics as a means of disabusing ourselves of the notion that our desires speak the truth about who we are, which is the type of individuality that has been constructed for us in the modern period. This hermeneutics of desire involves a relation to oneself whereby we attempt to discover the true nature of what we are by attaching ourselves to various human knowledges through our personal identity.

Foucault's historical construction of humans as desiring people is not new. Socrates, Plato, and Aristotle were aware of this facet of our humanity and discussed it a great deal. Even Augustine and other Medieval Christian thinkers were interested in this problem. Yet, Foucault's version sets this problem within a different historical context. In it, he implies that there is a direct relationship between what one does and what one is. By desiring things, values, people, and ideas, we move toward them, and we attach ourselves to them as we frame our personal identities. But in this, he adds a hermeneutics of truth to desire, for how we act on our desires speaks the truth about who we are. Most importantly, this truth is always embedded in relations of power. Experts, who make claims to knowledge, tell us who we are through the strategies of individuating power. Recall that individuating power categorizes humans of a society according to the claims of the human sciences, culture, and religion. The recognition of where persons are located in relation to the universe of human data makes individuals into subjects and each person recognizes himself as an individual with a personal identity.

Please note that there are two facets of this recognition: one by others and one by oneself, along with degrees of resistance and transgression.

One's personal identity has a relation to truth that carries with it substantial political implications. Foucault shows us that what passes for ultimate truth is dependent upon our historical circumstance and the power relations underlying them. Thus, we have regimes of truth that vary with historical time and place.[36] More importantly, these regimes force us to believe that the truth is at stake in whatever we do. This causes us to discover where we are located in relation to truth, playing real-life "games of truth."[37] Humans are led to believe that by attaining the knowledge about who we are we will be better equipped to transform ourselves. Foucault traces the histories of these truth games and how they are used as a basis for self identity and behavior toward others. His inquiry ultimately leads him toward ethics, and thus he says that his "problem is to know how men govern (themselves and others) by means of the production of truth . . ."[38]

It is the production of truth that constitutes who we are. For example, we can try to locate ourselves within the categories of psychopathology, relying on various measurement tools and practices such as the *DSM*.[39] Foucault argues that we are subjected to these games of truth by the power that individuates human beings. For him, "subject to" means that one is "subject to someone else by control and dependence," or "tied to his own identity by a conscience or self-knowledge." Both meanings suggest a form of power that subjugates humans to scientific knowledge.[40] Individuals are forced to into a connection with knowledge, and power makes certain that we are dependent on that knowledge for our identity. My subjectivity arises from the recognition of myself. Foucault shows us that in the modern era, humans see themselves primarily as sexual (desiring) beings. Therefore, we subject ourselves to the games of truth associated with our sexuality, thereby constituting our subjectivities through that sexuality. Recall that power creates docile subjects that are manipulated by these truth games. Yet, each of us can influence the way these games affect us. Thus each person, for Foucault, is divided into two components, a subject and an object. The objectivized self appears both socially and personally and is one part of the split subject that emerges from the dividing practices of the relations of power. It is these dividing practices, both on the social level and on the individual level, that objectify us and subject us to the process of normativity.[41]

There are two levels of dividing practices. There is the social level where individuals are divided from others at points where they deviate from the norm. There is also the individual level where individuals divide themselves into subjects and objects, in which the objectified realm emerges from the attachments of personal identity. Various discourses on knowledge arise because of the power formations in society. Those who espouse the truth of various claims to knowledge gain power over those who are subjected to that knowledge. Thus, when mental health professionals assert various truths they often alter the behavior of individuals who become subjected to the knowledge employed. A psychotherapist subjects his clients to a system of truth to which he or she is aligned. Yet, if one changes therapists one is subjected to a different brand of the truth, for instance, Gestalt therapy instead of Rogerian therapy, or self psychology instead of Freudian analysis. A different truth is raised by each new relationship to knowledge that a person creates for himself.

Recall our main argument that the methodology of contemporary psychology unduly restricts the phenomenological data of the human because of the Newtonian-Cartesian influence. In the main, our criticism is directed toward the dualist, spectator philosophy, in which the subject-object dichotomy objectifies humans, framing perceptual data about them in terms of a reductionistic theory. Foucault helps us understand the underlying political foundation of this tendency from a historical perspective. In an earlier chapter we utilized Sartre's theory of consciousness as an alternative to the psychoanalytic strategy of creating a substantial self. The cogency of Sartre's argument rests on the theoretical plausibility of his correlative concepts of the pre-reflective self and pure reflection. Nevertheless, Foucault's assertions about the relationship between power and knowledge, while limiting Sartre's theory, do not destroy its efficacy. Foucault believes that Sartre's theory speaks from the assumption of a self that can transcend its historical constitution and that Sartre is trying to define self-constitution for all humanity and for all time. Nevertheless, with Foucault's formulations about power, the traditional masterful subject is gone. Because power traverses everything, the categories of subject and object collapse as well.[42] Although Foucault's work ends in a self that cannot transcend the relations of power within its own history, it does open up possibilities for new forms of subjectivity.

Like Sartre, who presents freedom as our very ontological essence and a practical possibility, Foucault speaks of freedom as resistance to disciplinary forms of objectification, saying "at the very heart of the power relationship, and constantly provoking it, are the recalcitrance of the will and the intransigence of freedom."[43] This resistance to power is resistance to the Other's look and involves an individual's struggle to unfold his own image in the world. Whereas for Sartre, the very structure of consciousness implies the possibility of a radical freedom from objectification, for

Foucault we cannot escape it. The best we can do is to release
ourselves from the will to truth and, instead, creatively search
for new forms of subjectivity by living in the aesthetic mode
through our creativity. For Foucault, individual freedom
is limited by the field of power relations, which are both
intentional and nonsubjective. The subject that he tries to
destroy is the traditional, masterful self who controls the
"objective" world around him. This is the subject whose
consciousness remains on the interior, separate and apart
from the body, and who encounters an outside world. But,
for Foucault, this is the subject that is the result of biopower,
the force that creates subjects who define themselves in terms
of the positive sciences. By collapsing the oppositions of
internal and external, and subject and object, Foucault argues
against a sovereign subject who is radically free and whose
consciousness is independent from the world.

In the light of Foucault's notions about power, we must
reinterpret the Sartrean-Husserlian notion of intentionality
in terms of the discussion above. For Foucault, there is no
such thing as radical freedom, and individuals are not the
center of their own movement within culture. In contrast,
one's autonomy is decentered by relations of power that
pervade us to the very core. This means that we are not
radically separate and independent from the external world
or from other individuals, and therefore, all intentionality is
historically, culturally, and socially conditioned. Furthermore,
because Foucault's analysis of power shows that there can not
be such a thing as a masterful subject, it must also be the case
that there is no mastery of the "objective" as a totality. This
implies that an individual can never objectively interpret the
world because no one can ever step outside the network of
power. Each individual is always a part of that which is to be
interpreted, and each interpretation can be re-interpreted by
others, ad infinitum, in order to come to a final and objective

interpretation. But this is impossible, for there is no place to stop this process of re-interpretation. Thus, any science or body of knowledge that purports to explain a facet of human nature is always incomplete. We are always more than the sum of what science, culture, religion, and society say we are, a point we are going to take up in the next section on Marcel.

This does not render Sartre's notion of the pre-reflective self *effete*, for there are serious questions about who or what is doing the resisting in Foucault's conceptualization. After Foucault, we may not end up with a self that transcends an external world, yet he suggests we can "get free of ourselves" and believes that we can analyze our subjectivities in terms of the relations of power that bind us. This leaves us with more than the objectifications of the relational theorists and more than the kind of objectification Lacan espouses. Perhaps these new kinds of subjectivities are best left for individuals as a kind of mystery. Now, before we address Marcel, let us say a bit about Lacan, from a Foucauldian perspective.

The relation between Lacan and Foucault is a complex one that has been written about by a number of theorists.[44] For the purposes of this work, let us continue to keep in mind our main thesis that the reductive methodologies of contemporary psychology unduly limit the phenomena that we can examine. Further, let us also keep in mind that Lacan was a structuralist and was very opposed to the phenomenological notion of intentionality, even as modified by Foucault's pronouncements about power. In contrast, Lacan tries to reduce psychic phenomena to unconscious linguistic structures by removing human intentionality and meaning. By reducing the conscious subject to an effect of the signifier, Lacan precludes meaningful transformation. For Lacan, we are just playthings of the linguistic unconscious, which prevents us from using language as *praxis*. This is consonant with his position that there is no transcendent subject, in the Sartrean sense, who could possibly effect such change. Presumably, this also means that there is no Foucauldean subject who could effect change either.

Lacan's position is that language speaks us. As such, we are inert objects that are pure otherness and there is no chance for transcendence. As an inert repository of past *praxes*, language is always an invitation to *hexis*. Using language inserts us into a cultural order and, as a result, otherness inscribes itself into our own intentional projects. Foucault's position (and Sartre's) is that we can use language creatively and intentionally, subject to contextual factors that emerge from relations of power and knowledge. It is the creative aspect of language that Lacan avoids. Thus, Lacanian alienation is unsurpassable because it is this Otherness that has created me as a speaking subject. For Lacan, we always enter into a world that is filled with symbols and we can never return to a place that is outside the cultural-linguistic order. For Lacan, the most one can do is to understand that we are the playthings of the linguistic unconscious, that one is a signified rather than a signifer, an object pretending to be a subject. Thus, for Lacan, the signifier represents only a subject, but not a referent nor a signifier. He thereby defines the subject in terms of representation, as a discourse of the Other, in which each subject has himself represented by a signifier to another signifier. Further, each subject, though speaking himself amongst signifying chains, concomitantly absents himself from them, in the mode of being other than his identifying signifiers.

For Foucault, in the modern era, these signifying chains largely revolve around discourses of sexuality in which subjects recognize the truth of themselves as subjects of desire. Subjects of desire are located, for him, in terms of relationships to desire in which we form ourselves by distancing ourselves from that desire. As Charles Scott says, "desiring, then, is at a distance from the subject of desire, and this distance is structured by relations of power."[45] Each of us exercises these relations of power in our relation to desire, which gives each of us a certain relation to the truth of who we are. Thus, desire, truth, and power are fragmented into various discourses in the human and social sciences. As Scott rightly notices, Foucault's genealogy exposes a kind of surface freedom that accompanies the fragmentations that run through our constituted selves.[46] Within this line of reasoning, we cannot say what selves are, but we can talk about the kind of self that has formed within a certain lineage of subjection. That is, we stay outside of the metaphysical question about what we are and, instead, focus our inquiry on the line of subjections that define the range of selves we can become. We are fragmented across discourses and we are both subjected to, and resist the confining forces of the relations of power to which we belong and identify.

Freedom is, for Foucault, a freedom of fragmentation that comes from not being essentially anyone, a "freedom that accompanies the differences that constitute a lineage of loose alliances, relations of resistance and mastery and confederations of fluid interests, ..."[47] One position to take is that Foucault's idea of freedom does involve subjects at some level of intentionality, a position we write about in a previous work. Even though this resisting element may not rise to the level of a Sartrean transcending self, it is arguable that subjects have some locus of power to effect transformation in their subjectivities.[48] Even so, it is also arguable, and perhaps with more force, that freedom does not belong to subjects and that, instead, it means the kind of fragmentation and malleability that occurs within structure. This allows the Dionysian element to always have a play, in which selves are always in question and always problematized, and in which we come to ourselves by fleeing. As I argue in *Group Authenticity*, this play in structure allows selves to creatively re-arrange the elements that comprise their subjectivities. With regard to Lacanian structuralism, this is where Foucault parts company, for in Foucault's system, subjects have some power to influence the cluster of power relations that make up their personal identities. It is not so clear for Lacan that we can do anything beyond accepting our fate in strategies of "full speech."

Marcel

Next, we are going to review the problem of objectification in psychology from the standpoint of Gabriel Marcel, who has been alternatively labeled a Catholic metaphysician and a phenomenologist.[49] Gabriel Marcel's notion of the self challenges the received view of the relational psychoanalysts as well as the natural science model with its limiting constraints. We find him in the same camp as Binswanger, criticizing the idea of *homo natura* with its hypothetical constructions in favor of *homo existentialis*. Gabriel Marcel, just like Sartre (and Merleau-Ponty), has severe doubts about the metaphysical dualism that Descartes created and eschews all traditional forms of intellectualism and empiricism.

Marcel wants to provide an anthropology of man, but he does not think that the answer to this question can be found in abstracted, objectified categories of scientific thought, reflected upon by a so-called objective, incarnate knower. For him, we cannot penetrate into the deeper riches of what it means to be human through the Cartesian spectator philosophy and, instead, must discover ourselves through exchange and participation. He also rejects the assertion that we can provide a systematic and complete account of what/who we are, which has always been the aim of the contemporary schools of psychology. Marcel is concerned that our sense of value comes only from the functions we perform in society and no longer from the intrinsic quality of being a human being. When we say that a man is what he does we lose the ontological sense. Within this loss of the ontological sense the world loses its mysterious character and all things are explained by cause and effect relationships, which is the trap into which psychology has fallen. In this functionalized world we are always prey to despair which, for Marcel, comes from limiting reality to that which can be measured, understood, and controlled by scientific, functional thought.

It is not that Marcel is totally against technology, but rather that he is against technolatry, whereby it is believed that technical thinking yields the only valid knowledge about reality. In a technomanic view of reality, humans see themselves as the sole creator of meaning and value. Within this anthropocentric view, humans see the world as raw material to be transformed to meet his needs and desires. When this attitude prevails, humans admire only the products of their technology and trust only the knowledge that is within the limits of their categories of thought and possibilities for action. For Marcel, when this view predominates, we cut ourselves off from the kind of humility that fosters different understandings and expressions of reality. Yet, technology cannot overcome tragedy or death, and it disregards the substance of authentic life. It cannot provide the answers to ultimate questions about values and thereby creates a rootless, anonymous, and mass-produced society that is lost. Further, it only encourages the continuation of a collection of atomized and alienated selves whose science and technology are just hypostasized projections of our need for control, in order to have. In this light, consider the consequences of sophisticated psychological assessment tools and tests, as they gain control over the abnormal.

The alienation that results, Marcel believes, is directly linked to the spirit found in abstract thought, which completely bypasses the kind of concrete philosophy Marcel espouses. This is not to say that Marcel is against abstract thought, for he recognizes its necessity in all thought and action. What he is against is the valorization of it to the exclusion of the concrete life from which is emerges. For example, a schizophrenic can be understood as a whole person, separate and apart from the scientific categories into which he is placed; flowers can be understood as things of beauty, separate and apart from their functional categories. What he is against is our tendency to understand reality solely in terms of those abstract categories of thought that can be manipulated for power and economic gain. This mental reductionism, he thinks, comes from the avoidance of the resentment we experience when we cannot control the things around us, including ourselves, and is a life orientation toward having rather than toward being.[50] For Marcel, "being is what withstands — or what would withstand — an exhaustive analysis bearing on the data of experience and aiming to reduce them step by step to elements increasingly devoid of intrinsic or significant value. (An analysis of this kind is attempted in the theoretical works of Freud.)"[51] Marcel is concerned that the objective world that we attain through abstraction provides no guarantee against emptiness and despair. Consider the impact this may have on a psychotherapy that objectivizes.

Marcel's analysis of having — our need for control and possession — is a phenomenological analysis. In *Being and Having*, Marcel develops his distinction between being and having, which is at the root of other conceptual polarities

he advances.[52] In the transformation from being to having,
we also move from participation to objectification, mystery
to problem, presence to object, I-thou relationships to I-it
relationships, thought which is presenced to thought which
interrogates, concrete thinking to abstraction, and secondary
reflection to primary reflection. Marcel understands that
both modes are necessary, but he is concerned that the type
of thought that deepens participation in the mystery of being
will be lost as the possessive orientation to the world becomes
even more dominant over the other orientation. For to possess
is to render something to one's control. It is to have the power
to manipulate something, whether it is an idea or another
person. An act of abstraction is itself the effort to characterize
and categorize a concrete reality in such a way that it becomes
a manipulable mental possession. When I possess something,
I acquire a right of disposition over it, but there are dangers in
that possession.[53] Notwithstanding the ethical issues involved,
in the mode of having we trade a wider and deeper view of
reality, mystery in all its fullness, for a clear-cut view which is
certain, though limited and even dangerous.

For Marcel, being can never be totalized as a sum of discrete
elements. Thus, he argues that *"I am always and at every moment
more than the totality of predicates that an inquiry made by
myself — or by someone else — about myself . . . would be
able to bring to light."*[54] When we construct the world in the
mode of having, we concomitantly construct the self in the
same way. In the mode of having, we become attuned to our
praxis and thereby see ourselves in terms of our functions.
This, for Marcel, has created the idea of the "problematized
man" who is the product of our rational-scientific-industrial
culture, in which we are alienated from being, and therefore,
from fulfillment and joy. A functionalized world produces a
specialized self whose resources can be thoroughly tabulated
and utilized.[55] Unfortunately, the successes of modern man's

rational side have enabled him to become a manipulator of nature, of others, and of himself, perhaps even in the realm of psychology and psychotherapy. We manipulate that which we possess, yet we are limited within the mode of having.

Marcel is concerned with the problem of how to interpret basic realities and experiences that he does not believe can be logically demonstrable nor objectively describable. He believes that through participatory sympathy we can re-experience the lives of other human beings. His development of an ontology that is based on our being with others, along with his idea of participation, moves him away from solipsism. His methodology of an indirect and concrete approach to feeling out the meaning of an experience or concept is his phenomenological method. Thus, he advocates an intermediary type of thinking between the subjective and the objective, the private and the common, which amounts to an appreciative type of consciousness much like we have for works of art. Note that this notion conjures Foucault's notions about maximizing freedom by living in the aesthetic mode, even though Marcel's metaphysical assumptions are, of course, on a radically different footing. This aesthetic consciousness is not commonly available but requires a specific exigence and intention toward a specific otherness. Yet, it is not merely private either, for it bears on something other. It is not mere subjectivism because there is an opening to something that is really present for us. It is this presence that we must get back to, this original experience of other reality that is closed off by our secondary images and ideas that become idols for the real thing. In order to gain access to this otherness we must, like the novelist or the playwright, allow it to be present and not seek a mere illustration of general truths, which again, we argue, is the downfall of contemporary psychology. For example, I may want to know a flower, not just by its class, genus, and species, but in terms of its singularity and uniqueness. I want to know the present reality of this flower. The same goes for other experiences such as religion.

Marcel makes a distinction between two types of thought, which are primary reflection and secondary reflection. For him, the phenomenological method proceeds through participation, which can be approached through secondary reflection. Primary reflection, which operates through the mode of abstraction, emerges most prominently in science and technology, and is brought to bear on *problems*. For example, we can how this works in the case of treating depression with prescription medication. In this case, a "problem" is solved through drug intervention. Arguably, psychoanalysis also solves problems through primary reflection. In contrast, secondary reflection, which is the kind of thought more characteristic of art, philosophy, and religion, has as its purpose the deepening of our participation in the *mystery* of being. The problematic approach to understanding reality implies the separation of the subject from the object about which one asks questions. Marcel says: "A problem is something I meet, which I find complete before me, but which I can therefore lay siege to and reduce."[56] If, for example, I ask a question about the nature of cats or of the shape of the earth, the object about which I am asking is separable from myself and may be discussed apart from my feelings and subjective involvement. Problem and verification are complementary notions, and all problems yield verifiable solutions. If we can get sufficient distance from our own subjective, emotional, and biographical selves in order to pose an objective problem, we create the possibility of obtaining an answer that can be verified by all observers who go through the appropriate procedures of observation and testing. For instance, a group of psychiatrists may actually agree on a mental health diagnosis and its "solution."

Primary reflection is problem-solving activity which aims
at knowledge that is universal, abstract, objective, and
verifiable. It necessarily excludes the personal, the particular,
and the contingent aspects of thought, for example,
one's feelings about the nature of cats or the shape of the
earth, for they are irrelevant. Thus, we can argue that
even though psychoanalysis applies itself to individuals it
utilizes a conceptual, analytic machinery that is universal.
For example, object relations systems are closed systems
through which phenomenological data are interpreted by
the analyst. Primary reflection is necessarily abstract and
involves only a partial relation between the thinker and
his object. The object is not approached in its totality with
any kind of openness that allows it to reveal itself. Instead,
the object is forced to submit itself to the interrogation of
the interrogator whose questions and intentions reflect the
purpose of that interrogator. Here, one is reminded of the
American pandemic of "hyperactive" children along with its
solution, which is much to the delight of the pharmaceutical
companies. Instead of directing itself toward the highly
personal character of artistic, philosophical, and religious
thought, this type of thinking makes its primary stand with
modern science, forcing nature to answer our objectively
framed questions. With interrogation, the existential world is
not a concern. Gaining control is.

Let me highlight that Marcel is not criticizing primary
reflection itself, but only its misuse and overuse. It is true that
primary reflection allows us to possess and manipulate the
world more completely, and it can be argued, therefore, that
it is indispensable to our survival and growth as a species. We
must stand at a distance from the natural world sometimes in
order to objectify it, abstract it, and utilize it for our survival.
Yet, for Marcel, intellectual and moral confusion result when
those who engage in primary reflection claim that this way

of thinking is the only way to judge all knowledge and truth by criteria that yields objective answers to problems. When this happens, everything, including humans, is reduced to a collection of objects, science gives way to scientism, and the multi-layered texture of reality is forced to conform to a very narrow black and white logic of objectivity. Marcel refuses to give one aspect of our experience complete domination and, in contrast, advocates a broader view of experience, knowledge, and rationality. He gives an account of this broader view in his discussions about secondary reflection and mystery.

Secondary reflection seeks a wider and richer understanding of the meaning of human existence by returning to the unity of experiences including availability for others, fidelity, hope, and love within which the mystery of being can be appreciated. It seeks to recover the unity of experience by asking from within my own experience what meaning it has for me. It is a reflection on reflection that prioritizes participation over observation, encounter over objectification, and concrete existence over abstraction. In the case of the depressive or the hyperactive, for example, the approach would be to understand the meaning these existential conditions has for those particular patients, and then to generate therapeutic strategies that avoid interrogation and control. While secondary reflection does not deny the value of primary reflection, it does deny that primary reflection has any kind of finality or exclusiveness. Further, according to Marcel, secondary reflection involves recognition of the insufficiency of the categories that make primary reflection possible. The most infamous example of one of the problems raised by primary reflection is Descartes's conception of the dualism between body and soul, for it arises out of thought that emerges from the traditional subject-predicate logic. With these logical categories in mind, Marcel thinks that "we shall either be led to consider the body and soul as two distinct things between

which some determinate relationship must exist, some
relationship capable of abstract formulation, or to think of the
body as something of which the soul, as we improperly call it,
is the predicate, or on the other hand of the soul as something
of which the body, as we improperly call it, is the predicate. . .
But in both cases, body and soul, at least, are treated as *things*,
and things, for the purpose of logical discourse, become *terms*,
which one imagines as strictly defined, and as linked to each
other by some determinable relation."[57]

Recall that Descartes's starting point, the *cogito ergo sum*,
implies an isolated, thinking individual who is free to pursue
knowledge about external reality. Within his system, there
is a marked dualism between the thinking subject and the
objective, material world, which includes the human body.
The existentialist tradition had to grapple with this dualism
and, in contrast, has asserted that philosophy must begin
with the concrete individual who is fully engaged in the
world and thoroughly involved in relationships with others. A
concrete philosophy begins not with the certainty of thinking
but with the experience of immediate existence. Under this
view, existence precedes reflective knowledge of existence.
Thus, our assurance of our existence is not of a conceptual-
intellectual nature but starts from the sensation of our bodies
in the world.

Marcel rejects the mind-body dualism and argues that
incarnation is the primary given of metaphysics.[58] He believes
that only through incarnation do we recognize ourselves to
be subjects in the world and not mere abstract minds that
process ideas. For him, we come to know the world through
the body, and the way we relate to our body is the way we
relate to the world. Yet, as incarnate beings, we do not adopt
the materialist position that we are merely the chemical
and material components of our bodies. Idealism is wrong

because humans are not just minds accidentally residing in bodies. Materialism is wrong because humans are not bodies accidentally housing minds. In contrast, to be incarnate means that the only way we can think about the world is through our bodily insertion into it. We think about the world in terms of being incarnate. We think through our incarnate being, and it anchors us to the real.

Marcel thinks that we are also inseparable from the concrete situations in which we find ourselves. Recall that he disagrees with the idealist tendency to define humans in general and universal terms because he thinks that this ignores the particular circumstances of any one individual. The intimate and particular life which each of us inhabits shapes each individual consciousness in a way that universal descriptions do not capture. Adopting a purely objective stance toward my situation destroys the intimate connection each of us has with the world. Further, the fact that I am always an integral part of each situation I am in prevents me from ever being a totally disinterested and detached observer of my environment.

Furthermore, just as each individual is inseparable from his incarnated situation, he is also inseparable from his relationships with other persons. Here, we can see Marcel's anti-Cartesian position, for he insists, like Heidegger, that philosophy begins with a "we are" rather than an "I think," with *co-esse* rather than *esse*, with intentional consciousness rather than self-consciousness, with intersubjectivity rather than subjectivity. The individual is not an isolated, atomized monad to whom relations are added, and relations with others are creative of being. For him, the individual ego arises out of an intersubjective nexus. It is true that a person may purposefully cut himself from others and live within the confines of his own ego, but for Marcel this subjective isolation is a denial of the communion within which the mystery of being can be known. Thus, in his play *Les coeurs des autres*, "there is only one suffering: to be alone." His position lies in sharp contrast to Sartre's early vision of the world in *No Exit*, in which he claims that "hell is other people." Although Marcel does not deny that the self may become a hellish prison, but he refuses that this is the primary condition of the authentic human life. The imprisoned and isolated ego results from a refusal to heed the appeal to communion that arises from other persons. Thus, because intersubjectivity is the precondition of human consciousness, and communion the mode of authentic life, Marcel believes that philosophy must be an account of the meaning of "with."

Marcel also prefigures Buber by making use of the distinction between I-thou relations and I-he relations. To treat another person as a *he* rather than a *thou* means to treat him as an object. The parties in an I-he relation remain closed to deep creative interchange, are not with one another, and are merely two isolated beings who come together for pre-conceived purposes. In this case, the relationship operates in terms of pre-conceived categories, in terms of objective and sometimes scientized knowledge, and prevents a fuller relation from developing. In contrast, in the I-thou relation, the partners are present to each other in an attitude of openness and self-giving. Being with another person means to transform the dynamic of two isolated entities objectifying each other, to transform dialectic into dialogue, and to transform conversation and chatter into communion. When the other person becomes a thou for me, the relation established is an end in itself, and there is nothing beyond love and the communion that changes and enriches the lives of both. Thus, I become an I in the fullest sense only when I encounter a thou. Apart from the mutual giving and intermingling of such relations, I remain an isolated Cartesian ego that is prey to loneliness and despair.

Marcel implores us to train our thought on mystery, which
is only accessible through participation and not abstract
thought. The concept of mystery implies that we are not
mere spectators but are conscious participants in life who
are inseparable from the world and other human beings.
Only by a distorting act of abstraction can I pull myself from
my existential foundations in order to arrive at objective
knowledge. Authentic human life, therefore, exists in the
realm of mystery. Whenever one is involved in a mystery one
is involved as a total person in an intimate set of relations
that can never be grasped as something apart from one's
own self and held up as an object of knowledge. Recognition
of mystery necessarily involves a whole person and is as
much a matter of living one's self into the heart of mystery
as of thinking. Recall that a problem aims at a solution. In
contrast, recognition of a mystery does not end in a verifiable
solution but rather in the truth that each of us must discover
for ourselves the reality of our own meaning, freedom,
interpersonal love, and the way to deepen participation in
being. We can surely witness the other's calling out of his
own experience, but there cannot be any direct transmission
of the communion such relations generate. This is not to
say that Marcel is suggesting that there is a realm of human
experience that thought cannot penetrate, that is unknowable.
Rather, he believes that we can clarify the meaning of human
existence by deepening our participation in relations between
ourselves and the world. This deepening involvement in
participation does not generate knowledge in the traditional
sense, but it is not of the realm of pure feeling or subjectivity
either. It is, rather, an illumination that is interior to
participation, and it springs from the origin of our experience
prior to objective conceptualization and objectification.

Finally, the concept of availability (*disponibilité*) is perhaps
the central concept in Marcel, around which all others

relate. *Disponibilité*, which cannot be adequately translated into English, although "availability" seems the closest, is an attitude of the self that implies a turning toward something else. Thus, Marcel says that "it is essential to human life not only . . . to orientate itself towards something other than itself, but also to be inwardly conjoined and adapted — rather as the joints of the skeleton are conjoined and adapted to the other bones — to that reality transcending the individual life which gives the individual life its point, and, in a certain sense, even its justification."[59] Its opposite, unavailability, implies that a self is closed in upon itself, isolated from the presence of another, and unable to share in participation, more or less. To be unavailable means to be encumbered and occupied by the self in such a way that there is no room for anyone else. For example, a narcissistic person who is totally enamoured with his appearance cannot be attentive to others around him and thus misses the revelation of their being. Living in the mode of having rather than being is an indication of unavailability, for availability is an opening to the presence of another, not a way of accessing goods he has. Instead of being entirely with me, the unavailable person only gives me a loan of resources he has at his disposal. Marcel is arguing that we render ourselves unavailable when we treat our lives as a having, in some way measurable, which can be wasted or used up. Further, when we live in this mode, we develop an anxiety about losing the things we do have, and it is this anxiety that paralyzes us and precludes us from being available to the other.

Being unavailable renders us incapable of presence to the world and especially to others. It prevents us from allowing ourselves to pass into the world toward others and also prevents their presence from influencing our own life. This sealing off of experience closes the doors between people so that experience becomes fixated on the old and thereby resistant to what is new. It is a withdrawal into the self and

involves a fixation on old categories of thought through
which we view the world. This wall that the encumbered
erects hardens with time and locks out the world as it
isolates him from it. This wall hinders free movement and
creates a heaviness that, in our culture, is exemplified by
depression. If we crystallize our experience into one world
we miss the richness that other worlds could bring. In this
case, our experience becomes unavailable for fresh life and
new forms of experience. By not availing ourselves to new
experience, we become unavailable for others. Marcel thinks
that moral egocentricity also contributes toward the state
of unavailability. He describes moral egocentricity as the
illusion "that I am possessed of unquestionable privileges
which make me the centre of my universe, while other people
are mere obstructions to be removed or circumvented, or
else those echoing amplifiers, whose purpose is to foster my
self-complacency."[60] Because the egoist throws up barriers
between himself and others, he is unavailable to himself, as
well as to others. He ends up not knowing himself or others.[61]
This state is opposed to its contrasting condition, which is
availability (*disponibilité*).

Availability implies such phenomena as self-presence,
receptivity, and welcoming. Self-presence is the "particle of
creation which is in me, the gift which from all eternity has
been granted to me of participating in the universal drama,
of working, for instance, to humanize the earth, or on the
contrary to make it more uninhabitable."[62] For Marcel, there
is a convergence of self-presence with the presence of the
other. Self-presence appears where the presence of the other
is recognized. Love is the revelation of self-presence, with
the presence of the other. Availability is the attitude that
permits this revelation. When we are open to ourselves we
allow ourselves to be open with others, and when we are open
with others we are open with ourselves. Availability means

that we are receptive and ready to welcome the other. The paradigm case is to receive someone into our house, but we must be at home in order to receive. It means that we must be at home within ourselves, or present, in order to receive the other. The human meaning of receptivity is to introduce the other into a zone of our experience, a region that is our own, which we have prepared by investing something of ourselves in it. Receptivity is the active power of opening ourselves and responding to the appeal of the other.

In contrast to an object that we can grasp, manipulate, and control, in presence this is not possible. Presence rises from intersubjectivity, which is an opening from one subject to another. It is that zone of mystery that we have just mentioned within which the distinctions between "before me" and "in me" collapse. This does not mean that there is an identity between the subject and the object of normal human discourse, but rather that the distinction becomes insignificant because of its limitation in revealing being. Marcel does not assume that the "I" is a primitive and self-evident datum of experience, nor that we know others in terms of reasoning by analogy. Instead, for him, the "we" is more original in experience than the "I." We can only constitute ourselves as interiority as we recognize the reality of the other. The conception of the "I" as a monad, independent and without real connection with other beings, is false, for we are never alone nor are we one. The "we" reveals itself as more phenomenologically profound than the "I," for whenever the bonds of intimacy are broken, for instance through betrayal, the ego appears to consciousness as independent and alone. Yet, the intersubjective level is the foundation from which this isolated ego emerges. It is the background or horizon against which the "I" and the "thou" stand out. This horizon of intersubjectivity constitutes the condition of the possibility of communion, and of every communication. It also constitutes the radically mysterious nature of intersubjectivity.

I submit that any psychology that bases itself on the kind of de-presencing that occurs with objectification of humans prevents the kind of availability and participation about which Marcel writes. We assert that this kind of psychology is inadequate because it stands in the way of understanding human behavior, consciousness, motivation, and related elements. In this light, when we take stock of Marcel we can see how concerned he is about the kind of social engagement we prioritize in our culture, and we can see how it emerges in our psychological science. Let us now discuss his relation to Sartrean phenomenology as well as to Lacanian structuralism. Then we will make some final remarks about the status of psychology and suggest a new direction. In our final discussion, it is fitting to go back to the spectator philosophy of Descartes, for all individual and social alienation in psychology perhaps starts here, although this condition most surely receives its fuel from Newtonian-based, determinist methodologies. We think it clear that the tendency toward objectification in contemporary psychology makes it a psychology of alienation. As such, we must ask ourselves if this is the kind of knowledge we want to acquire about ourselves. We must also scrutinize the kind of value this sort of knowledge has for ourselves, individually, socially, and culturally — and psychotherapeutically.

People typically think of Sartre as a philosopher of alienation and of Marcel as a philosopher of communion. Yet, it can be shown that Sartre, more or less, overcomes this charge. No one disputes that his early philosophy is a fierce argument that social life is nothing more than a conflict of gazes in which each person attempts to master a present situation. His famous quotes such as "hell is other people" or that "the other is a gun pointed at me" demonstrate his absolute commitment to dualist ontology and an alienating dynamic. In order for there to be a masterful subject there must also be an objective world — including other people — which can be mastered. He has an unquestioning belief in a foundational subject-object dichotomy. He assumes that humans can objectify anything that one is and can, therefore, always make oneself other than what is objectified. Consciousness itself is just this fundamental alienation which manifests itself individually. What is more, in his analysis of the "Look," Sartre shows how this subject-object dichotomy plays out in the social realm. Narcissistic love, Sartre argues, is an attempt to overcome our fundamental alienation, but this pursuit fails because is it impossible to overcome the subject-object duality in our being.

Nevertheless, even Sartre seems to overcome much of the alienation his Cartesian-styled theories imply. For example, with regard to individual alienation, the very idea of the pre-reflective self, when brought to the forefront of human experience through pure reflection, seems to transcend the antagonism and alienation wrought by the other's gaze. Giving up the God-project in which we try to become the foundation of our own freedom through narcissistic attachments to others, and replacing this by the project of radical freedom, promotes an authentic self relationship, as well as authentic political community. Further, at the social level, though Sartre never gave up his dualistic ontology, he makes great strides toward the overcoming of alienation with his cogent theories about the transformations of group consciousness in the *Critique*. Hazel Barnes does a fine job of explaining that positive reciprocity, through the Look-as-exchange, is possible even given Sartre's early ontology. Additionally, in a late interview, even Sartre recognizes the possibility of positive reciprocity in love, through the appeal of the Other, saying that "I wrote *Saint Genet* to try to present a love that goes beyond the sadism in which Genet is steeped and the masochism that he suffered."[63]

Finally, in *Being and Nothingness*, Sartre suggests that empathy ought to be the primary tool in existential psychoanalysis; in *Search for a Method* and in the *Critique of Dialectical Reason*, the proper method is comprehension, which implies an ability to understand the Other.[64] Thus, even though he fiercely clung to his dualistic ontology, we can see Sartre stretching it to the limits as he attempts to overcome the inevitable alienation his theories imply, moving closer and closer to a Marcellian social position.

With regard to Lacan's alienating structuralism, he believes the best we can do is accept that we are determined by the linguistic unconscious. For Lacan we literally take the other for ourselves and we can never overcome this fundamental alienation. For him, both the self and the other are objects, never subjects, which prevents any kind of positive social transformation. In fact, the Lacanian ego is otherness absolutely and completely, and this means that there is no transcendent consciousness or Foucauldean intentionality that can reflectively alter or develop the ego. By placing the source of otherness inside the linguistic unconsciousness, Lacan considers normal the kind of alienation Sartre describes in his concept of *hexis*. For Lacan, the most one can do is to understand that we are the playthings of the linguistic unconscious and that one is only an object pretending to be a subject. It is the Cartesian subject that is also the subject of the humanist tradition that Lacan calls into question. He believes that the philosophical *cogito* is an essentialist illusion and argues that the centre of the human being is no longer to be found in subjective experience. Recall that Lacan advocates the reconstruction of the signifying chain by which a person has been constructed. The goal is full speech that occurs without the disrupting intervention of ego identifications. It differs from empty speech because it realizes that subjectivity is an illusion. In order to understand oneself as a product of the discourse of the Other, one must understand that one is integrated into its circuit, lost in it like objects, where our future is already determined by the chain of signifiers into which we are inserted. The best we can do within this condition is to understand our destiny within discourse.

The problem for Lacan is that no genuine *praxis* is possible in a system where the conscious subject is merely an effect of unconscious signifiers and there is no possibility for resistance. His tenacious grip on the Cartesian dictum, even though reversed, implies an absolute attachment to the will to truth — and to objectification, and perhaps this is where Marcel would respond first. By attacking subjectivity as an illusion, Lacan confirms it as one part of the dialectical tension in any kind of dualistic distinction between mind and body. Recall that Descartes's starting point implies an isolated, thinking individual in which there is a dualism between the thinking subject and the objective, material world, which includes the human body. The existentialist tradition quarreled with this dualism by arguing that philosophy must begin with the concrete individual who is fully engaged in the world and thoroughly involved in relationships with others. A concrete philosophy begins not with the certainty of thinking but with the experience of immediate existence. This is one major place where Marcel parts company with Lacan. Instead of turning toward the aesthetic realm like Foucault does, Marcel turns to the body's primordial participation with being. By letting go of the will to (scientific) truth (in terms of dualist ontology), Marcel avoids the kind of objectification into which Lacan lands.

Recall that Marcel rejects the mind-body dualism and argues that incarnation is the primary given of metaphysics. He believes that only through incarnation do we recognize ourselves to be subjects in the world and not through abstract minds who process ideas. For him, we come to know the world through the body, and the way we relate to our body is the way we relate to the world. Yet, as incarnate beings, we do not adopt the materialist position that we are merely the chemical and material components of our bodies. Idealism is wrong because humans are not just minds accidentally residing in bodies. Materialism is wrong because humans are not bodies accidentally housing minds. In contrast, to be incarnate means that the only way we can think about the world is through our bodily insertion into it — through participation, availability, and presencing. Our incarnation anchors us to the real. Perhaps it is here in the foundation of incarnation that a new psychology could begin.

Final Remarks

We have traveled a good distance, from Freud and the early drive theorists to the relational theorists and then to Lacan. We have examined the evolution of psychoanalytic thought from the standpoint of phenomenology and structuralism. We have shown the problems resulting from Descartes's spectator philosophy and how this leads to the illusion of a substantial self. Based on some of the theoretical questions we raise, it would be interesting to engage an empirical investigation into the ways that a psychology of objectification does not lead to the good nor to living well. It would also be interesting to construct a full-length study into a new direction for a unified psychology whose phenomenological presuppositions were better thought out, not borrowed, and richer. In these future studies, it would be imperative to re-define the objectives of psychology, and this raises the importance of Dilthey even more. Hugh Silverman wrote a great book that addresses the question of what we ought to do after phenomenology and structuralism, and formulates a position he calls "hermeneutic semiology."[65] Perhaps a new psychology needs to wait until

we have re-synthesized these two polarities. It does seem
clear, however, that we ought to carefully interrogate — and
perhaps this is the wrong word — our own motivations
and our vision about what it is that we wish to find in our
own phenomena. We cannot help but think that we must
take Nietzsche's admonitions about the balance between
the Dionysian and the Apollinian seriously, that we ought
to pursue a Heideggerian psychology more rigorously, and
finally, that we ought to re-think the ethical. One thing is
for sure, and that is that Sartre has taught us about the
jeopardy in which we place ourselves when we construct
a dualist ontology, even if there are interpretations of the
objectification of others that imply a virtuous psychology.
Marcel's pronouncements about participation are potent
and, we believe, signal us that all roads — in a new
psychology — lead to Levinas.

Notes

1. See Kevin Boileau and David A. Boileau, *The Algebra of History* (New Orleans: Loyola University, 2004).

2. Gabriel Marcel, "Reply to John D. Glenn, Jr." in *The Philosophy of Gabriel Marcel, The Library of Living Philosophers*, Volume XVII (La Salle, Illinois: Open Court, 1991), 551.

3. This is a concept explored at length in Kevin Boileau, *Genuine Reciprocity and Group Authenticity* (Lanham, Maryland: University Press of America, 2000).

4. Michel Foucault, "Philosophy and Psychology," in Rabinow, P. (Series Ed.), *Essential Works of Michel Foucault*, Volume 2 (New York: The New Press, 1998), 249.

5. *Ibid.*, 251.

6. *Ibid.*, 255.

7. Michel Foucault, "Madness and Society," in *Essential Works*, Volume 2, 341.

8. Michel Foucault, "Philosophy and Psychology," in *Essential Works*, Volume 2, 255.

9. *Ibid.*, 257.

10. See K. Boileau, *Genuine Reciprocity and Group Authenticity*, Chapter 2, for a discussion of how these standards emerged in the domains of the penal system, the hospital, and in mental health care.

11. Michel Foucault, "Psychiatric Power," in Rabinow, P. (Series Ed.), *Essential Works of Michel Foucault*, Volume I (New York: The New Press, 1997), 47.

12.   *Ibid.*, 48.

13.   See the earlier work by K. Boileau, *Genuine Reciprocity and Group Authenticity*, for extensive discussion of Foucault.

14.   Michel Foucault, *Discipline and Punish: The Birth of the Prison*, trans. Alan Sheridan (New York: Vintage, 1979).

15.   Hubert Dreyfus and Paul Rabinow, *Michel Foucault: Beyond Structuralism and Hermeneutics* (Chicago: University of Chicago Press, 1983), 7

16.   Michel Foucault, *The Birth of the Clinic (An Archaeology of Medical Perception)*, trans. A.M. Sheridan Smith (New York: Pantheon, 1973).

17.   Michel Foucault, *Madness and Civilization*, trans. Richard Howard (New York: Vintage, 1988).

18.   Michel Foucault, *Discipline and Punish: The Birth of the Prison*, 28.

19.   Also see Michel Foucault, *The History of Sexuality: An Introduction*, Volume I, trans. Robert Hurley (New York: Vintage, 1980) for advanced discussion.

20.   K. Boileau, *Genuine Reciprocity and Group Authenticity*, 27.

21.   Michel Foucault, 143.

22.   David Couzens Hoy, "Power, Repression, Progress: Foucault, Lukes, and the Frankfurt School," in *Foucault, A Critical Reader* (New York: B. Blackwell, 1986), 123-147.

23.   Michel Foucault, *History of Sexuality, Volume I*, 94.

24.   *Loc. cit.*

25.   *Ibid.*, 93.

26. *Ibid.*, 94.

27. *Ibid.*, 95.

28. *Loc. cit.*

29. *Loc. cit.*

30. Michel Foucault, "The Subject and Power," in *Michel Foucault: Beyond Structuralism and Hermeneutics*, p. 220.

31. *Ibid.*, 221.

32. *Loc. cit.*

33. See K. Boileau, Chapter 3, *Genuine Reciprocity and Group Authenticity*, for discussion about the Christian influence on this pastoral, individualizing power.

34. Michel Foucault, "The Subject and Power," 21.

35. Michel Foucault, "Sexuality and Solitude," in David Rieff (Ed.) *Humanities in Review I* (New York: Cambridge University Press, 1982), 10.

36. See my earlier discussion of Kuhn on this point.

37. Michel Foucault, "The Ethic of Care for the Self as a Practice of Freedom," in James Bernauer and David Rasmussen (Eds.), *The Final Foucault*, (Cambridge: MIT Press, 1988), 1.

38. Michel Foucault, *L'Impossible Prison*, Michelle Perrot, ed. (Paris: Editions du Seuil, 1980), 47.

39. *Diagnostic and Statistical Manual of Mental Disorders*, 4th (Washington, D.C., American Psychiatric Association, 1994).

40. Michel Foucault, "The Subject and Power," 212.

41. *Ibid.*, 208.

42. The collapse of these categories is part of the postmodern movement. Nietzsche masterfully portrays this view in *Thus Spoke Zarathustra* (Baltimire: Penguin, 1975). It is difficult to view these radical separations in others ways, i.e., where we could view two subjectivities belonging to two different individuals as not so radically separate. Our continued need to see in terms of these distinctive dualism stems from the radical individualist element that accompanied the Enlightenment project. Foucault and Nietzsche both demand that we try to see how historically embedded and contingent these radical oppositions are.

43. Michel Foucault, "The Subject and Power," 221-2.

44. With regard to the relation between Foucault and Lacan, see: John Forrester, *The Seductions of Psychoanalysis* (New York: Cambridge University Press, 1999); also see: John Rajchman, *Truth and Eros: Foucault, Lacan, and the Question of Ethics* (New York: Routledge, 1991).

45. Charles Scott, "The Pleasure of Therapy," in Sonu Shamdasani and Michael Mümchow (Eds.), *Speculations After Freud: Psychoanalysis, Philosophy and Culture* (New York: Routledge, 1994), 211.

46. *Ibid.*, 212.

47. *Loc. cit.*

48. K. Boileau, *Genuine Reciprocity and Group Authenticity*. Since the publication of that work, I have retreated from that position somewhat and willing to entertain that freedom may come indirectly from the malleability in structure. This, to some extent, obviates the need for a voluntarist position.

49. See our prior work, *The Algebra of History*, for a fuller discussion of Marcel.

50. Friedrich Nietzsche, trans. Walter Kaufmann, (Ed.), *On the Genealogy of Morals* (New York: Vintage, 1989).

51. Gabriel Marcel, *The Philosophy of Existentialism* (New York: Citadel, 2002), 14.

52. Gabriel Marcel, *Being and Having*, trans. Katherine Farrer (Boston: Beacon Press, 1951).

53. Gabriel Marcel, *Being and Having*, 134, 158-9.

54. Gabriel Marcel, *Metaphysical Journal* (Chicago: Henry Regnery Co., 1952), 199.

55. Marcel, *The Mystery of Being*, Vol. I, *Reflection and Mystery*, trans. G. S. Fraser (Chicago: Gateway Edition, Henry Regnery Co., 1970, Chapter 2; also see: *The Mystery of Being*, Vol. II., *Faith and Reality*, trans. G. S. Fraser (South Bend, Indiana: St. Augustine's Press, 2001), 42; *The Philosophy of Existentialism* (New York: Citadel, 2002), 9-12.

56. Gabriel Marcel, *Being and Having*, 117.

57. Gabriel Marcel, *The Mystery of Being*, Vol. I, 115-116.

58. Gabriel Marcel, *Being and Having*.

59. Gabriel Marcel, *The Mystery of Being*, Vol. I, 201-202.

60. Gabriel Marcel, *Homo Viator*, trans. Emma Crauford (Chicago: Harper & Row, 1965), 19.

61. Gabriel Marcel, *The Mystery of Being*, Vol. *II*, 8.

62. Gabriel Marcel, *Homo Viator*, 132.

63. Jean-Paul Sartre, "An Interview with Jean-Paul Sartre," in Paul Arthur Schilpp, (Ed.) *The Philosophy of*

Jean-Paul Sartre, The Library of Living Philosophers, Vol. 16 (La Salle, Ill.:, Open Court, 1981), 13; also see: Sartre, *Saint Genet*, trans. Bernard Frechtmann (New York: George Braziller, 1963), 327-8.

64. Jean-Paul Sartre: see earlier references to *Being and Nothingness* and to the *Critique of Dialectical Reason*; also see: Sartre, *Search for a Method*, trans. Hazel Barnes (New York: Vintage, 1968).

65. Hugh Silverman, *Inscriptions: After Phenomenology and Structuralism* (Evanston, Ill.: Northwestern University Press, 1997).

Existential Psychoanalysis: Sartre's Phenomenological Dialectic between Self-Deception and Moral Development

Introduction

In *The Critique of Dialectical Reason, "CDR,"* Sartre presents a theory of groups that he thinks provides a foundation for authentic political community that is comprised of positive and constructive social relations. One of the problems with which Sartre leaves us concerns how we can create the conditions under which individuals will actually promote the kind of authentic political community that he envisions. This requires that we investigate three different domains of freedom: 1) the abstract/ontological; 2) the concrete/practical; and 3) the psychological/psychoanalytic. In this essay, we will investigate the third aspect of freedom by focusing solely on Sartre as a way to bridge discourses between authenticity and morality. My goal is to explore the relationship between Sartrean psychology and authenticity. I will then explore the relationship between authenticity and morality, from a Sartrean point of view. My overall objective is to illuminate aspects of the moral development of a self that avoids self-deception. By looking at both Sartre's earlier ontological formulations as well as his later work that is based on concrete conceptualizations of the socio-political world, I hope to illuminate how moral development can be impeded by relationships that abrogate our freedom and radical responsibility. To this end, I will sketch a preliminary outline of how the methodology of existential psychoanalysis can overcome personal and social dysfunctions in moral development.

Sartre's Phenomenological Self & Authenticity

The basis of Sartre's notion of the self largely comes from his early ontological work and theory of value in *Being and Nothingness, "BN,"* although we will see important modifications in his later work. For Sartre, nothing possesses intrinsic value. Instead, humans create values by freely choosing them. In order to explicate these ideas, we will discuss his ideas about freedom, bad faith, our situation in the world, the role of others in the constitution of that situation, and our objective encounter with values in the world. We will also argue, like Sartre, that implicit in *BN* is an ethics that can liberate individuals from living in bad faith by means of a reflective comprehension of human reality. This ethics is based on a self-recovery, which is the pursuit of authenticity, whose ideal is the development of a morally autonomous individual who chooses freedom as his ultimate value.

For Sartre, consciousness has two fundamental characteristics. First, it is intentional, in which it is always conscious of something. Therefore consciousness itself has no content.[2] Second, it is self-conscious.[3] I can never stand completely behind myself in order to view myself clearly as an object. I can never completely capture my subjectivity. It is an implicit awareness of myself without taking myself as an object. On the other hand, reflection is a secondary act in which the reflecting consciousness posits the consciousness reflected on as its object. Sartre's contention is that "there is a [non-positional] pre-reflective *cogito* which is the condition of the [reflecting] Cartesian *cogito*."[4]

Unlike consciousness, which is a lack of being, i.e., nothingness, Sartre characterizes being-in-itself as solid, as a coincidence with itself. In contrast, being-for-itself, which

is the human reality of consciousness, establishes itself
against being-in-itself, which includes the givens of one's
situation. The for-itself exists as the process of negation of
that which has already been established. We have an original
negative relation designating an object as that which is
not consciousness. Thus, for Sartre, negation is the *a priori*
foundation of all experience. There is an upsurge of the for-
itself as presence to an object that it is not.[5]

The for-itself determines itself by means of what it is not.
This nihilation of being is an internal negation which reveals
the in-itself while determining the being or defining the
internal structure of the for-itself. In this way it founds itself
as a lack of being. Lack always implies a surpassing of the
in-itself toward a totality that it is not. For example, the first
few pages of this manuscript reveal themselves as a lack, as
incomplete. Negating behaviors include imagining, doubting,
questioning, and any other mental operation that nihilates
the status quo. By making one thing stand out, I relegate
other objects in its proximity into the background. Together,
these other objects become nothingness. Being-in-itself is an
undifferentiated mass from which specific objects emerge in
consciousness.

For Sartre, the existence of human desire proves that human
reality is a lack, that desire itself is a lack of being. For him,
human reality is never what it is. The for-itself is not identical
to itself because the for-itself lacks a self that is substantial
being, i.e., one that does not draw its existence through
nihilation; it lacks being-in-itself. Thus, the *cogito* is haunted
by a mode of being it can never reach and this constitutes the
origin of transcendence. He, therefore, believes that "human
reality is a perpetual surpassing toward what it lacks, . . .
toward a coincidence with itself which is never given."[6]

A synthesis between the for-itself and the in-itself is impossible, for Sartre, because it would have to combine the incompatible characteristics of the full positivity of being-in-itself with the self-surpassing self-awareness of being-for-itself. Sartre believes that we have hypostatized this impossible synthesis as transcendence beyond the world, which we call "God," who is self-identical, self-conscious plenitude. While he thinks that the for-itself and the in-itself are radically contingent, he characterizes God as a necessary being, "the necessary foundation of himself."[7] Because it lacks and desires this self-identical and necessary being, the being of human reality is suffering: "(Human reality) rises in being as perpetually haunted by a totality which it is without being able to be it, precisely because it could not attain the in-itself without losing itself as for-itself."[8] Later in this essay we will see how central the God-project is to both self and social dysfunctions that result in an impairment in moral development.

For Sartre, value is "the lacked," and forms a dyad with that which is a lack (the for-itself). Together, these two elements make up human reality. In this schema God is the supreme value: "The supreme value toward which consciousness at every instant surpasses itself by its very being is the absolute being of the self with its characteristics of identity, of purity, of permanence, etc., and as its own foundation."[9] Value is what pulls the for-itself into a particular direction. Thus, each for-itself lacks a particular reality; with each nihilation emerges new possibility.[10] There is an implication here that I always have the possibility of choosing and re-choosing myself in the world, as an original project. As a corollary, I am always haunted by the possible coincidence of my for-itself with my in-itself. For Sartre, the meaning of all my individual values is derivative from my original choice in the world. For most individuals, this original choice is deeply buried in consciousness in such a way that we don't see it without great effort. Because we are radically free to re-choose our original project, and because this freedom causes us anguish, we attempt to flee from it.

Value emerges as the freedom of the for-itself. The very existence of values is contingent on my freedom and since "my freedom is the unique foundation of values and that *nothing*, absolutely nothing, justifies me in adopting this or that particular value, this or that particular scale of values."[11] Because the structure of the pre-reflective *cogito* precludes us from ever being self-identical, we are always striving for unrealized possibilities. In addition, because brute things in the realm of the in-itself can always be interpreted in many ways, value always arises in terms of a situation. The values of objects change depending upon the nature of my project within a situation that includes such an object.

In a pure ontological sense we are absolutely free because the being of human reality is freedom. We limit this freedom through the ways that we interpret our situation; these interpretations set the framework of action, and for their limits. Further, even though Sartre believes that nothing possesses intrinsic value this does not mean that our freedom is unconditioned. According to him our freedom has limits and is conditioned. We can only be free in relation to a state of things.[12] Situation, for Sartre, is the contingency of the in-itself and freedom, taken together. This raises the paradox that there is freedom only in a situation and there is a situation only through freedom. Resistances and obstacles have meaning, therefore, only in and through the free choice that human reality is.[13]

The given that human reality illuminates by its choices includes factual items such as my place of birth, my physical body, my past, my environment, and the other humans around me. Within these aspects of my situation I encounter obstacles that are not absolute. Instead, they reveal their adversity in terms of my specific projects. Further, these projects always exist within the context of our historical-cultural milieu. I come into a world that already has meaning embedded within it, independent of my choices.

According to Sartre, the usual state of humans within this situation of radically free choice is bad faith.[14] When we are born into the world, we are thrown into a constellation of meanings and values, each of which is a demand upon us. The collective activities of others who have already established meaning are, together, the foundation of objective values. Values do not come from nowhere. Each for-itself is always conditioned by the meanings established by others, and we will see as we progress through this essay how this affects each person's relationship with himself and others. For now, let us say that in Sartre's view, we are free to accept, reject, or modify the valuations that are already present in the social world. Yet we conceal this fundamental freedom of choice from ourselves, and it is this concealment that is bad faith.

For Sartre, our projects are always called into question by the freedom of the for-itself, subject to the limits created by meanings that have already been established. Yet, the consciousness of humans is basically unreflective. It is a consciousness of the already collectively defined valuation by others in the social world. It is not a reflective consciousness of my relation to those structures, which would include their dependence on the constitutive activity of consciousness and my freedom to modify those structures. In bad faith, I conceal my original relation to values, whose meaning for me is derived in relation to my original projection of myself in the world. Because everyday consciousness does not recognize that values depend upon freedom, individuals do not experience anguish in this mode. It is through the reflective apprehension of freedom in which I distance myself from the world that anguish arises.[15] In this mode I realize that values can always be questioned and modified.

According to Sartre, we place limits on ourselves through strategies of self-deception, or bad faith.[16] Consciousness, recall, exists as a lack, in terms of its possibilities. We comprehend ourselves as incomplete, which motivates us to obtain the objects of our desires. Unfortunately we never coincide with those desires. We are always at a distance from our creations and driven by our possibilities. This means that consciousness cannot exhaust itself by an achieved arrangement in the world such as a role or a position. In good faith we understand, in contrast, that our nature is a demand but not a certainty. The ego is neither the cause of my actions nor a pattern to guide them; it is not a fixed self without the possibility of change. This also includes a demand that I clarify the temporal categories of the past, present, and future for my self.

The experience of freedom is dizzying and full of anguish as we realize the great responsibility involved in making choices. We try to flee from our anguish by engaging in one of the patterns of bad faith, which are the mental mechanisms that place an individual at a distance from his real condition as a free being. These cloud my ability to contemplate my possibilities. One type of bad faith occurs if I believe myself compelled to act by forces that are beyond my control. In this case, a criminal might believe that early environmental influences in his life compel him to break the law. He gives up his autonomy and responsibility and gives over his freedom to an essential nature or some kind of determinism. This kind of person believes that everything is pure externality thereby denying any kind of sovereignty and the ability to transcend one's situation. This attitude is exemplified in positivist psychologies that describe an individual in terms of what has happened to him or her. Another type of bad faith occurs when a person denies his surroundings. In this case, he denies the reality of his body as an object in the world and posits himself as pure freedom. This results in alienation and isolation from the world. A final type of bad faith is like the first in that an individual becomes what he is expected to be, defined by what others think he is. This individual believes that he is without a horizon of possibilities.

Humans maintain themselves in bad faith by polarizing their attitude between believing that they are completely determined by their past or social role or by believing that they are pure freedom. Yet we ambiguously are both elements. When we are not in bad faith we spring forth in the world from a foundation of actuality and move toward our possibilities. We are more than the roles that are heaped upon us, and we live in the world through mind and body. Instead of having a fixed self we have a self that is temporally dispersed. This is a self that can never totally identify with any role or knowledge, one that can never totally identify with oneself. The for-itself always leaps beyond the in-itself, for our subjectivity is dynamic and not static. We can be in bad faith when we unthinkingly accept traditional judgments and social arrangements as truth. In good faith we are a synthesis of facticity and transcendence, each mutually limiting the other.

For Sartre, the risk of bad faith is part of being human because of the ontological structure of the for-itself. Recall that human reality is a lack and with it comes the desire for an impossible synthesis of the for-itself and the in-itself. Yet, if we seek this impossible goal then all our efforts are futile. When we are in a mode of bad faith our underlying motivation just is this impossible synthesis of becoming the objective foundation of our values. However, there is implicit in *BN* an ethics designed to liberate us from living in bad faith through a reflective comprehension of our condition. This ethics of self-recovery — authentic existence — springs from a pure, reflective consciousness that attempts to develop moral autonomy.[17] An individual living authentically is aware of the ambiguity of the human situation, that one can never be self-identical. In bad faith we try to deny one side of the ambiguity. Sartre's notion of self-recovery is a focused awareness of this ambiguity.

In *The Transcendence of the Ego*, *"TE,"* Sartre distinguishes between reflective and unreflective consciousness. The latter type is the positional consciousness of an object other than itself, along with non-positional self-consciousness. In contrast, the former type is positional consciousness of itself as another act of consciousness, along with non-positional self-consciousness. At the unreflective level, objects appear as though they have a kind of power over us.[18] Impure reflection can grasp consciousness in such a way as to prolong this state of the power of objects over us, whereby we do not see our free choices. Pure reflection, on the other hand, can occur in such a way as to grasp the true nature of consciousness as freedom.

Sartre argues that the consciousness of impure reflection, which is unreflective about the true being of consciousness as freedom, "imprisons itself in the world" by believing that the ego is foundation to one's situation. In fact, the ego is merely a choice.[19] The bad faith of *BN* is this impure reflection along with its patterns of flight. In contrast, pure reflection recovers and knows the true being of consciousness. Objects, including the ego, no longer have power over us because their relation to and dependence on consciousness is apprehended.

In pure reflection, consciousness understands its fundamental freedom and its absolute responsibility for itself. For Sartre, this opens up the possibility of an ethics distinct from everyday morality.

Nevertheless, we have seen that the very structure of the for-itself renders the impure reflection of bad faith a permanent possibility. According to Sartre, though, through the method of existential psychoanalysis an individual can become aware of his "original choice" of himself in the world.[20] "By a *comparison* of the various empirical drives of the subject. . . we try to discover and disengage the fundamental project which is common to them all. . . . each drive or tendency is the entire person."[21] There are two levels of choice here. There is the original, non-positional choice of myself that is completely unjustified by anything else because there is no base of support outside of the choice itself. All of my lived values derive their meaning from this original projection of myself into the world. Existential analysis enables us to become aware of this choice by moving from either the immediate, prereflective plane or the plane of impure reflection to the level of pure reflection.

Pure reflection is a moral consciousness because it cannot arise without simultaneously disclosing my valuations as choices. This is where the second level of choice becomes operative as voluntary deliberation. This is a deception at the level of non-positional choice because such choice is prior to logic and principles of decision-making.[22] At the reflective level particular choices are justified by reference to the fundamental choice and the totality of meanings it includes. At this level, a decision has already been made as to what will count as a reason; it is always in terms of the fundamental choice. Pure reflection allows me to evaluate my lived values through affirmation, denial, and modification.

Even though the structure of the for-itself always risks the possibility of bad faith, through Sartre's methods of analysis and pure reflection, which focus on the reflective comprehension of our condition, we can liberate ourselves from this bad faith. Viewed in this way, the opaqueness of bad faith can be contrasted with the transparency and lucidity of pure reflection, i.e., good faith. It is this reflective comprehension that provides justification for our choices. To be in good faith means to reflectively comprehend that the human condition is the source of all values. It means that our choices are not arbitrary while in this state. Sartre himself says that individual authenticity "consists in having a true and lucid consciousness of the situation, (and) in assuming the responsibilities and risks that it involves . . . it (authenticity) demands much courage."[23] His ethics of authenticity demands that I acknowledge my freedom to choose my values and that because of this freedom I must act in accordance with it. We will see later how this ethics of authenticity serves as a foundation for overcoming dysfunctions in moral development, leading to positive and constructive social relations.

Because the project to be God is futile and because we can see that freedom is the source of all values, we can set aside the pre-reflective God-project in favor of values chosen on the basis of a reflective awareness of the human condition. In addition, we must choose freedom as our primary value.[24] Because freedom is the source of all values, the choice of values entails a prior valuing of freedom. We cannot value anything that comes from a free choice unless freedom itself is also valued. Sartre's ethics of authentic existence is the reflective development of a morally autonomous individual. By substituting freedom as our primary value, we adopt "a constantly renewed obligation to remake the *Self* which designates the free being."[25] Authentic existence means to engage in an ongoing process of remaking the self, mediating an unstable equilibrium between engagement in situation and a distanced reflection. Thus, this freedom for reflection means that in the authentic mode of being we choose to be at a distance from ourselves even though we are engaged with the world, instead of attempting to collapse the for-itself and the in-itself into pure being.

Clarification of Sartre's Construction of the Self

Husserl's ideas had a big impact on Sartre because they allowed Sartre to bypass the opposition between idealism and realism for a concrete relationship between consciousness and the world.[26] In this concrete relation, consciousness is always intentional, pointing to a real, remembered, or imagined event. Sartre goes further than Husserl, denying the existence of the transcendental ego, and therefore arguing against the possibility of withdrawal from the world by bracketing one's intentionality. For Sartre, we must try to grasp our fundamental project in the midst of being in the world and not in some transcendent state apart from it, although we can attempt a pure reflection in order to gain clarity about our motives and inner states.

In *BN*, Sartre's descriptive ontology attempts to describe Being, especially as it relates to human being-ness. It is more than a cataloging of events, for it pursues an understanding of the meaning and significance of human phenomena. Against Freud, he denies the existence of an unconscious. Thus, a meaning that is unconscious is not a meaning at all. Consciousness is not the same as the will, and it is influenced by emotion and imagination. His theory also explains all those self-deceptions that are phenomenological evidence for the unconscious. Moreover, Sartre's theory can investigate the present as well as the past and the future as the ground of human meaning and reality.

For Sartre, spontaneous or prereflective consciousness is not just a part of consciousness.[27] Rather, Sartre believes that consciousness is all of one fabric without compartments. Reflective consciousness, seen in this way, is prereflective consciousness making an object out of its past, directing itself inward instead of outward toward the world. It is here that the possibility of self-deception arises because a gap emerges between the reflecting consciousness and the consciousness reflected on. Consciousness is not a thing with substance and structure as it is for Freud. For Sartre it is a translucid rather than an opaque openness toward Being; it is a desire or lack of a future fullness rather than a self-contained, intra-psychic system. In order to be present to other objects, consciousness brings into being a nothingness or gap between itself and its objects. A human being is not a bundle of drives but is rather a position on Being, implying a world. It is intentional in the sense of always being aware of objects.

Consciousness is always directed toward objects and into the future. It lives through awareness of a movement out of the past towards those objects that it intends. It is always nihilating itself from objects as well as from a future that it projects and intends.[28] It is because consciousness inserts itself into the heart of Being that it can conceive of a future that is different from the present. Moreover, we perceive objects in terms of our projects. That is, we interpret the furniture of the world in terms of our intentions. For example, a forest appears one way to the owner of a lumberyard and a different way to a poet. We each create hodological maps in which we organize objects of the world in terms of our plans and projects. Thus, my nearness to or distance from objects can help reveal my fundamental project in the world.

This fundamental project includes tastes and habits by which I define myself. On the level of prereflective consciousness we find a person in those choices that clarify his project of being. This project is not to be found behind these concrete choices but right within them. The value of things and their temporal and physical relationship to me is, for Sartre, an outline of my fundamental choice of being. These prereflective choices may never have been reflectively conceived. Yet, according to Sartre, all of my concrete choices about being, doing, and having each reveal the meaning of my fundamental project of being in the world.

The primary categories of being, doing, and having, by which I define myself in the world, are ontologically related to each other. Doing is a mode of having and having is a part of the attempt to be, to achieve a substantial sense of self. By examining these primary categories we can reveal and understand a person's fundamental project and individual character. Sartre proposes a type of psychoanalysis of things and offers the example of slime, whose quality can be applied to the human world as well as to the material world. For him, it suggests an anti-value in which the facticity of the world threatens to swallow up consciousness, in which matter absorbs freedom. Inauthentic being always involves the possibility that the materiality of Being might annihilate consciousness.

My attachments to things reveal the way in which I construct meaning in the world. Yet the meaning of my various ways of doing, being, and having may be reflectively misconstrued if they are part of a project of self-deception. For example, I may be aggressively warm and generous, and this is revealed in the way that I am warm and generous. It may be the case that I manipulate others with my warmth. Thus, for Sartre, our acts inform us of our intentions if we would only attend to

Circuit of Selfness

our underlying motivations. However, all too often we choose not to see certain aspects of ourselves, instead perpetuating myths such as the one that we are warm and generous.

Self-deception is possible because of the gap between prereflective and reflective consciousness. Although a person spontaneously acts and then reflects on those acts, these two movements are separated by the same nothingness that separates consciousness from objects in the world. It is only by virtue of my not being my past spontaneous self that I can reflectively conceive of myself as past. This is where the possibility of bad faith or self-deception emerges, for in the reflective mode I can deceive myself and give myself attributions that are distortions. I can, however, move back into the spontaneous mode and rename those same attributions.

Sartre thinks the pursuit of meaning through future oriented value-creating activity is the prime focus of humans. This process, for him, takes place through our lived, bodily experience as subjects and not as objects. In contrast, the body of scientific investigation is an object that cannot express meaning. Scientific categorizations of body parts, for example, do not express meaning, as attempts at transcendence of the world through lived experience do. Conscious experience is lived as a connection with the world through which we create meaning and value. We all use the world to gain a sense of self, which Sartre calls the "circuit of selfness."[29] This is the process of consciousness perceiving its possibilities in a forward-looking way in the world. My need for love, for example, transmutes into affection and attention toward a particular person. Each human action has a teleological meaning that is motivated as an attempt to create a kind of self. My choice of myself in the world and my discovery of the world are identical.

Consciousness is desire or lack of a particular kind of future fullness. Yet this lack discovers itself outside in the world. It is motivated by a desire for Being. Each person has a different and unique fundamental project. Ontologically speaking, this desire is for a substantial self and yet to remain a free consciousness.[30] This is the God-project we discussed earlier, which attempts to combine substantial being with a transcending consciousness; it is freedom within material fullness. However, this is an impossible goal because of the very nature of consciousness. The capture of substantial being is illusory; at the very best it is ephemeral and is lost in an instant. Another way of articulating this phenomenon is that once we complete a project, this completion becomes the background and context for the next, as consciousness propels itself forward. Thus, consciousness can never coincide with itself. Unlike material objects, consciousness is always propelled forward as lack. This creates anguish because I can never establish myself once and for all time as a certain kind of person.

We try to create a self in everything we do in the world. Our fundamental project is always a solution to the problem that consciousness can never coincide with itself. This solution is always one that we live every day in all our concrete acts. As long as we are always future oriented and realize that there is no destination, there is no lack of authenticity in the pursuit. Yet, when we pretend that we have arrived at who we are, by playing a role to the hilt, by *being* that role, we are in bad faith, deceiving ourselves. In the inauthentic mode the ego is my reflective view of myself as having a particular character; that I *am* a certain way. Within the structure of consciousness, however, the reflective mode is always susceptible to distortion and bad faith self-deception. While these distortions can take a variety of forms, they always involve the God-project in which my consciousness tries to coincide with itself; to integrate freedom with materiality, a fullness of being that is transcendent. These are always an escape from freedom and responsibility.

Escaping from our freedom is bad faith, an ontological rather than ethical category, although it has ethical reverberations. As we stated, it takes one of two basic forms, which coincides with the two sides to human reality. First, there is my facticity, which is the contingent world that I did not create but within which I must choose a way to live. This includes my history as well as present external circumstances. Second, there is my freedom, which is my choice of objects in the world as a way of realizing my own project of being. There are no values except those that I create through my free choices. I fall into bad faith if I pretend either to be free in a world without facts or to be a fact in a world without freedom.

If I desire to escape my facticity, I might deceive myself by thinking that I am absolutely free in being able to act in ways that have no connection to my past. I cannot escape a connection from my past just by hoping it to be so. If I desire to escape my freedom, then I desire to make the world, my past, and my character determinative factors in my life. This is the spirit of seriousness held by those individuals who treat the world as being more significant than they, themselves, are. This way of thinking creates cognitive sedimentation in which we take ourselves for objects instead of subjects; the opposite attitude is the spirit of play in which we discover ourselves free in every action. In play we do not attribute our actions and our situation to nature, circumstances, or the past. In play we do not seek the position of the Unmoved Mover in which transcendent freedom is coincidental with the inert materiality of the world. Instead, we release our subjectivity into a position of responsibility and bring to the forefront of consciousness the reality that what we do is always conscious choice.

Freedom within situation is not rationalist voluntarism because we often choose emotional, imaginative, or other irrational modes of being. Further, choice is not the same as will. Prereflective consciousness is basic intentionality and this is different from will, which is reflective. What passes for decision-making is really just the surface manifestation of deeper motivation. For Sartre, all basic intentionality is conscious and therefore we always end up doing what we want to do. For example, humans often say they intend to do one thing but end up doing another. For Sartre, these individuals were simply not reflecting accurately on their intentions. For him, if we focus sufficiently we can clarify these deeper motivations.

There is another way that we can distort our ability to reflect. This can come about in my awareness of myself as an object for another consciousness. We come to be aware of the Other through the Look. The Other's Look reveals another subject because it reveals to me my own object status beneath the gaze of another. This awareness of the Other can lead to a contamination of my reflective process; it can give me the hope of recovering substantive freedom. If I can incorporate the Other's view of me into my free project then I imagine that I will become that integration of materiality and freedom in which my consciousness is reflexively coincidental. The problem is that in doing so I abandon the position of good faith in which I accept the ontological failure for a position of bad faith in which I attempt to make substantive freedom itself an ideal motivation. I will always be a lack in the value-making process.

Even though it is true that I cannot overcome the Other's freedom to this end, I may still make the attempt; if the Other does so as well then we will create a conflict of consciousnesses in which we both try to use each other to create substantive freedom. The attempts always fail because each individual is a separate freedom and we cannot incorporate each other into one's own consciousness. Even though I cannot incorporate the Other into my consciousness I could try to mimic the Other's view of me in my own reflective consciousness, further alienating reflective awareness from prereflective experience. For example, a child mimics his parents, but to the extent that the child is not seen accurately, he will carry it into the future as a distortion in his reflective project.

Sartre uses the term "self" in three main ways as he develops his early ontological constructions into more practical under-standings of social exigencies and finally into a recognition of the power of deep socio-structural conditioning.[31] First, there is the self of prereflective consciousness (present stream of consciousness). Second, there is the self as reflected-upon ego (past oriented). Third, there is the self as value (future oriented). Understanding these different usages will advance our account of a more comprehensive definition of self, especially as it relates to bad faith and authentic political community.

With regard to the self of prereflective consciousness, every self is self-consciousness, for consciousness is always aware of itself as consciousness. This follows from the fact that in being aware of an object, consciousness knows that it is not that object. There is, therefore, an awareness of a distinction between awareness itself and an object. Sartre himself uses the idea of nihilation to express this removal of consciousness from the objects of which it is aware. To nihilate is to be conscious of something as an object not identical with consciousness or with the background from which the object emerges. There are two elements in any act of consciousness. There is, first, the consciousness of an object and second, an act of self-consciousness. This is consciousness's awareness of itself as being aware. Further, this awareness of being aware does not have personalizing qualities. It is, rather, the condition of all consciousness rather than the differentiating selfness of a particular consciousness. This consciousness is individual but not personal, and thus retains the emotional dimension without being accompanied by any sense of I or me. It is pure intentionality directed toward an object.

Prereflective consciousness is egoless. By separating it from that part of the self that is thought of as personality, Sartre postulates a radical freedom from psychological determinism. It is prereflective consciousness that makes the original choice of being, our fundamental project by which we relate ourselves to the world. It is this non-personal level of consciousness that gives us the uneasy realization that there is nothing fixed or necessary in this fundamental choice; we could always make another.

The second usage of self by Sartre is the self as ego. This familiar personal self is not part of the structure of consciousness but is, rather, its product. This product of consciousness is backward looking and imposes a unity upon past experience. At first glance the unity itself seems to imply an agent but on second glance the true agent is the original prereflective consciousness. It is comprised of qualities amassed through its experience with the world. This is not the Freudian Ego, which is only part of the psychical structure. Instead, the Sartrean ego is the whole of the psychical structure; as such it refers to all of the mental and emotional objects of the reflective consciousness instead of to the original prereflective consciousness. This is the self of the natural attitude and includes both the "I" and the "me." It is the structured personality, manifested in the multitudes of past acts. It is my permanent, enduring self, which is distinguishable from all other selves. Yet, its existence is purely ideal, a formal unity that a present consciousness imposes on its past and future.

If we are considering the ego as past then the essence of what I have been is a part of my being-in-itself that I drag along with me. It is the self of one's personal history that is the object of impure reflection. This involves the ordinary introspection that we do when we try to interpret and understand ourselves in order figure ourselves out. This involves a psychological analysis of our different mental states, categorizing them as though they were things in themselves; this analysis is carried out in terms of our fundamental project. Nevertheless, this method is dissatisfactory because we apprehend an object where we sought a subject. The original self-consciousness is not the personalized self. Instead of searching for what kind of self I am I should re-direct my search in terms of what kind of self my consciousness has created. More importantly, for a consciousness to look at its own product and pass judgment on it is an original ethical act. It is on the level of pure reflection that we posit morality.

The problem with pure reflection is that consciousness cannot know itself knowing. For Sartre, knowledge is consciousness's direct presence to an object. The self of prereflective consciousness cannot become the object of knowing at the same time that this consciousness is the reflecting agent. When we are conscious of our consciousness of self, these two consciousnesses are different; every act of consciousness nihilates the consciousness reflected on from the instant act of consciousness. Thus, we cannot make of our consciousness an object without falling to the level of impure reflection.

Pure reflection is, therefore, a modification of prereflective

consciousness by making me aware that I have an outside
for others. Here, I become my own witness in my pure
reflection about a spontaneous act of consciousness. In
pure reflection we attempt to examine our fundamental
choice of value as it was when it was made, not in terms of
associations we come up with after the fact. The purpose
of this sort of reflection is not to discover the self as object
but to free it from the overlay of the ego. The focus is on the
spontaneity of prereflective consciousness instead of on the
ego, which becomes a constant creation of that prereflective
consciousness. As we will see, the function of the ego in many
respects is to cover up one's own spontaneous consciousness,
which protects against a fear of freedom. More importantly,
bringing the spontaneous self into full view and attention
helps us understand that there is no substantial self and that
a free consciousness has never been identical with the self
it has made in the past or the self it projects into the future.
We will later see how strategies of bad faith keep us locked
into sadomasochistic, psychosocial dynamics that affect at a
profound level one's ability to grow morally.

The third main use of the self for Sartre is the self as value.
This is the future dimension. Recall that the ego is the ideal
unity imposed on all psychic activity, both past and future.
Yet the future does not belong to being-in-itself. It depends
upon the nihilating activity of the for-itself, which transcends
the present. This self has a purely virtual existence and there
is no way to predict exactly who that "I" will be that I project
in a forward-moving way. When we speak of a future self
we hypothesize that a consciousness will continue to create a
self that can only be grasped retrospectively. This third type
of self is always in process, does not belong to the ego, and is
never realized.[32]

Sartre believes that the for-itself that pursues value is a lack of being that seeks to achieve being. For him, consciousness is a process, not a substantial entity, and it is always directed toward something that it is not. It is not a self but as a self-making process it pursues a self. Thus, it attempts to come to and coincide with itself. This future self is a self of desire. It is value because it is always the unattained object of my desire. As we have seen, each consciousness wants to be simultaneously a desire as lack and a desire fulfilled. The ultimate desire is that I would be the self that I have to make. This is, again, the self-contradictory God-project in which a consciousness seeks to become an Unmoved Mover, self-caused, and fully self-coincidental.

It is impossible, as Barnes says, to have "both an unrestricted freedom to grow and a built-in program."[33] If a consciousness is a continuous self-project, it is impossible to say what that future self might ever be. Looking toward the future, pure reflection can stay vigilant to keep the future open to a free consciousness. Pure reflection can consistently inform me that my prereflective consciousness is not trapped by my ego and that I do not have to make of my future a repetition of the past through fear or anxiety. As Barnes asserts, pure reflection "regards the future as provisional."[34] Living in good faith means that one keeps the temporal categories of one's life separate and clear in one's attitudinal choices. In good faith we realize that the ego is a product not a cause. We realize that because the ego is not a fixed self, although it can temporarily become sedimented, my prereflective consciousness is responsible for each choice, past and future.

Sartre and the Other: Sadomasochism

The problem of whether or not I am alone in the universe has been paramount to Western culture and important to Sartre.[35] This problem of solipsism is epistemological because it concerns how one can know that there are other consciousnesses. According to the traditional view, which Freud takes, we have no direct intuitive awareness of the Other as other consciousness. The idea that another person is conscious becomes an inference that we draw from his or her behavior. This inference is different from the immediate awareness that we have of our own consciousness.

In contrast, Sartre addresses solipsism by asserting that I know the Other exists as a consciousness not by inference but by direct experience. We do not first experience the Other as an object. Neither do we deduce the Other's subjectivity from our own. Instead of constituting the Other we encounter him through his Look. We know him directly by being an object for his gaze. For Sartre, it is not my experience of the Other as an object that establishes my certainty about his existence as a consciousness. Rather, it is my experience of myself as an object beneath the Other's gaze that gives me this certainty. It is an immediate awareness that gives us this certainty. Sartre's famous example of the Look is a man who, with his eye glued to a keyhole, hears footsteps and suddenly becomes aware that he has an outside and that he is being watched. He experiences shame and, as with fear and pride, he intuits the Other's subjectivity as threatening.

In shame we recognize the Other's power over us, to use his knowledge of my subjectivity against me in some harmful way. It is the Other who looks at me and names me as an object in the world. For myself, I am only a pseudo-object within a reflective consciousness that can never fully grasp that which it attempts to contemplate; I cannot at the same time see and be the object of contemplation. The aspect of shame that Sartre contemplates is ontological and non-thetic, for it does not matter what we are doing when we are caught within the Other's gaze. This basic shame relies on being seen in the first instance. The Other's Look is an original fall that degrades me as sovereign subject and makes me an object for an Other's world. Furthermore, I can never fully understand my objectivity as it appears to the Other within his Look.

Recall that the basic goal of all humans is to create a self that is an object like other objects in the world while still remaining free, i.e., substantive freedom. This is not bad faith if it is merely a non-thetic value-making process. Unfortunately, humans incessantly attempt to make the process of self-creation refer to a created self, on a reflective level. This is bad faith. In contrast, a good faith attitude implies the acceptance of the impossibility of achieving substantive freedom while engaged in spontaneous self-creation.

The presence of the Other can cause me to believe in the possibility of the missing God because it is the Other who shows me that I have an outside. Yet, I can never be another for myself like I can be for another human being. I can imagine that if I could grasp this object that I am for the Other that I would understand myself as object. If I could then integrate the Other's knowledge of me with my freedom I would become a Being-in-itself-for-itself, i.e., self-coincidental consciousness. I would be a free being with a substantive nature. This fantasy encourages me in three ways. First, I might be motivated to submerge myself into the consciousness of the Other through a strategy of masochism. Second, I might be motivated to manipulate the Other into submerging himself in me through a strategy of sadism. Third, I might become indifferent to the Other by treating him as a mere object like other objects.

Most important is Sartre's (and my) core assumption that part of our nature as humans is to use the Other to achieve a substantial self.[36] It is a futile attempt to create the fullness that is missing because of the very nature of consciousness. Although I may directly experience the Other's Look I can never directly grasp the object that I am for the Other as I exist for him. When I attempt it, the Other ceases to be a subject, becoming an object for me in his pure externality. I can never directly apprehend and possess the Other as a perceiving subject.

The Other is a different kind of object than other objects because he is also a subject. Through the Other's Look I quickly understand how the Other is also a subject with his own center of reference for meaning, perceptions, and behavior; these are different from mine. This causes me to be interested in the Other's intentions and motivations toward me, in terms of my own future-oriented projects. I come to understand that his world and his future are different and perhaps conflicted with my own.[37] Because the Other is already and always a subjectivity that can turn me into an object, this possibility can motivate me to keep this ontological dynamic in place by holding him as object.

Perhaps one treats the Other as object because of the continual threat of being objectified by him. This treatment of the Other, however, is often reciprocated, and can lead to deep conflict. In this case, according to Sartre, we adopt, except for the position of indifference, one of two main attitudes. We either attempt to overcome the Other's transcendence by our own, in the attempt to subsume his freedom, or we attempt to incorporate the Other's transcendence within oneself without removing from it its character as transcendence.

These attitudes of sadism and masochism form the circle that we mentioned at the beginning of this essay; each is unstable and contains within it the other as opposite. Typically, a consciousness contains both as thesis and antithesis, in a master-slave dynamic.[38] This creates a dynamic in which a consciousness oscillates between looking at the Other and being looked at by the Other. According to Sartre, it is ontologically impossible to recognize simultaneously both the Other's freedom and facticity, or the Other ours. This implies that two subjectivities cannot approach each other simultaneously, but rather that the subjectivity of one requires the objectivity of the Other. Without the Other I lose the means to found my objective being. Likewise, if I try to recover that objective being by identifying with the Other's freedom as its foundation, I discover that the separation of consciousnesses prevents me from doing so. The Other always remains an alien freedom that I can never quite absorb into my own consciousness; as corollary, I always remain a freedom without substantive being. I also learn that I cannot absorb the Other as a subject because he can easily recover subjectivity by looking at me. On the plane of bad faith there is no possibility of escaping this circle.

I agree with Sartre's belief that what we call love is usually motivated by the desire to be loved. On a deeper level, it is a desire for the beloved love object to provide a justification for one's existence. To do this, one must assimilate the beloved's freedom as the foundation for one's existence. One wishes to be the love object not transcended. This sort of love attempts to overcome the danger implied by becoming an object for the Other over which I lose control. This sort of love is a strategy for the God-project and for consciousness to become self-coincidental by becoming object for the Other's freedom. Any aspect of the Other's psyche that is not directed toward me goes largely unnoticed or becomes the subject of frustration as I attempt to capture his freedom.

Feeling possessed by the Other's freedom I want to absorb

my beloved's time and attention. I want to absorb that which
possesses me. I want to reduce the Other's freedom to a
freedom that is subject to my own. Yet I do not wish the Other
to love me from duty. I do not want the Other's freedom as
an enslaved freedom; in contrast, I want the Other to want
me and to make me his or her ultimate value by willing her
captivity, eternally. Nevertheless, this is an impossible goal
because I am only one object among many others for my
beloved. I can never be the sole object of his or her attention.
Further, I can never successfully use the Other to create
substantive freedom, precisely because he or she wants the
same thing from me. This conflict is created because each
of us wants from the other a love that is not reducible to the
project of being loved. We want an unselfish love without
reciprocity. We ultimately discover that the Other can never
be a pure subjectivity that founds my objectivity.

The sort of love described above is futile and may lead to
masochism. In this attitude I give up the project of justifying
myself by assimilating the Other as witness to my free project
as object. Left with only my subjectivity and no justification,
I might try to induce the Other to make me be as an objective
freedom. In this state I get rid of my futile subjectivity and
instead try to make myself into a pure object without any
transcendent qualities. In this strategy I adopt the position
of pure instrumentality in order to be used by a radically free
Other; by identifying with his freedom I immerse myself in
my objectivity as justification and foundation. Unfortunately,
this strategy will fail, too, because I simply cannot apprehend
for myself the object that I am for the Other. I can never be
that object I am for the Other, and the more I try to be that
object the more I engage my own free subjectivity.

The other strategy I may employ, either through failure of
masochism or as an original project, is sadism. In this strategy

I attempt to commandeer the Other's freedom, and the
Other's objectification of me, in the Other as object. Here,
I induce the Other to incarnate himself as consciousness so
that I can possess not just his body but his body as flesh. In
my desire I attempt to realize the incarnation of the Other
through my own incarnation. Solitary desire is suffocating,
a kind of vertigo that attempts to drown me in my own
facticity. Because desire always has interpersonal implications
it includes the language of the caress. It is a shaping of the
Other's body as passivity for my desire; this motivation can
work in both directions, and in the caress, inert body parts
inevitably touch each other as pure facticity.

The meaning of desire, especially sexual desire, comes from
the possibility of using the Other as a means to create a self,
for Sartre. This is an ontological interpretation of sexuality
that focuses on one's original upsurge into a world of Others.
In sexual desire there is a reciprocal, double incarnation of
desire as both individuals appropriate the Other's flesh. Yet
the mutuality in this double incarnation does not last, for each
subject fails to capture the Other's freedom in his or her body.
Through pleasure I can lose the ability to see the Other as
object. The pleasure of caressing is thereby replaced by the
pleasure of being caressed as I become absorbed in my own
incarnation.

This failure can lead to masochism if I seek to become
absorbed as object into the Other as consciousness, thereby
becoming a flesh swooning beneath the Other's Look. It can
also lead to sadism if I break the reciprocity of incarnation by
appropriating the Other's flesh. Here, the Other as incarnated
consciousness disappears as the Other as he or she becomes
object. At this point I become an instrumental organization
directing a flesh. The sadist reacts to the rupture in reciprocal
incarnation by attempting an instrumental appropriation of

the incarnated Other. As a transcendent subject, the sadist tries to capture the Other as flesh.

The sadist's attempt to capture the Other's consciousness through his incarnation as flesh is done to produce pain rather than pleasure, triggering a reflective consciousness that focuses on enslavement. It is done to make the Other's freedom subject to the sadist's will. Sadism is also unstable, for when the Other is reduced to an enslaved freedom his facticity reappears. The submissive body of the Other ruins the sadistic project because the only way to keep the Other as flesh is to enter into that state, too. The emergence of the sadist's desire renders his sadism futile.

Further, one Look from the submissive victim can demonstrate how out of reach the appropriation of another's freedom ultimately is. This Look prevents the sadist from being the sole subject in this dynamic and re-establishes the victim as subject confronting the sadist as object. One Look from the victim and the goal and meaning of the sadism collapses. I can never establish myself as pure transcendence by annihilating the Other. Furthermore, killing the Other fixes my being in the past, something I can never overcome. The sadomasochistic circle is a position into which all relationships can fall, more or less. This way of interpersonal being triggers questions about ethics and moral development. One wonders whether there is escape from the sadomasochistic oscillation into interpersonal relations that are mutual, positive, and constructive. We wonder whether this bad faith dynamic can ever be overcome in the quest to develop morally and cultivate virtuous behavior. This essay explores such a possibility.

As we discussed earlier, Sartre himself does speak of a radical conversion to good faith and authentic human relationships by the valuing of freedom itself, especially with regard to the treatment of others. Sartre believes that positive reciprocity is a genuine human possibility.[39] This radical conversion implies that a renunciation of the belief that substantive freedom is possible. It implies a rejection of all attempts to coerce, manipulate, or degrade the Other so that she or he might provide me with a substantive sense of self. This sort of renunciation does not lead to despair or hate but rather leads to a valuing of the value-making process — freedom itself — while renouncing the aim of creating a substantive self. This renunciation leads me to freely respect the Other as another subject just like myself; in this new orientation, even though the Other may have different desires, views, and life projects, I avoid subverting him to my own ends.

In this new project, I remain open to the Other, freely accepting that he affects me just as I him. By accepting that we do affect each other in a factual way in any case, we can begin to release ourselves from the project of using the Other to create a substantive freedom, i.e., the impossible God- project. As I discussed extensively in an earlier work, Hazel Barnes points out that there are two other possible Looks that Sartre does not emphasize in *BN* but which could provide the kind of socio-ontological orientation leading to the overcoming of sadomasochistic dynamics.[40]

The first of these alternative Looks occurs when two people look at the world together in a common project. More importantly, perhaps is the second of these alternatives, which is the "Look-as-Exchange." This is not a union of subjects but a mutual affirmation of respect for the Other as a subject. Even though subject-object dualism is retained, there is a motivation to understand the Other's world in a positive and constructive way in order to proactively enhance the lives of both. It is a mutual receptiveness that is similar to Marcel's notion of "availability."[41] This exchange lies at the heart of positive reciprocity and authentic love.

Even negative reciprocity, in which we try to dominate each other in conditions of scarcity, implies a comprehension of the Other as subject. Fortunately, however, this comprehension could theoretically lead to a positive comprehension of the Other in which care, love, and regard play a prominent role. In fact, in a late interview with Michael Contat, Sartre argues vehemently for "absolute transparency" between people instead of secrecy.[42] What is most intriguing is his assertion that this kind of transparency can only come from the illumination of those dark regions in our souls; most importantly, it is only by illuminating these dark regions to others that we illuminate them to ourselves.[43] This requires commitment to an attitude of freedom as its own project and a willingness to bear the different experiences of others, including the fact that they might see us differently from how we'd prefer.

Sartre presents a love that moves beyond sadomasochism in his biography of Genet, asserting that it is the appeal of the Other that makes the reality of love.[44] Love is a shared experience and a joint undertaking that is quite different from the sadomasochistic solipsism of Genet. Love goes beyond the attempt to make the Other love me so that I have a foundation for my being. It may involve the virtue of empathy, which cognitively amounts to the successful attempt to understand and comprehend another human being. Perhaps it is one's relationship, as object, with historical, important subjects in one's life that has the most profound effect on one's motivation to use others to create a substantial self. One's relationships can then be interpreted as attempts to struggle with and resolve earlier ontological relational deficiencies, or at least one's idealized version of the perfect union, i.e., substantive freedom. This can allow the insight that the demand that the Other be a part of my quest for whole being be renounced and a more genuine reciprocal relationship be substituted. This would imply the acceptance of the Other as different. This is perhaps the beginning of mature moral development that overcomes the impulse to manipulate and control, or adopt attitudes of submission, indifference, or avoidance of genuine intimacy.

Sartre's Understanding of Pure Reflection

Recall that Sartre speaks of the self as prereflective consciousness, as ego, and as future value. He takes issue with the traditional, essentialist view of the self and instead advocates for an existentialist view that is on radically different footing. Aristotle's ideas about potentiality, sometimes called the "acorn theory," lie at the bedrock of the received view of the self. Here, the self starts as an acorn of sorts, with structure and matter, and has a certain potentiality that it can actualize. This might involve, for example, overcoming paralytic emotional residue, or disabusing oneself of false beliefs in order to free a "true" self.

In contrast, according to Sartre, the self as prereflective agent does not have structure or substance. At the heart of being human is prereflective, free choice, not the realization of some a priori potentiality. Thus, we recall the famous adage that "existence precedes essence." We are radically free to choose our attitude and our orientation toward our circumstances in the world; there is no pre-defining essence that limits the development of these free choices. Under this view, a self's ego is given form and substance by that same self but from its perspective as a prereflective agent. This ego becomes an image of consciousness but is not the real experiencing self. The self as value, in the form of coincidental consciousness, can never really exist although it drives us forward as the meaning of our present actions.

The prereflective self is not an agent that realizes potential; rather it meets its interactions in the world with radical possibility for interpretation. Possibility involves imagining future value and choice for myself. Thus, human reality is always a lack, which leads to desire. Consciousness is always aware of the distance between itself and the objects of its world. Through its intentional structure it orients itself toward these objects as ways to attempt to meet its desire. At the prereflective level, the self does not have personality traits; it is a translucid awareness of itself existing temporally, its objects toward which it moves intentionally, and the distance between self and these objects. Sartre says that at this level, I am "all lightness, all translucence," all openness to being.[45]

In *TE*, Sartre maintains that the "I" and the "me" only appear in the reflective process. These forms of the self are objects rather than subjects. The consciousness that formulates them is always beyond the object being characterized through language. Furthermore, the reflective judgments we make about ourselves unify themselves into what we know as our ego, through time. Sartre's ego is opaque and, in contrast, prereflective consciousness is translucid. The ego is actually outside in the world[46] like any other object; thus, personality traits are a product rather than a source of one's reflective view of the self. As an object of reflective consciousness, the ego is the "transcendent unity of states and actions."[47] It is consciousness standing back from its objects that creates an ideal whole out of its past actions and states.

The ego is the "I" pole of past actions as well as the "me" pole of past feelings/actions. There is an important distinction, too, between states of mind used to describe what are really cloaked feelings. For example, I may feel anger toward someone, but built up over time this may transform itself into an attributive state of hatred. The descriptive feeling is ephemeral and temporary; the attributive state implies more of ego permanence. I might then attribute to myself a personality trait of having some kind of disposition toward the ego state. For example, I attribute to myself the quality of being spiteful or loving. These hypothetical qualities[48] are thereby viewed as potentialities within ourselves when really they are just reifications of repeated feelings and actions. They exist only *a posteriori*, not *a priori*. Again, the ego is not the source of the qualities and actions and states that define it. Instead, it is a product.

When we take this account to the realm of the future, we can also fall into the trap of believing that the ego has a claim on it as well. Here the self as ego connects with the self as value, with bad faith, in order to construct an illusion of a substantial or secure future. We fear our own radical freedom; we are anxious of our spontaneity. We fear that our future self could betray our current self. Thus, for Sartre, "perhaps the essential role of the ego is to mask from consciousness its very spontaneity."[49] Thus, by making believe that we are just ego, a substantial self, we provide a "false representation" of ourselves.[50]

The attempt to reify consciousness as a potentiality for actions and character involves accessory reflection; it is always self-deceptive. As I create and develop my ego I always run the risk of trying to turn my consciousness into a thing while still remaining free. The ego always tends to distort the truth that I am spontaneous consciousness with radical freedom. One cannot simultaneously see and be the consciousness reflected on. Perhaps this is why we are so tempted to use the Other's view of us in place of our own. Reflection enters into the value creating process when we try to characterize ourselves as something, moving toward the future. Yet, when I make myself believe that I will become a future self that I value, or that I have no connection to my past self, I fall into deception. I must realize that my ego is not the source of my states of mind and behavior. I must also realize that I will never bring into reality my future self as a substantial self because it is always beyond my grasp.

For the Sartrean existentialist we never are quite what we seem to be. The prereflective, spontaneous self is always free to make new choices and to see the world in new ways. Thus, we are always in the position of creating value. It is something that we choose, not something that we find somewhere. We are, then, always responsible for making a self that never gets made. Instead of searching for an ego, Sartre propounds that we aim away from seeking a substantial self. We are always at a distance from ourselves and, as such, we cannot ever fully coincide with ourselves. When we reflect on who we are, we move away from our prereflective self; when we move back into our spontaneous, non-reflecting self we lose focus on ego. So instead of seeking a true self we must, for Sartre, look for ways to live authentically. Under this view the self is more of a process than a thing, a translucidity and temporality rather than an entity. When we see the futility in using the Other to create a substantial self, we can then begin to confront the real nature of the prereflective self and its relation to the ego.

In theory, pure reflection attempts a relation between a reflecting consciousness and a consciousness that is reflected on; yet, we see that these two consciousnesses are different, separated by a nothingness between them. He maintains that it is possible to discover oneself as prereflective spontaneity[51] by keeping "to the given without setting up claims for future."[52] At the end of *BN*, Sartre argues for the possibility of an ethics that is based on a philosophy of radical freedom that averts attempts to use others to create substantive freedom.[53] Pure reflection reveals the past as spontaneous choice rather than as an emanation of the ego. Impure reflection conceives of the self as a static object through time in which states of mind are attributed to the ego; recall that in actuality, these "states" cloak underlying emotional experience. Thus, although I have feelings I am not the underlying ego to which they can be attributed by transformations in language. An example of this is the conversion of feelings of anger into language of hatred. The language of hatred is language that implies an ego engaged in impure reflection.

Pure reflection is at the foundation of profound psychic change. It involves the clearest possible view of one's ego commitments, past and future. Through our own assessment — and distance of the prereflective self from our ego — we can make new choices through nihilating interpretations about our immediate past ego selves. Objectivizing the past allows us this perspective so that we can attach, detach, and reattach to our formulations of value in a progressive-regressive manner. In addition, as we formulate new present projects with new choices of being, our past experience can take on new meaning and even original meaning if it was never reflected upon. Even though the facts of the past never change, our interpretations can, in terms of how they serve our projections into the future. Because I can always move beyond myself with even a small shift in my fundamental project, the goal of substantive freedom is never possible.

The possibility of radical change raises anxiety because it necessitates letting go of the weight and burden of a past project with which we have become familiar. Trading familiar misery for an unfamiliar future can be a terrifying project;

it also requires letting go of the motivation to use an Other to create an illusion of a substantial self. It is possible to free myself from falsely identifying with illusory ego states and instead understand the choices that I have made and continue to make. Consciousness is translucid; it has no content. By freeing ourselves from the pursuit of a reified self we can stay more wholly in pure reflection, thereby understanding our ability to reinterpret the past and steer toward a different set of value choices in the future.

Recall that each of us has a relationship between one's prereflective consciousness and one's image of oneself, i.e., one's ego. In various ways, most of us suffer from a crushed, tempered, or diminished spontaneity; a decreased sense of personal freedom. This manifests itself in a sedimented ego that, through strategies of bad faith, pursues a substantial self. The quest for authenticity at a basic level must concern new ways of being with one's prereflective self instead of developing (ego) structure.

As we have mentioned, this may require a new basic choice of orientation in the world that recognizes one's radical freedom. Being a subject who pursues authenticity requires one to give up the illusory project of creating self-objects through accessory reflection. It requires one to look for the reflective distortions of spontaneous experience. This requires us to look at the choices we made in the past and understand why we made them. This also requires us to look at the voices of important others that have become part of our reflective selves. Attributions we make about ourselves through our reflective personal identity can be discharged if we discover that they negatively affect spontaneous experience. We can discover that there is no fixed self.

Sartre's Views about Authenticity

Much has been said and written about Sartre and the notion of authenticity. I have written about it extensively.[54] It is not my intention here to write a compendium of the subject or to do a contemporary, postmodern analysis about it even though I believe that this is important in its own right. What I plan to do here is to trace a rough outline of some of the questions Sartre wrestled with concerning authenticity, especially about its relation to morality in general. We can take the core of this discussion and use it to help us understand how moral development is affected by one's ontological relationship to the God-project.

In the years that followed the publication of *BN*, Sartre came to believe that his early project was futile. In late conversation with Benny Levy, Sartre asserted that his work was a failure because it had led to a contradiction in *BN*.[55] When Sartre realized that his ontological approach to authenticity was unsuccessful, he shifted focus to the socio-material conditions of the world, railing against the kind of structures that lead people to treat each other as objects, i.e., to act in bad faith. After his early, ontological period, he argued that the ideal of authenticity was possible in a city of ends in which people treated each other as both subjects and objects.[56]

Sartre criticized Heidegger, showing that the ontological, individual search for authenticity was futile. Instead, he argued, we must each take part in a socio-political revolution that changes deep social structures in a way that allows for mass transformation toward authentic existence. Heidegger denied that any particular ethic could be incompatible with authenticity. For Heidegger, authenticity is foundational to any morality. In contrast, Sartre, views moral systems in opposition to authenticity. Initially, Sartre agreed with Heidegger's view of the primacy of authenticity over any particular moral system. In some of his thoughts that he penned during the war, Sartre said, "I can't really see anything but a moral code based on authenticity." However, he added that with regard to authenticity he could not but strongly "feel our inconsistency, as beings without a God, yet not authors of ourselves."[57]

After becoming more politically involved, Sartre reversed the priority of authenticity over morality. He argued that only a just and non-oppressive society whose members do not treat themselves as instrumental objects could foster free and authentic individuals who are the authors of their own lives. This could also overcome the human tendency toward bad faith, leading him to state that "one cannot be converted alone . . . ethics is not possible unless everyone is ethical."[58] On this point, in a late interview with Michel Sicard, he mentioned a new ontology of consciousness that would leave "nothing of *BN* and even of the *CDR* standing," but would lead to an ethics of "We" in contrast to the individual "I."[59] The "We" that Sartre is referring to is not the anonymous one that serves as the antagonist of authenticity. Instead, this is the "We" that Levinas spent his whole life trying to account for, which raises the questions of philosophical anthropology. We take up this question directly in another work on Levinas, ethics, and humanism.[60]

According to Sartre the radical conversion to authenticity does not mean that we can radically escape from the clutches of bad faith, but it does mean that we can execute a self recovery of being that leads to an ethical restructuring of oneself and possibly a whole society. In *CDR* Sartre shows within his concrete ontology of concrete human relations, that we live in a world of social alienation.[61] In his interview with Levy,

"Today's Hope," he was seeking "the deepest relation between men . . . which binds them together beyond the relations to production".[62] Further, he stated that this kind of relation exists in a family whose members have a common goal.[63]

For Sartre, the ontology of human reality does not lead to authenticity but bad faith can be avoided by restructuring social relations in a way that goes beyond normal relations of production. Sartre's plan for political reform shows us how to create a morality that can protect justice and equality even though these might not rise to the level of authentic being. However, through the anthropological methods of existential psychoanalysis, there is a possibility of gaining authenticity by creating ourselves as works of art.[64] Thus, he shares that "the moral problem which has preoccupied me till now is basically [that] of relations between art and life.[65]

While under Heidegger's influence, Sartre believed that phenomenological ontology could establish authenticity as a valid moral ideal. For example, his phenomenology of emotion aimed at purging consciousness of all content until what was left was pure spontaneity, within an aesthetic model of authenticity. In *TE*, Sartre argues for a non-egological, intentional theory of consciousness. Anything that we normally think of as some content of consciousness is actually just an object that consciousness presences and toward which it directs itself. This includes emotions, motives, and values. Further, because consciousness is intentional, it always transcends the objects it creates.

The ego, too, is an object constituted by consciousness.[66] Consciousness is a pure transparency and openness to the world. It is a pure spontaneous process without psychic dispositions, character, or emotion. Sartre uses the phenomenological method to attack Descartes' *cogito*. There is, for Sartre, no "I" that thinks, only reflection upon thought. This allows Sartre to conclude that there is no original, authentic self or ego. Instead, authenticity lies in the creative process itself. The ego is not isolated but is instead outside in the world. He thinks that this maneuver avoids the solipsism to which Husserl's transcendental ego fell prey. Authenticity is founded in this flight out into the world. It is a refusal to exist as substance and an attempt to overcome facticity. This purification of consciousness, for Sartre, operated as a moral foundation because it is at the very bottom of the creation of the self.

Consciousness is an intentional, creative process that produces transcendent contents, including our egos, in the world. Authenticity is something that occurs in the inter-subjective world and not in some isolated, alienated hiding place. Authenticity is defined by consciousness because it is the outcome of intentional acts. Consciousness is pure spontaneity because it cannot be directly influenced by the external world. Freedom is, therefore, a relation of consciousness, not the ego, to the world. Every intentional act is spontaneous, self-originating, and radically free. Because of the nature of consciousness, Sartre does not believe that introspection can lead to authenticity.[67] One cannot introspectively access one's self if there is no immanent self to access. The quest for authenticity must occur outside in the social world because my ego does not belong exclusively to myself.

Authenticity is a product of reflection and action. Recall that there is no "I" on the un-reflected level. The intentional act of directing one's consciousness toward a world of objects in not reflective. Yet reflecting upon it produces an ego. Thus, the reflected consciousness generates the "I" that becomes the transcendent object of the reflective act. Because each autonomous act occurs only in a present moment, the ego itself is a fleeting entity. Because we are always more than what we can possibly reflect on, we constantly live in a future of possibility. The "I" is also an object but also ephemeral. To think of it as a rigid, permanent entity is self-deceptive, given that I can always re-choose myself from moment to moment. Likewise, the "me" has the same danger of falling into bad faith.

Because all objects of consciousness are outside consciousness and only consciousness is certain, all authentic states transcend consciousness and are capable of deception. The more intensely I reflect on my consciousness the clearer I can become about my self that emerges. Yet this hyper-reflection diminishes or even destroys my spontaneous consciousness, thereby rendering precarious and fragile my authentic state. Because of the structure of my consciousness, it seems that I am condemned to be my creative self and condemned to be the creator of that self. Furthermore, because the ego is in the social world and therefore public, "authenticity is a duty that comes to us from outside and inside at once, because our 'inside' is an outside."[68] More importantly, one "can and must in authenticity assume the objective transformation of [one]self."[69]

In his work on emotion, Sartre attempts to sketch a phenomenological psychology whose premise is that each of us is the sole author of his emotional states.[70] His main assertion is that there is nothing "accidental" or passive in consciousness or in life.[71] Instead of contents of consciousness ever being accidental or involuntary, we actively and intentionally create them. We are the sole authors of our lives and are thus completely responsible for them.[72] I am always free to shape the contents of my consciousness and free to determine my aims in life. We see here Sartre's strong assertion that there is intentionality in consciousness even at the level of emotion.

For Sartre, introspection is not necessarily a straightforward process because self-deception is always at risk. Yet, in our pursuit of authentic thinking, feeling, and behavior we must try to lay open and correct the deep recesses of our pathos through phenomenological thinking and experiencing. This requires us to explore directly what we create in consciousness. Emotions make life bearable but they can take us into magical, deceptive realms and render us paralytic. This is so because in emotion we sit and feel but often do nothing. In fact, for Sartre, this is the unstated cleverness of emotion: we are not required to do anything more.[73] They are escape routes from a direct confrontation and each of us chooses them intentionally. Thus, the task is to directly analyze and explore the "things themselves" and move past the illusory reality that emotions and fantasies create.[74]

Sartre's reluctance to give up the Cartesian [75] and his notion of authenticity as spontaneous activity play an important role in his attack on traditional (Freudian) psychoanalysis. Recall that for Freudian analysis, unconscious emotional states play causal roles in attitude, emotion, and behaviors, thereby introducing passivity into explanations of human behavior.[76] This type of explanation also undermines the possibility of spontaneous self-creation because by definition we cannot control that which is not conscious. Sartre is very clear that traditional psychoanalytic theories and therapies cannot lead to authenticity, because of their anti-Cartesian premises. Yet, he did hold in common with the analysts the idea that emotions intentionally sought transformation of the world when direct and realistic courses of action are barred because of weakness or fear.[77]

Emotions are a creative but passive solution to an uncompromising world. Instead of changing the world or transforming a state of affairs — an object — through external, social, and political action, consciousness acts upon itself.[78] By transforming itself through emotion, it necessarily changes the objects that appear to it. This is, therefore, a type of bad faith that operates through emotion. Sartre uses his phenomenological analysis to reveal the magical and deceptive character of emotional experience in order to delineate a lucid, Cartesian understanding of our situations and realistic strategies for coping with them. Liberation can only come from a purifying reflection or an abandonment of the emotion.[79] The authentic frame of mind can only be arrived at by a lucid and unemotional evaluation of one's situation because only a clear assessment can lead to a conversion of one's self away from the God-project and toward freedom. This can always lead to routes out of social sadomasochistic dynamics because we are no longer attached to the utilization of the other for a state of immanence-transcendence, in which the other operates as sole foundation of personal value. Emotion is frequently the gateway into acts of bad faith toward another person.

Authenticity involves spontaneity, mental lucidity, assertive and active process, self-sufficiency, and originality. We cannot create ourselves authentically by introspection or by indulging our emotions. Only through outward-moving activity within the social world do we have a chance for moments of authentic being. As Sartre shows in one of his early novels, it is possible to author a self much like a novelist creates a piece of literature.[80] Here, Sartre shows that humans can never be an object like a rock or a chair. We will never have a well-defined essence in the same way a non-conscious object does. This explains why the main character, Roquentin, is nauseated about the unattainable desire to be sure about what and who he is. His focus on external objects highlights that as a pure consciousness a human being is fluid and lacks definition.

Nausea itself is a foundational existential category that
seizes us in its grip.[81] It is a symptom that reminds us that we
cannot escape our freedom and responsibility for authentic
self-creation. It is a by-product of the search for authenticity,
which have to each do alone. More seriously, nausea reveals
that we are absolutely contingent and therefore constantly
have to justify our existence, i.e., to make it seem necessary.
Yet in our most lucid moments we can accept our contingent
nature and play with the absurdity of the world. In this
lucidity we can accept our distance from objects and utilize
them to define who we are. Sartre identifies the bad faith
of the bourgeois in terms of their self-regard as serious and
solid objects. In contrast, Roquentin attempts to create a self
against this monolithic world of the crowd. He does so in an
aesthetic way as a strategy to overcome nausea as well as the
lack of a firm foundation for value.

In his aesthetic strategy for self-creation, Roquentin expresses
total acceptance of every event in his life, total acceptance of
his authentic life. In creating one's self we become artists as
well as works of art. This becomes the strategy for justifying
one's existence. This search for self-creation is opposite to a
weak, fear-based person who flees from his freedom to carve
out an identity for himself. This fear-based person lives life
as a copy and draws his identity from well-worn, dogmatic
stories; this person accepts what others have made of him and
runs from an aesthetically-based life. This kind of individual
escapes freedom to such a large degree that authenticity all
but disappears. With regard to the moral question, which we
take up following our discussion of authenticity, for Sartre it
is not something that is found but rather is something that is
spontaneously created.

As we have stated earlier, authenticity implies a clear-headed
view about oneself and one's situation and the acceptance of

full responsibility for acting. Because authenticity is not a state but a quest, we cannot be authentic but we can pursue it. Note that the wish to be authentic is the wish to be God, who is self-identical and self-caused. He is the only necessary foundation of his own being. In the Greek vernacular, having *auctoritas* means to possess an authority over oneself, to be the sole source of one's own being. Only a necessary, self-identical being could be authentic, on this interpretation. However, humans are different and therefore simply cannot *be* authentic because they are always more (in the future as possibility) than they are (in the present). As such, we can pursue authenticity.

Even though we cannot actually be God, for Sartre, we can and must create ourselves within the factual limits of our situations. This requires us to face our life situations directly rather than project ourselves toward unreal fantasy, especially through emotion. For Sartre, the very idea of God is a human creation, an anthropological product. Recall that human consciousness is comprised of two different elements, the for-itself and the in-itself, and that it is impossible to be both simultaneously, coincidentally. Furthermore, because my consciousness is always independent from the constructions I make of myself, its essence cannot be given beforehand as a substantial form that has realizable potential. Instead of attaining self-identity, which we cannot, according to Sartre, we can pursue constant and selfless becoming. Thus, in our pursuit of authenticity we can never gain essence but we can affect our range of freedom.

According to Sartre, "authenticity has to do with what I will . . . It is "the refusal to define myself by what I am (Ego) but instead by what I will (that is, by my very undertaking, not insofar as it appears to others — objective — but insofar as it turns its subjective face toward me."[82] Further, he shares that "the grasping of the authentic self is not based on being, it is a willing."[83] Because this kind of authenticity is based on spontaneity and not intentional reflection, it cannot be attained through reflection but only through action. The self is that which emerges out of those acts, authentic in character to the extent that is the product of authentic actions. Yet we cannot simply seek to be authentic for that sort of intention would not be authentic.[84] Humans cannot be authentic the way that God is; further, in the human realm authenticity is nothing. Yet we can become authentic like God though an aesthetic strategy of pursuing freedom.

Given that we can never be coincidental with ourselves, we must realize that we can never own our transcendent self. I am simply not what I am, in the mode of having possibility toward an unknown future. We are always inescapably free, which mandates our radical responsibility in everything we do. Because we struggle to bear this freedom and cannot renounce it, because it is so difficult to be conscious and not exist as a thing, we live in eternal dread about what to do next. We have discussed bad faith earlier in this essay as the futile attempt to deny either the subjective aspect or the objective aspect of being human. It involves a relentless pursuit of substance by the for-itself, which in-authenticates the nothingness of human consciousness. It is a self-deception that refuses to recognize the self as both transcendence and facticity, which leads to a dislocated freedom, a spirit of seriousness, or treating oneself as another person by playing a role.

In *BN*, Sartre does not give us an account of authenticity but argues that like other values it is neither justified nor unjustified. In his 1946 lecture, "Existentialism and Humanism," he considered two problems that had beset his ontology.[85] First, if freedom is solely a form and if authenticity as a value is completely unjustified, then why is this value supreme to all others? Second, how is it possible to make the transition from the realm of theoretical ontology to the realm of everyday existence and concrete action? Sartre has trouble providing satisfactory answers to these questions. If he could objectively ground value judgments and account for their application, he could utilize authenticity as a moral ground and derivatively as a socio-political theory.

After this project failed, Sartre never repudiated the viability of the ideal of authenticity. Nor did he repudiate his aesthetic model of the self. He, however, acknowledged the importance of one's actual life situation in coloring possibilities for freedom. In his later writings, Sartre set ontology aside and concentrated on the aesthetic model. He strenuously argued that we could make room for the freedom of all but only through radical change in the nature of social and political relationships.[86] In his biographies he also argued that we could stimulate our will to self-creation by discovering suitable role models. Thus, even though he came to an ontological impasse about authenticity, Sartre kept his ideal alive through his method of existential psychoanalysis, which we mentioned earlier in this essay.

The method of existential psychoanalysis can expose the patterns of bad faith to which we have become attached. It can reveal the specific way that an individual attempts to become the impossible synthesis of transcendence and facticity/immanence by looking at one's original choice of being in the world. Through an existential conversion, we can accept, change, or modify our original choice in the world that operates as the ultimate reason or sense of value for everything that we believe in, feel, and do. In his extended biography of Flaubert, Sartre examines his notion of authenticity in exquisite detail.[87] Because he believes that we are radically free, Sartre tests his assumptions about the possibility for authenticity under difficult initial conditions. For example, an idiot becomes a genius. In his study of Genet, as we mentioned earlier, a rogue and a thief becomes a brilliant playright. Sartre's point is convincing: we can take even the worst of conditions and transform one situation into another. Even the worst of facticities can be overcome once we let go of those interpretations that maintain our passivity.

One's original choice in life shapes the overall meaning and trajectory of one's behavior, emotions, and thoughts. Every single thought, deed, and feeling emerges from this primary choice and is filled with its being. But we must remind ourselves of the incompatibility between his ontological conclusions as to the impossibility of authenticity and its viability at the anthropological level. Existential psychoanalysis is an objective method that brings to light one's first subjective choice by which he makes himself a life. In order to reconstruct the life of a person, this sort of analysis deciphers and interprets any and all objective pieces of evidence that may shed light on the original choice.

Even though I have some consciousness of my fundamental choice I may not have conceptual knowledge of its meaning. Pure reflection sees everything at once, which may prevent a useful understanding of one's position, unless there is help from another. Reflection itself can bring to light the primordial content of one's overall situation, but we still need to gain critical perspective about it through existential psychoanalysis. As Thomas Anderson says, "The analysis and conceptualization of knowledge is necessary to interpret the complex experiential aggregation of acts and to determine which are peripheral, which more significant, and ultimately, which act of choice is absolutely fundamental."[88] Even though the objective knowledge of the analyst cannot get at the subjective experience of the individual being analyzed, this knowledge can help him to clarify his own reflective process.

It is through an intuitive awareness of the individual whether the analysis has really gotten to the core of his orientation in the world. In the end, it is the individual's recognition, along with the evidence, that is decisive, for at the very core of each of us is an understanding of who we are. Most interesting is that Sartre implies that this type of objective understanding does not degrade one's subjectivity like the other types of objectification he lays out in his ontological studies. This sort of awareness is a comprehension of the Other that does not fall prey to degradation or oppression, presumably of oneself or another. One important feature of this line of thinking is the importance of the Other in constructing an authentic comprehension of the self that overcomes bad faith.

As we mentioned, in the final section of *BN*, Sartre makes some important comments about the ethical implications of his ontology. Ontology itself cannot tell us which sort of ethics is best suited to human reality. Ontology tells us that values come solely from our free choices; they are not transcendent givens. Yet they are unconditional demands upon us, as free beings, to make them real. Yet if it is human freedom that makes values exist, this relativizes and paralyzes ethics, for it means that there are no absolute or objective values. Any ethics that attempts to set forth objective norms is a futile project from the beginning. Unfortunately, this reasoning seems to lead to the legitimacy of any values whatsoever.[89] Further, it is possible that one may authentically act in bad faith, and others authentically submit to it in bad faith, results that are counter-intuitive to a solid foundation for an ethics.

The purpose of existential psychoanalysis is to help us realize that there are no objective values in anything, including being God. By shifting our goal from the God-project to the primary valuation of freedom, through the process of pure reflection, we can approach action authentically. We must note that the value to be God is most often lived non-reflectively. We simply take it for granted without question. For Sartre, we do this in order to avoid the anguish we would experience by understanding that our freedom alone is its cause. In reflection, we can direct our attention toward these un-reflected values. Even though we might desire to pursue the God-project we may deliberately and reflectively choose another sort of project.

Sartre never abandoned his idea of an aesthetically-based morality in which we pursue radical freedom; in contrast, as we have outlined, there are severe ontological limitations to authenticity as a moral compass. Sartre's notion of authenticity is ultimately negative, despite its creative aspect, because it has no meaning apart from society. More importantly, it requires the liberation of society from bad faith. However, by transforming the basic structures of society we can overcome alienated forms of humanity.[90] This, in turn, provides the resources for individuals to become free and creative subjects in a society that practices social relations of genuine reciprocity. Generosity becomes the chief moral virtue.

Even though we cannot change the ontological impossibility of authenticity we can, therefore, weaken the social and political forces that perpetuate living in bad faith. This requires us to secure universally a realm of freedom for each individual. The ontological impasse that Sartre ended with served to propel him into political activism as the ultimate force that would create a kingdom of ends in which each of us acted for all of us, all the time. Sartre's political conversion operates on both the individual and social levels. Individually, we avoid bad faith projects; socially, we adopt egalitarian strategies that overcome the reductive sadomasochistic dynamics in which individuals are treated like objects. In a positive sense, sadism and masochism are strategies of revealing the Other. Political conversion and individual transformation render these dynamics inert.

In this new social structure each of us would attempt to promote and assist others to engage in creative growth and expression. Economically, the reduction of scarcity and unjust conditions that force us to treat others as instruments would create a new basis for social relationship. This new kind of relationship could not overcome Sartre's metaphysical dualism in which we are both subjects and objects, but the new way could promote a kind of social reciprocity that overcomes the instrumentalization of each other. Authentic relationships become a source of joy[91] and include authentic loving[92] and other relations where each person regards the Other as an end in itself and not just as a means of furthering one's own projects. As we said earlier in this essay, this involves a different kind of Look than the annihilating type expressed in the early ontology. Instead of one person objectifying another in an inauthentic relationship, both individuals respect, honor, and promote the ends of each other even though they might not be profitable for oneself. This means that we see the Other as a subject, too, just as we see ourselves. In genuinely reciprocal relationships, each member can become an essential element in creating and expressing the Other's authentic self. I choose to help the Other by not trying to dominate him but by regarding him as an autonomous person who is both subject and object in relation to me. Instead of assimilating the other into my own projects, I accommodate his or her difference.

Authenticity and Morality

Let me make it clear that in this essay I am not going to examine Sartre's Marxist ideas in *CDR*, which in great part together are the foundation of the *Notebooks*.[93] I will leave to a future project an expanded version that includes this important work. Suffice it to say that Sartre was constantly moving from a pure ontological position on the self to an understanding that was more sensitive to the concrete factors involved in human subjectivity. This is true of *Notebooks for An Ethics*, *"NB,"* as well, where he presents a more realistic view of humans than pure subjectivity and radical freedom. Here, he shows how we are tied to our body, to our facticity, and to our concrete immersion in the world. Later in the essay I will address additional contributions he made to this more concrete morality in the 1964 Rome lecture.

However, even though we are tied to our facticities, he shows in *NB* that we can still surpass and transcend these limitations. We can persistently disengage from what is and withdraw from every one of our established interpretations of the in-itself aspect of our nature. Yet we always seem to drag our facticities along with us, for we cannot detach ourselves from our societies or our bodies; thus, transcendence is always colored by the given. The givens, for Sartre, include the economic, political, scientific, and technological forms that are the foundation of the concrete milieu of situated freedom. Thus, even though he rejects simple determinism, he freely admits that the technological and economic aspects of our culture prescribe limits beyond which it is very difficult to go. This trajectory of his thinking started in *CDR* and continued throughout the rest of his life; for him we must change the structures of society that limit freedom in oppressive ways.

The notion of a situated self allows Sartre in *NB* to make the distinction between abstract and concrete morality. Abstract morality is the kind of morality that Sartre outlines in his early ontology, showing how we are always radically free no matter what our situation. Yet abstract morality only focuses on the part of human reality that is concerned with freedom, and nothing else. It is formal and without content because it does not concern itself with specific circumstances. Unfortunately, this focus on radical freedom at the ontological level misses all the important aspects of a particular person's facticity. So, for example, a person who is poor and lives on the street has a radically different situation than a person who eats well and sleeps safely. Most importantly, abstract morality does nothing to change the status quo and is, therefore, full of inertia and paralysis.

A morality that is abstract, for Sartre, presupposes that moral salvation is possible in some transcendental realm.[94] In contrast, concrete morality focuses on human beings in their cultural and historical situation with the goal of identifying and promoting goals directly in the realm of concrete human freedom. As is well known, Sartre proposed massive and radical re-structuring of society in accordance with socialist and classless views.

Within this concrete interpretation of morality, as we have stated earlier, freedom replaces the God-project as the dominant value. If we seek the impossible goal to be a self-caused, necessary being, we fail and our existence is useless. However, Sartre indicated at the end of *BN* that we could give up this futile goal and replace it with freedom as the primary value, which involves pure, not accessory reflection. In *NB*, Sartre takes this up directly. Reflection is not contemplation. It is not a passive observation of the un-reflected upon. Instead, all reflection is a project with a goal; it is action oriented.

Impure or accomplice reflection is the natural tendency
in humans, according to Sartre.[95] Accomplice reflection
originates in and is the accomplice of the natural attitude and
non-thematic project of prereflective consciousness. Because
reflection in the first instance is derived from the God-project
at the prereflective level, it [reflection] has an initial tendency
to duplicate the God-project.

Accomplice or impure reflection fails in bad faith just
like its nonthetic, prereflective origin. Nevertheless, this
failure of accomplice reflection, along with a prereflective
consciousness of freedom, can motivate a person toward pure
reflection. This is a kind of reflection that resists the God-
project and thereby becomes an antagonist of the nonthetic
project to be a self-caused being. Pure reflection accepts
the failure of the God-project through a radical conversion
toward a commitment to radical freedom. Thus, even though
it is true that on a prereflective level we are naturally drawn
to the goal of being a self-caused being, it is also true that we
can choose, at the reflective level, a new primary value.

In his early work on the two types of reflection, Sartre implies
that pure reflection is necessary for a realistic ethics.[96] *BN* was
written from a bad faith, impurely reflective point of view.
This means that the whole ontology is from the perspective
of humans living in bad faith, each pursuing the God-project,
each pursuing a substantial self, and each generating and
adopting sadomasochistic social dynamics in the process.
In contrast, Sartre is clear that *BN* was a pre-conversion
ontology and that pure reflection is foundational to an
ethics.[97] In pure reflection, I accept that I am not a substantial,
necessary thing but instead am a contingent, gratuitous
freedom that must constantly question itself about its purpose.
In pure reflection I fully accept that there are no transcendent
values and nothing whatsoever that confirms my life.

This new choice of oneself as free, unjustified, and unnecessary is a radically different way of creating a self than the primordial, natural way of accomplice and bad faith reflection in which one pretends to be a necessary, self-justifying sort of being. This new way is an authentic orientation that transcends the "dialectic of sincerity and bad faith."[98] Authenticity is the way to radically escape bad faith because it does not reproduce pursuit of the God-project at the reflective level. In *NB*, Sartre attempts to clarify previous formulations of authenticity. The person who pursues authenticity takes full responsibility for his nature as an unjustified and unsubstantial being. This new attitude comes to the forefront of one's thinking, feeling, and behavior.

The person who pursues authenticity understands what it means to be condemned to be free. This person accepts full responsibility for the charge to justify and re-justify his or her choices. This implies that he accepts his nature as a creating being as the foundation for his freedom. To be creative means to be generative, and to be generative means to be generous. By way of illumination, in Marcel's thinking, this means to be available to the mystery of the other as well as to the mystery of oneself.[99] This implies a process of pure reflection in which I fully embrace my accountability to re-justify my values. This responsibility is extreme, as Sartre holds by saying "authentic man never loses sight of the absolute goals of the human condition [which include saving] the world and [making] freedom the foundation of the world.[100] This is a very substantial responsibility.

For Sartre, human freedom creates all the meaning and value in the universe. Meaning comes solely from freedom. In relation to being, meaning comes from human consciousness taking the undifferentiated plenitude of being and carving it up into constellations of objects. We are not creators of the world but we are the creators of its ontological structure that cause a particular phenomenal world to appear out of the full positivity of being. The very structure of freedom condemns us to create. The authentic person fully accepts this and will proactively and deliberately express his creativity and generosity. In ontological terms, it is our destiny to reveal being by imposing meaning on the world. Recall the original bad faith desire to be God, a necessary and self-justifying being. In creation, at whatever level, I bring joy to myself. Insofar as I am the creator of a world that has meaning and purpose I feel a certain level of sovereignty over it. I interpret myself not as an unjustified contingency but as a necessary foundation and essential cause of a meaningful universe.

Through the experience of aesthetic joy, the facticity of the world is transformed into an imperative so that I feel the "essential and freely accepted function of my freedom is to make that unique and absolute object which is the universe come into being."[101] There is an implication that the joy we feel in creation is a sign of positive and constructive generosity, both in art and in life. Just as the goal in "What is Literature?" is the recovery of the universe through meaning-giving activity, the authentic individual in *NB* recovers his freedom to be the foundation of the world. Through our experience of joy we come to understand that our existence has meaning and purpose as foundation for a meaningful world.

Thus, even though human beings can experience this joy of meaning-giving activity as a quasi-divine privilege, still we must accept that we are not essential and necessary, self-caused beings. This is a further insight about the kind of generosity that we can experience in the mode of pure reflection. We can recognize with total clarity that we will never reach the self-caused status of divinity. Yet, life in this mode is no longer the kind of "useless passion" accounted for in the bad faith ontology of *BN*. At its foundation, human life is neither meaningful nor meaningless. We can, however, give it a meaning that we choose, and for which we take full responsibility. For Sartre, the primary value is this meaning-giving, free activity.

He argues that the only way we can achieve inter-subjective unity is by making freedom the primary value. There is an important implication here that perhaps no one can achieve the kind of freedom he postulates unless and until society is re-structured. In a society that has class distinctions, those with privilege may be just as alienated from freedom as those who are oppressed. In that case, both sides are oppressed, thereby creating the kind of sadomasochistic dynamics we are discussing here, *writ large*. Sartre's point is well taken though. We must choose for each and everyone, every time. This is the only way we can develop the infrastructure needed for individuals to develop selves. As he says in his ethics, "the person is his goal in the form of an ecstasies [i.e., freedom] and a gift."[102]

We are each creators of the world which, for Sartre, is the absolute end of human existence. In his hierarchy of values he places generosity, which is our ability to create, at the very top. The basis for his ranking is the degree of freedom that is immanent in each value; all values must "lead to" or converge on freedom.[103] Pure reflection obviously rejects God and takes freedom for its end. *EH* states that our ultimate goal is the quest of freedom.[104] In his late piece on literature, he clearly identifies the city of ends with "the reign of human freedom."[105] In the *NB*, there are constant indications from Sartre that the reason humans create a world, conferring meaning on being, is to obtain meaning and justification for their own existence.

Because we are ontologically grounded in Being, it
[Being] can have meaning only if we give it that meaning.
Derivatively, we humans ground our meaning in the meaning
we first give to Being. Sartre asserts that freedom is the
highest value precisely because we are freedom. This implies
that human existence itself is our highest value and goal.
To justify something is to give it a foundation, an absolute
meaning and purpose. For Sartre, human freedom is the
ultimate foundation and source of any and all value that
we possess. For the meaning of anything to be absolute, its
source and foundation must possess absolute value. In the
case of humans, my act of reflecting on my freedom gives it an
absolute foundation of meaning and value.[106] Inasmuch as my
justified freedom is an absolute source of meaning and value
for myself as a free being and for others as free beings, our
common reality is also justified as foundation. Thus, because
we freely will our freedom, absolutely, our creations are
absolute.[107] By choosing my freedom and justifying my own
existence I become a sort of God, in a "weak sense."[108]

For Sartre, since human freedom alone can supply an absolute
foundation and justification for its and everyone else's
existence, we must accept this freedom as our highest value.
As he says in *EH*, because human freedom is in fact the only
(thus the absolute) source of all meaning and value, "strict
consistency requires that it be chosen as the primary value."[109]
If we do not value freedom as the first value then our choices
and creations will not possess an absolute meaning and
purpose; justification would then stand on shaky ground.

Let us now talk about freedom as a primary value in relation
to the possibility for authentic human relations in which one's
choices are always socially mediated. In *BN*, Sartre paints a
bleak picture of human relationships. Yet, he also points out
that through the conversion away from the God-project and

its inauthentic nature the character of these relations could change measurably.[110] Let us make it clear that in *BN* Sartre was not presenting any kind of necessary ontology.[111] After conversion two people can actually engage with each other in a non-adversarial dynamic.

The kind of individual [and social] conversion Sartre presents is one that overcomes domination and conflict; attempts at control are given up. The fact that I might still be an object for the Other does not alienate me from my being unless the Other refuses to see any subjectivity in me. If both the Other and I reject the God-project and choose our mutual freedom as our goal, any objectification of each other is not necessarily oppressive but can be positive and constructive. Cooperation is possible in an inter-subjective system in which each party facilitates each other's projects. While it is true that on a social and economic level Sartre is referring to socialist, classless society. On an individual level, which is more of our direct concern here, it is in our generosity that we authentically will the freedom of Others. Moreover, this also means that we accept that we will become an object for Others and that we cannot control how they will objectify us.

Anything we create, and this includes ourselves, can be taken away by Others. We simply do not have mastery over how Others utilize our creations. This actually works for a person who has moved away from the influence of the God-project, for he has little or no attachment to being his own self caused being. Instead of clinging to his objectivity by attempting to control it he accepts that Others may want it; in fact, in generosity the authentic person welcomes and encourages the Other to his objectivity. Furthermore, the authentic person helps Others obtain their own goals by acknowledging their freedoms and not interfering with them. Instead of focusing on some abstract moral formula, he acknowledges and promotes the concrete freedom of the Other that operates through a specific facticity. We promote specific people living in specific circumstances. This is the way of valuing freedom. This kind of promotion of the other's freedom Sartre calls "authentic love," for in it we unveil the Other's being in the world, and experience joy in it without appropriating it.[112]

This leads us to the important question of why we should value and promote the freedom of Others. Sartre was always adamant that one freedom was not superior to another because they were always of equal weight. He says "I am obliged to will the freedom of others at the same time as mine."[113] This is not a Kantian move because he is not appealing to a universal rule. Rather, he is saying that when I choose the man I want to be, I am choosing based on a certain image of man that I have.[114] I am creating in my choice an ideal of what I want man to be. There is an implication here that there are common goods of humanity that are universal. What is good for me is good for all. Perhaps this is not true, but it is still true that when I choose my freedom as my primary value I am proposing that Others choose in this way, as well.

For Sartre the reason that I should choose my freedom as my primary value is because it is the source of all my other values. But this does not hold true just for me. Actually, it is a universal human condition and I am no different. I am using myself as an instantiation of a quality about all humans. Moreover, if I will that others choose freedom as their primary value then I must impliedly will that they not be impeded by me in their efforts. I must then will that they have the freedom to act. This means that I must not interfere with the Other in his goals. It is more difficult to say that I must also act affirmatively to promote the Other's freedom and, if so, how much effort I am obliged to give. It also seems problematic to contemplate a conflict in freedoms, for if I value my freedom and another's equally, resolution seems tricky.

Nevertheless, Sartre offers suggestions that we might use to overcome these seeming problems. He has a strong belief that there is an interdependency of freedoms. They simply do not exist in isolation and, in fact, are dependent upon the rest of them, together. This means that ultimately I cannot get what I desire unless I not only have my own freedom but that any others involved have freedom, too. I need another person's freedom in order to secure my own![115] For simple pragmatic reasons I need the Other and his freedom for my own. In return, he needs mine. This is the concept of genuine reciprocity, the social possibility of which Sartre wrestles and struggles his whole life.[116]

One could object that a person with a great deal of power might not have to abide by a policy of non-interference with another's freedom, for he can get what he wants, in fact, by enslaving others. Although this seems true to some extent, it still is the case that I need some cooperation by others even in their enslavement. Further, for some of the important intangible goods of life, i.e., emotional, spiritual, and intuitive, I do need the Other's freedom to secure them. In fact, the joy that I feel in being generous can only come from respecting the freedom of another person. The joy I experience in being grateful for another's promotion of my freedom can only come if the other actually has the freedom to promote mine.

This interdependency of human freedoms has both a sociopolitical and personal psychological dimension. While the sociopolitical level is very important, we want to focus away from it and attend to the personal psychological dimension. Recall that the very foundation of our work here is to explore the relationship between moral development and the kind of psychology that Sartre espouses. There is, I believe, more at stake here than the very important practical interdependency of freedoms Sartre advocates. Very strong arguments can be made for sociopolitical interdependency, but we will not focus on these here. Very strong arguments can be made that I need the Other to attain very important intangible goods; these are the sorts of goods that directly involve emotion, spirituality perhaps, and other states of being that are highly personal and necessary to human flourishing. Nevertheless, we believe that at a deeper ontological level I may need the Other for my very existence and sense of self. Therefore, the issue of how I treat the Other takes on paramount importance. This issue is directly relevant to the ongoing discussion about how my treatment of Others may fit in with my bad faith God-project. Again, we want to say that in this essay we are concentrating on dyadic relations between two people, which intentionally avoids the issue of broader sociopolitical change and my responsibility in it.

These conclusions lead us to the position that I must act affirmatively to secure the freedom of the Other. I must not merely avoid interfering with his freedom. Instead, I must actually do things — I must act in ways — that promote the Other's freedom. Sartre even takes the position that we need the Other to help us become more aware of ourselves.[117] This position coincides with the pragmatic underpinnings of existential psychoanalysis itself in that we need the analytic encounter to obtain more self-awareness and understanding. Even though Sartre never fully retreated from his early ontological position that in prereflective consciousness we are always fully aware of ourselves, he does counter these notions to some extent in his notebooks.

Sartre believes that I can be lied to in such a way that I become confused about my own freedom. Further, he acknowledges that when we are in a position of relative powerlessness this process of enlightenment can be very difficult.[118] If others can limit my awareness of my freedom or even take it away, they can also promote it. Yet Sartre is not explicit on this point until he writes his work on Genet a few years later. Here, he illustrates the point that the way a family and a society treats a person is very causal and to some extent determinative of how a person develops. Without the kind of genuinely reciprocal relationships that promote love and respect for the other, a person's developmental processes can be, in short, derailed. This is not to say that a person cannot overcome what others make of him, but that the identities and objectifications others bestow upon us are very influential and significant in the developmental process.

Recognizing the value of freedom for others means that we must act in ways that promote it. A contemplative acknowledgment might satisfy one's intellectual cravings but a full-on recognition must include action. Recall for Sartre that a move toward authenticity always includes action. Thus the value of freedom for Others depends upon how I value it for them; as a corollary, the value of freedom for me depends upon how Others value it for me. We [meaning] all of us as community must recognize this value of freedom together. Furthermore, as I encourage another person in his freedom, his ability to encourage me in my own freedom is strengthened. To the extent that a person's freedom is dampened, he or she is unable to recognize a greater freedom in Others.

On the dyadic plane, we can see how significant this reciprocal facilitation of freedom can become. It is logical to suppose that the more I do not recognize the other's freedom and the more I actively contribute to its decrease the less freedom my dyadic partner has to recognize and respect my own. The arrest of one dyadic partner's freedom means the arrest of the other, within the dynamics of the relationship.

The arrest of both together through sadomasochistic relationship curtails the freedom of both. This, we have seen, occurs through pursuit of the God-project by attachment to the Other. When both parties pursue a substantial self within the confines of the relation, using each other as a way to fix one's self, the result is a bad faith arabesque that includes a loss of freedom and a denial of responsibility. Because Sartre advocates a concrete morality based on one's phenomenal field, the interdependency he talks about must spring from and within one's community. Surely the kind of sociopolitical changes he espouses require support for Others that we might never meet. At the personal level, though, my concrete acts of morality are critical, not only for the other, but for me and the other together.

Let us probe a little deeper now into Sartre's position about objectification of the Other. In his early position in *BN* he makes it clear that objectifying another subject was, on its face, a degradation of the other into a thing-like object. He denied the possibility of simultaneously apprehending another's subjectivity [freedom] and objectivity, together. In a penetrating analysis of the Look,[119] he claims that social life is primarily a struggle for mastery over the objectification of the Other. He went even further to claim that ontologically it was impossible for two people to recognize each other's freedom in the same stroke. One always had to be objectified.

In *NB*, to some extent, Sartre continues to claim that objectification involves adversarial conflict, oppression by the Other, alienation from one's spontaneous being, and a degradation of freedom. More importantly, it involves a process in which one person is created as substantial object, which is the very process we described earlier in this text. Where one person is chasing a substantial self we can always find evidence of it in the way he or she objectifies others in his or her social relations. This process of reification fixes another human through the exchange of Looks and can quickly take the form of sadism or masochism, or both. Yet, in a movement away from his early ontology, in *NB* Sartre argues that objectification of Others need not lead to forms of oppression. Merely being the object of Others does not imply being degraded in value or reified as a fixed self.

In the pursuit of authenticity through purified forms of reflection, we can and must accept our objectification by others.[120] An authentic person, according to Sartre, generously gives himself, as object, for Others to utilize for their own ends. Being an object, therefore, is not by itself oppressive. In fact, when others objectify my being by using my acts and my creations, they enrich the world. Moreover, they give an objective meaning to my existence that goes far beyond any subjective meaning that I give to myself. The threat in objectification only arises if others refuse to see, acknowledge, and respect the freedom in my being, i.e., my subjectivity. In a society full of these sorts of reciprocal meaning-giving relationships, the community as a whole deepens its embeddedness in meaning.

Unlike *BN*, in which there is a conflict of Looks and shifting subject-object relations, in *NB* Sartre believes that each member of a dyad can see the other as an object and a subject at the same time. If this is true then there are great opportunities for moral development that move beyond sadomasochistic dynamics. This is not to say that a person whose development has been distorted through oppression by others is able to see himself or the Other as a free subject. Yet it does open discussion about the effects of self-growth on one's ability to recognize his subjectivity and that of Others. Thus, the rigid social dynamics of *BN*, through a conversion to pure reflection, can lead to a social transformation that opens up new possibilities of relating.

This social space for individuals to recognize each other's subjectivity is, in Sartre's terms, a "reciprocal comprehension" of freedoms.[121] Unlike knowledge that purely objectifies from a position of distance, comprehension engages empathy, grasping the Other and his freedom by sympathetically acknowledging and facilitating the pursuit of his goals. Comprehension is not a passive, spectator-like contemplation of the Other at a distance. Instead, I anticipate in myself the action of the Other toward his goals. In addition, I actually participate in these goals without adopting them as my own. By willing a realization of the Other's freedom, I allow myself to become an instrument for that freedom. By freely willing them I am not objectified precisely because I do will them as subject. In like fashion, I do not reveal the Other as object or subject, but as a freedom moving toward his goals.[122] This ontological position can be thought of as a primary revelation of the Other that is preliminary to its ripening either as subject or object. Another way to view it is that the Other is revealed both as subject and as object simultaneously. In either case, this overcomes the conflict-ridden Look in *BN*.

This sympathetic engagement appeals to a shift in consciousness that apprehends the Other, not as an antagonist, but as the same. In this new dynamic there is a unity between two humans that Sartre did not portray in *BN*. This unity is not an ontological fusion of individuals but it is a "kind of interpenetration of freedoms"[123] where each freedom is wholly in the other one."[124] In this interpenetration of freedoms, for example in relations of love and friendship, there is a unifying process that occurs between two people. There seems to be, as Sartre explores in groups in *CDR*, a parallel shift in consciousness for both individuals in a dyad, whereby they become in some sense the same.

214

This sameness in consciousness operates on the practical but
not the ontological or ontic levels. There is an experience
of unity through consciousness. It is a shift from radical
otherness to radical sameness in consciousness, will, and
action even though both individuals remain individual.
By identifying with the interest of the Other and by him
identifying with mine, even though we cannot be unified
into one super-being, we can be unified by will and action.
Any objectification I make of the Other in this state does not
alienate him from his freedom; instead, because I am the same
in will, it is like taking a position on myself while remaining
sensitive to my own subjectivity. Sartre's *NB* holds a view
about human relations that has evolved significantly beyond
the rigid, antagonistic categories in *BN*. Human relations in
NB are not inherently adversarial and in fact can ultimately
promote an inter-subjective community that promotes the
freedom of all.

More Thoughts on the Circuit of Selfness

What we have covered so far is a preliminary look at the major
ideas of Sartre's transition from an abstract ethics to a concrete
ethics. Shortly, we will take a look at his Rome lecture of 1964
and his very late and final musings about ethics. We will see
if and how these later positions add to his development as a
moral theorist, and second, to see how they might add to the
basic discussion about the moral conversion toward freedom
first mentioned in *BN*. Please keep firmly in mind that we
are discussing the manifestations of bad faith within human
relationships. A careful reading of *BN* reveals a number of
Sartre's examples of bad faith. Recall that in bad faith we try
to deny the ambiguous nature of our being, including both
our facticity as well as our transcendence. In bad faith we
deny the facts of our situation or our freedom to alter them or
reinterpret them. In bad faith we may reject the ambiguity that

we are both for ourselves but also for others, calling one true and the other false. Thus, not only are we subjects but are also objects, subject to being looked at by others.

Sometimes we try to flee our freedom and responsibility when we recognize aspects of ourselves in others. The look of the Other can threaten our fundamental ambiguity because he may see only our facticity or only our transcendence but not both. Not seeing our transcendence negates our possibilities; not seeing our facticity ignores our limits. Moreover, the Other's Look may reveal something that is being denied, for example, an individual's object side. By revealing what is being denied, the Other's Look threatens the continuation of a bad faith strategy. As a corollary, because we feel anguish about our freedom we may attach ourselves to another's Look that only sees our facticity. These essences that others may make of us can be appealing because if we attach to them we can avoid the dizziness that comes from confronting our freedom directly.

The Other's Look can give rise to two attitudes toward the Other. First, the one being looked at can re-establish his freedom by looking back and thereby turning the Other into an object. Second, the Other's Look can be appealing because it destroys the ambiguity the individual in bad faith tries to escape. For example, the Other can see an individual solely in terms of his facticity, bestowing an essence on him. In reaction, the individual in bad faith may incorporate the Other's view inside himself in this sort of attempt to create a substantial self. Of course, each attempt fails but the attempt drives one into its opposite. Within the dynamic of a relationship, this creates a circle of relations with others. It is a negative dialectic because it destroys part of the totality of what a person is; it is relentless because each strategy contains its opposite at its core. We must try to understand why it is so difficult to break out of this circle.

In the first attitude, which includes love and masochism, we try to recover the being that we are for the Other. The Look by the Other may alienate us from this aspect of our being. As transcendence we can try to overcome this alienation by absorbing the Look and by identifying oneself with being looked at; for example, a lover tries to capture the freedom of the Other's Look. Yet, this project fails because of the alienation of the freedom it demands. What the lover wants is a similar alienation on the part of the Other but the Other remains transcendent. In this game of seduction each person tries to identify himself with his object side but does so to produce love in the partner, always a failure. For Sartre, to love is a wish to be loved. To wish for love from the beloved is to wish that the beloved want the lover to love him. This is an ideal that is impossible to attain. There is, in this kind of love, always dissatisfaction and destabilization because the lover can always re-establish himself as transcendence, making the Other into an object.

In this failing dynamic, individuals try to lose themselves in objectivity, in their being-for-Others, but without success. Inevitably they are reminded of their subjectivity. They can push this even further by becoming masochistic and denying their subjectivity completely. Yet the harder a person tries to deny his subjectivity the more he is reminded of his complete nature. This failure can propel an individual toward attitudes such as indifference, desire, hate, or sadism. The strategy is opposite to that of masochism. Instead of identifying with being looked at, one can confront the Other's freedom by looking back and regarding the Other purely as an object. This looking back at the Other pays the price of losing any justification one draws from that other. The loss of this quasi-essence pushes an individual into a direct confrontation with his responsibility for making oneself. The opposite strategy would be to become desirable with the goal of possessing the transcendence of the Other.

Desire will always fail. By incarnating itself it may lose sight of the incarnation of the Other which is what it wanted in the first place. For example, the pleasure of touching someone may transform into pleasure of being caressed, possibly becoming masochism. In contrast, this failure may motivate sadism, which is an attempt to incarnate the Other. With desire I use my own flesh to awaken the flesh of the Other; with sadism I don't reveal my own flesh to do this. Although the sadist does not oppress his victim's freedom he does want to force the Other to identify with his flesh. Yet the sadist always fails because it is up to the victim to determine when the pain becomes unbearable. Furthermore, when the sadist achieves his goal of totally incarnating the Other, he loses the freedom of the Other that he has tried to master; all he has left is pure materiality. The goal of constraining the victim's freedom to will freely what the sadist wills of him is always futile; one look from the victim accounts for this.

Love and desire are bad faith projects that fail. Further, these two attitudes are fundamental in all approaches to the Other, according to Sartre, not including hate. They show us the circle of relations with the Other. Love fails and desire arises which, in turn, collapses as love emerges. There is a circle of relations in which we approach the Other as object, then as subject, and so on. The circle arises because of the nature of the Other. He is always part object and part subject. He is always a transcendence that is transcending and a transcendence that is transcended. As we have shown, for Sartre, one can never apprehend both of these aspects simultaneously. Hate does not break us out of this circle either for in hate we try to murder the Other out of desperation that our former attempts within the circle have failed. Hate's rogue attempts at absolute freedom without facticity fail, as well, because it is impossible to bring it about that the Other never existed.

This circle of relations, as we have discussed, is motivated by the bad faith desire to create a substantial self and derivatively to capture the Other, who will not allow this. Capturing the Other, one way or the other, is always in service of this fundamental pursuit of a self. Both sides of this circle of relations keep the other in place, and both are motivated by bad faith. Without exercising the will and choosing the moral conversion toward authenticity, there is no way of escaping this circle. Part of the reason why it is impossible to break the circle without conversion is that individuals caught in it simply do not recognize reasons against what they are seeking. Because they seek what they may even recognize as impossible, their frustrations and failures do not push them to see and acknowledge those reasons that would motivate them to escape the circle.

The alienation caused by the Look of the Other cannot be overcome if an individual remains within a bad faith foundation. Recall that what we demand here is a simultaneous apprehension of the Other's freedom and objectivity. We want to assimilate or negate the freedom of the Other. Yet to become aware of the Other as object is to destroy the Other's freedom. The dilemma is to try to become aware of the Other's freedom and subjectivity as object through indifference, sadism, or hate. We can also try to become aware of the Other's objectivity as freedom through love, language, and masochism. As we have shown, both poles of the circle, objectivity and subjectivity, exclude each other and will never coincide with one another. Importantly, Sartre believes that there is no dialectical process that can motivate a person out of the circle. There is no way to think oneself out because the self in bad faith simply does not recognize reasons against its position.

In bad faith all evaluations are made within the original bad faith determination of value, thus creating the circle. Lack of success in attaining these values does not register against the values themselves, and we keep trying, oscillating from the subjective to the objective pole of the Other, if our bad faith strategy includes an active relation. The value of all choices and projects can always be traced to an original foundation value, a primary choice of what is to count. For Sartre, nothing can count for or against one's ultimate value commitments. They determine what is to count for and against other choices. They are, therefore, invulnerable to dialectical attack. Individuals in bad faith deal with the futility of their projects by reconciling themselves never to be satisfied. Impossibility becomes a familiar ending.

Conversion

For a person who pursues authenticity, alienation is inevitable. These individuals fail to coincide with their goals, with themselves, and with others with whom they may try to involve themselves. They remain free and are therefore never identical with their projects, with what they are, or with each other, whatever their relationship. They remain what they are not, with their facticities and their being for Others. The Look of another can always alienate them from part of their being. Yet, although alienation is inevitable there is a kind of alienation that can be overcome. Authentic individuals can always overcome the sort of alienation perpetrated on them by Others. Those who live in bad faith are opposed within themselves in a way that an authentic individual is not. They cannot allow themselves to see clearly what kind

of being they choose. In their attempts to deceive themselves
by chasing a substantial self, they alienate themselves from
what they are in a way that an authentic individual does not.
Nevertheless, some levels of alienation may be so structurally
deep that authentically-oriented individuals can overcome
it only by engaging in a radical re-structuring of society. In
contrast, the type of personal alienation that comes from bad
faith can be overcome through acceptance of freedom and
the limits of the human condition. Let us delve a little more
deeply into what Sartre means by moral conversion.

Generally, conversion means to realize that one is fully
situated in the world; that we must claim full responsibility
for this situation; that we must refuse any sort of excuse
for ourselves. Authenticity moves from being a purely
ontological category and becomes part of a discourse about
sociality. It requires a lucid recognition that we must live
our unjustifiable freedom and take responsibility for it no
matter what. The authentic person rejects flight, as well as the
sedimented values of society by reflectively choosing to value
the unsettledness of one's non-substantial consciousness.
Because of the non-coincidence or ambiguity at the core
of being human, we are always susceptible to bad faith
attempts to fill its nothingness. Nevertheless, human freedom
can radically convert; it can deliver itself from bad faith
attitudes and through a reflective, willed choice, enjoy its
ambiguity, spontaneity, and contingency while accepting full
responsibility for all of its choices.

The act of conversion goes from an awareness of one's
ontological freedom to the deliberate and intentional valuing
of that freedom. It is a moral conversion, moving from
one's falling into a world of facticity into a recovery of a
non-substantial self. In spite of human reality's initial quest
for being, it is possible for a human being, in good faith, to

confront and affirm its freedom without losing out to bad faith flight. For Sartre an authentic consciousness converts itself from the natural attitude of fleeing one's freedom to an attitude of affirming and valorizing the radical freedom to which it is condemned and for which it is responsible. Most importantly, conversion is a function of will, and will is a part of reflective consciousness. The will, in conversion, attempts to recover itself as a spontaneous nothingness rather than to continue its prereflective project of fleeing in the direction of its facticity, toward being.

In *NB*, Sartre shows how, in authenticity, consciousness is an unveiling of being through modes of non-being. The act of reflection is an unveiling of freedom because it constantly calls itself into question.[125] This reflective process ultimately renounces appropriation and reveals that part of the self that is unable to be appropriated. This is the part that is identity-less freedom, manifesting Being/facticity. Further, he shows that the transformation brought about by purifying reflection can liberate an individual from primitive alienation. If a person transforms his contingency into autonomy he takes on responsibility for himself, others, and the world, thereby overcoming facticity.

Sartre asserts in *NB* that a new ethical respect for freedom leaves undetermined the relation we must have with the content of that freedom.[126] Yet, by making freedom the highest value he wills a norm by which appropriation of that freedom by another can be judged inauthentic and immoral. By creating a city of ends whose members promote freedom as the highest value, individuals avoid the kind of aggression that results in exploitation and destruction; they avoid the kind of harm that results from social relations that are dynamically sadomasochistic. It is this reflective willing of our spontaneous freedom that results in the moral dimension of human beings.

Authenticity is closely related to the way that we approach our human condition. We are always faced with the task of motivating ourselves to *be* in some way because we are free. Each human being is an instantiation of nothingness without foundation, but this motivates us to create one. For Sartre, our goal is not necessarily happiness or self-preservation, but instead is to pursue a self. Because we seek to become our foundation, human reality becomes moral. What is exhausting is this relentless requirement of re-creating ourselves anew every moment. In this search for future substantiality we become tired, which causes us to conceal the fact that we must motivate ourselves solely from within.[127] Inauthenticity just is the seeking of a foundation in order to move away from the sheer absurdity of our facticity. In our relationships, as well, and even more strongly, we desire the Other to pull us out of our facticity.

In the moral conversion, we accept our situation that we are without excuse. By not only accepting our freedom, but by actually willing it, we make it ours. By converting this radical freedom into a freedom that we own, we become fully and completely responsible for our choices, for everything. In this conversion we assume complete responsibility for our situation no matter what it is. Our anguish comes in each moment because we are faced with questioning everything, constantly. This process is obviously never completed. We are always faced with the temptation to fill out our consciousness with being.

It can also be said that Sartre's pure reflection results in a kind of phenomenological reduction like Husserl's. The natural attitude of flight and impure reflection can be bracketed and overcome in which consciousness recognizes its failure in providing ready-made values. In this attitude we break from our normal attachment to objects in the world. The bracketing itself is tantamount to a conversion as purified consciousness accepts itself as a self-motivating, groundless entity. Both purifying consciousness of the "I" and disengaging from bad faith provides a foundation for a positive and constructive ethics. It creates a basis for moral agency by taking full responsibility for creating values for all humanity. Because Sartre's ethics turned away from an abstract system toward a concrete approach, and because his method is phenomenological, we will take a look at how his ethical focus changed later in this essay. For now, let us explore a bit more his thought on conversion, especially as it relates to the unveiling of authenticity. We will now turn directly to NB for this exploration.

Sartre says "authenticity consists in refusing any quest for being, because I am always *nothing*."[128] By refusing being, an authentic human constantly reveals to itself the sheer force of its freedom by calling itself into question and by explicating its concrete situation. This is a direct, reflective confrontation with oneself, making it clear that absolutely nothing justifies oneself except for oneself. This is a move away from any excuse or determination from the outside, dialectically opposed to one's facticity. This reflective assumption of my freedom as mine justifies myself inwardly and reveals that part of my being that is unable to be appropriated by myself or anyone else. I am not a fixed being, unlike the world of objects, and this sort of unveiling reveals this truth to me. Thus, this reflective process makes truths appear.[129] It is a process of revealing Being, but this can only happen through the type of being that a human is; non-being reveals the truth of Being.

For Sartre, what *is* is illuminated by what is not. This, for

Sartre, is the "structure of truth."[130] It is nihilation that
lights up Being against an undifferentiated background. In
these acts of disclosure, a human being illuminates Being by
interpreting his situation and giving it meaning. In contrast
to the bad faith attempt to be a self-caused being, in the
unveiling process of authenticity an individual embraces the
nothingness of his consciousness and creates from nothing
a foundation of meaning. This involves my refusal to define
myself by what I am, as ego, but instead by what I will as a
reflective questioning of myself. In this way an individual
changes his relation to Being. He becomes a project that
loses itself, as ego, in order to save himself as a consciousness
always at a distance from himself. Conversion involves a
reflective refusal to define myself as a thing and instead to
choose to affirm myself as a being with ambiguity, gratuity,
non-coincidence, and radical questioning.

Although authenticity refuses to pursue being, it cannot
by conversion absolutely suppress it.[131] Thus, there is no
absolute moral conversion. Furthermore, any deliverance is
not from human reality, but toward it, viewed in a different
light. Purifying reflection maintains the tension at the heart
of being a human being. It changes the attitude toward
which we live this tension, valuing our own non-coincidence,
embracing our radical responsibility. With this new resolve,
an individual frees himself from all of the values and identities
he had created in bad faith, and learns to maintain himself
at a distance. It is, as he says, a matter of "willing the Good
(in the un-reflected upon) in order to be ethical."[132] But this
requires us to give up a belief in transcendent values and
instead make freedom the highest value. If God, the *causa sui*,
does not exist, then we "have to decide by ourselves [even]
on the meaning of Being."[133] As we have said, this is a grave
responsibility, for ourselves and for all others. When I will
freedom as my highest value, I must imply that this includes

the freedom of all Others, as well. On this point, Sartre believes "the being of the Other is *my affair*."[134] Keep in mind the sheer gravity of this charge. For Sartre, who wills a city of ends in which each person respects the freedom of each other person, to ever denigrate or refuse the freedom of another is to behave inauthentically because it destroys freedom, which is the highest value.

The duty to respect the freedom of each other person means that, because we exist in situation, we must interpret this highest duty in terms of what a situation calls for concretely. This means that we must strive to transform the Other into a "pure, free subjectivity."[135] This requires me to adopt the Other's ends as my own; practically this requires me to [authentically] will that the Other's end be realized. By valuing the Other's freedom, I adopt his ends only in terms of how he wants them, which precludes me alienating my will or the Other's freedom. Instead of seeing each other in terms of the conflict of Looks in *BN*, through purifying reflection and authentic motivation, we each adopt the Other's freedom and ends. This new attitude embodied in a city of ends overcomes primitive alienation starts to develop a morality by pushing us toward a deeper recognition and comprehension of the freedom of the Other. This requires the virtues of empathy, generosity, and openness toward the situation and plight of the Other.[136] Also included among genuinely reciprocal inter-subjective relations is the beginning of a criterion that can be used to distinguish between morally justifiable and unjustifiable behavior. This does not mean that Sartre is attempting to create an absolute moral principle because that would violate the spirit of bad faith seriousness that we accounted for earlier in this essay. This is so because value is not a being; it is a choice.

The conversion from bad faith to purifying reflection

constitutes for Sartre the moralization of human consciousness. This transformation into authenticity marks a deliverance from our original fall into the world. It marks a break from our attachment to things as well as from the domination by the facticities of our situations. Authentic choosing and reflective conversion lead to a coherent self. This is a self that is integrated in its value commitment to freedom. The conversion to authenticity becomes a moral foundation.

Sartre's Rome lecture, the Flaubert Study, & His Late Ethics

Now that we have covered the main points of Sartre's first, abstract ethics, and his later corrections that led to a more concrete morality, let us add a few comments about the Rome lecture and the Flaubert study. This will help us understand more about the evolution of his thought that led to a concrete ethics that focuses more on the specific historical, familial, and social situations in which we find ourselves.[137] This can also shed some light on how to overcome the pursuit of a substantial self and the kind of sadomasochistic dynamics toward which this pursuit pushes us. We will also acknowledge a few of his very latest and final comments on morality that brings him toward a position that is close to Levinas' views.[138]

In Rome on May 23, 1964, Sartre gave a lecture at the Institutio Gramsci at a conference entitled "Ethics and Society" that further clarified his idea of a concrete, materialist ethics.[139] He criticized abstract moralities and argued that every morality is dialectically conditioned by basic social structures. For him, this meant that we must engage in the moral exploration of real humans existing in concrete historical circumstances. This approach must be limited as well, so that we do not preclude some general moral principles that apply universally. He undertakes the phenomenological analysis of moral experience and centers on ontological structures present in all of this type of human experience. He argues that the experience of moral norms is unconditional; that it demands obedience no matter what the circumstances, and that this is an experience of human freedom. Here, the norm itself requires me to freely create my future self independently of my past and present circumstances. To ignore this obligatory character of the norm implies a disregard for the ontological structure of the moral requirement.

In his discussion about the connection between moral norms and class structure, Sartre asserts that the exploited do not often know that integral humanity is what they seek; he argues that they often do not understand what it would mean to live a totally human life. He believes that most of the moralities that have operated throughout history have been alienated moralities because they are not based on structures that facilitate concrete freedom for all. The task for Sartre is to discover the roots of the ethical in the very depth of human reality. This root, for him, is located in human needs. It is our needs that cause us to experience moral norms as obligatory. Needs demanding to be satisfied cause their goal, which is a satisfied organism/human being. Further, these needs are not chosen; they are given, which is a notion that moves away from Sartre's early pronouncements that we choose all value/ends.

By rooting morality in human needs, Sartre provides himself with an ontological basis for analyzing alienated moralities. For him, true moralities are at the basis of all alienated moralities. It does not matter what the characteristics of a particular moral system are, for every human moral system possesses an unconditional normative character. This is not because it is rooted in an absolute principle but because it is concretely rooted in the needs of human beings in all kinds of societies and cultures. He thinks that humans from all cultures have the same basic needs even though their socioeconomic systems vary. Human fulfillment is the goal of each and everyone no matter what the culture. In contrast to alienated moralities, true morality is rooted in the most fundamental needs of humans. In his notion of direct democracy, human beings are transparent about their basic needs and work together to overcome structures that oppress some individuals.

In *The Family Idiot*[140] Sartre acknowledges the tremendous amount of social conditioning of human individuals. He believes that parents and families condition their children, and that we externalize this conditioning in adulthood. Instead of retreating to a position of determinism, which he soundly rejects in his early ontology, he adopts a later position of predestination. Here, he allows for a small amount of freedom in response to previous conditioning. This position is far from the kind of radical freedom he espouses in BN, but he never succumbs to the charge that we are totally conditioned. Humans get a chance to make something from what was given to them. Integrated fulfillment of basic needs is the goal, and our predestination toward this end is based on the degree to which we receive love and generosity during key developmental stages in our lives.

We also need Others in order to gain self-knowledge; otherwise, we might become alienated from ourselves by the imposition of false consciousness. This can occur if we occupy a passive position, like Flaubert did, whereby we do not believe ourselves a moral agent capable of changing reality. By becoming passive, a person who lacks the ability to act and feel as an agent will be unable to satisfy the need to seek evidence in order to verify the truth or falsity of what is proposed about his or her world. What is clear is that by the time Sartre engages in his Flaubert study he has moved far away from his early position that each consciousness is lucidly transparent to itself prereflectively and that it can do this on its own without others. By this time, Sartre has come to realize the profound impact that Others, both specific and anonymous, can have on our self-knowledge.

The Flaubert study makes human needs central to an ethics. In it, Sartre shows the overwhelming importance of the human need to be valued and loved and therefore the complete dependency we have on each other in attaining human fulfillment. He shows that we are deeply conditioned by our families and society and that we live with severe limits on our freedom and our awareness of it. Moreover, he shows in concrete fashion how social structures and relationship structures can prevent us from developing fully. In this study, however, Sartre continues to maintain his early position that it is completely up to us to place meaning on the world. This also means that humans have complete freedom, subject to our mutual interdependence, to strive away from bad faith attempts to gain a substantial self.

Sartre's later moral position begins with a phenomenological analysis of everyday moral experience with the objective of ascertaining the ontological structure of its norms and values. He admits that there is a given objective character to true moral norms. He believes that this objective character is not reducible to the values and obligations held by a particular society or culture. This position is in contrast to his early position in which he argues that all values are freely chosen projects of individuals and rejects the view that some values possess a kind of intrinsic value. His matured position accepts some objective moral values that are dependent solely on

human need and not on human choice. This allows Sartre
to argue the position that there are some universal values
and needs of all human beings. This also figures prominently
in our own discussion because of the structural opposition
between alienated moralities and a true morality.

Alienated moralities are based on distorted thinking about
needs and values. In contrast, true morality is based on
Sartre's concept of integral humanity. The opposition triggers
the epistemological issue between appearance and reality,
and therefore, self-deception/bad faith. Social structure
that oppresses creates alienated moralities. Likewise,
sadomasochistic relational dynamics also create alienated
moralities in which the freedom and integral humanity of
the relationship partners is threatened. Through a reflective
and interpersonal process each of us can struggle with
understanding the infrastructure, both familial and social,
that results in distorted perceptions about promoting the
freedom and humanity of others with whom we are involved.
This strongly suggests that we use his method of existential
psychoanalysis, as modified by the replacement of radical
freedom with the value of integral humanity. This project in
itself, I believe, would require a new book project to carefully
delve into its process and methodology, but for now we can
make a few points that ought to be explored and developed.

In my judgment, humans continue to pursue a substantial
self, most often through relationships with other people. As
we have seen, this involves a bad faith oscillation within a
circuit of selfness, moving back and forth between sadistic
and masochistic orientations toward the Other. By examining
how our bad faith pursuit of a substantive self results in
degradations of promoting freedom and integral humanity,
we can begin to develop a method that can aid in making
moral corrections. For the last section of this essay, I want

to highlight some of the more important issues involved in pursuing an authentic orientation in the world that avoids chasing a substantial self.

Now that we have taken a look at how Sartre moved from an abstract ethics to a concrete ethics that promotes human fulfillment as well as freedom, we need to say a few words about his ethical pronouncements that he made close to his death. In his ontological accounts he never gave up his notion of the fundamental split between individuals. There was always a gulf between consciousnesses that could never be bridged except in a practical way through common projects in which we viewed each other as the "same."[141] Nonetheless, if we look at the totality of his life work, and the trajectory he was on, coupled with his very late comments that we will look at shortly, it seems that he was on the verge of breaking with his early ontology. With *CDR* and the *NB*, along with the implications of the Flaubert study, it seems clear that he believed we could never completely know ourselves, maximize our freedom, or achieve human fulfillment without a strong moral responsibility to each other and to our community.

In the very last phase of his career and life, Sartre taped a number of interviews with Benny Lévy entitled "Power and Freedom," which indicate a shift in position on ethics that is close to Levinas's views.[142] In contrast to the Rome lecture in which Sartre argued that moral experience is the experience of obligation to a norm, in his late ideas he argues that the moral experience is the experience of another human being. Instead of it being a relationship to a rule it is a relationship to another person. Instead of freedom being the predominant value, the phenomenal presence of the Other in my consciousness takes priority. Further, Sartre suggests that the Other is an already-existing value merely by virtue of being in my presence.

This very late moral conception of Sartre's overcomes the rigid polarization between two instantiations of an "I." This is the morality of the "We," in which consciousnesses are not isolated from each other but ontologically meet each other on some plane. This is a natural extension of his work in *CDR* in which he argues that there is a practical but not ontological meeting between consciousnesses. Here he argues that there is fraternity and solidarity between humans merely because we belong to the same species and have the same ends.

This overlap in consciousness is hard to understand from a traditional Western epistemological stance but it may exist on pre-discursive dimensions that include emotion, intuition, and spiritual-mystical union. It is more of a sensing of unity than a question of knowledge. Most importantly, Sartre adopts the position that this basic solidarity of the "We" exists at the very firmament of our sociality, a position that seems very Levinasian to us, although it would be important to investigate this. Furthermore, just like Levinas, Sartre adopts the position that this basic bond between people lies below the level of relations of production, which are more utilitarian in scope and imply a Cartesian ontology. In Sartre's mind, this new conception pursues the goal of complete human beings who do not have power over each other and who live with each other in a completely interdependent way, grounded in freedom.

Final Remarks

We have investigated the psychological-ontological aspect of the kind of authentic political community that Sartre envisioned. By tracing some of the main lines of his moral thinking and interpreting them in terms of his early and late formulations of authentic orientation in the world, we have illuminated some of the challenges involved in overcoming bad faith social relationships. It is the struggle against the God-project that leads to authentic selfhood and authentic

community. On the individual level, attaching ourselves to
ideas, places, objects, and the like creates the illusion of a firm
foundation for value. On the level of social relationships, it
creates sadomasochistic psychological dynamics that impede
both freedom and integral humanity that fully respects the
objective and subjective needs of everyone involved. For the
balance of this essay, let us reflect a bit on what is at stake
in the quest for authentic social relationship. Then, we will
make some final comments about possible direction for the
development of Sartre's method of existential psychoanalysis,
in terms of his later, concrete moral position, as well as his
final pronouncements about a different sort of social ontology.

The flight from our existential responsibility into the
absorption with particular entities is the essence of bad
faith. As we are absorbed by beings through our flight in the
world we become isolated. Here, we lose focus on the whole
of Being and instead focus on particular things that have
discrete and manageable boundaries. Yet, this strategy does
not dispel our fundamental anxiety. This anxiety in the face
of Being emerges when we recognize the illusory security
brought by attachment to particular entities. This anxiety
comes when we realize that our whole life's focus on the false
security of particular entities has been an entire project of
ignoring the ambiguous structure of consciousness and our
responsibility to our radical freedom and integral humanity.

Through the existential conversion process, we can turn away
from the pursuit of substantial being and face directly the
sheer fact of our overwhelming freedom to choose value and
to recognize needs. When we fully appreciate our existential
freedom we can begin to ask the questions about the purpose
and meaning of our lives. It is through anxiety that we place
our trust in particular beings. However, as we realize that
this will not bring us ontological security and fulfillment, we

can turn toward acceptance of our existential situation as a whole. Here we fully accept all of our being in the quest to maximize all our potentialities. Here we allow the totality to unfold. Moving to this state means to move toward a more and fully authentic being. Our authentic being, our existential continuity, is also disrupted within the dimension of the way we participate with others. We turn to an examination of what authentic being-with-Others means.

Just as we are alone in our perceptions, thoughts, judgments, and feelings, we are also in the world with Others, as Sartre shows throughout his oeuvre. The root of all inauthentic manifestations of being-with-Others is the attitude of self-concern. Here, we reduce our central value to self-concern and, as we have seen, this can take many forms within sadomasochistic polarization. This can occur even in a person who thinks he is being altruistic, for his motivation could ultimately be self-satisfaction. Self-concern, when it is our primary motivation, prevents our essential being-with-Others from full and genuine expression. It is a distorted actualization of the possibility of our being-with, for even in the midst of the Other we turn away from him. Because the development of a type of human possibility is hindered, the growth of a whole person is thereby thwarted.

Let us explain further. Self-concern usually has as its main feature a reduction of the presence of others to mere objects, and is born of a childhood in which we were unwitting members of a sadomasochistic process. In our [unconscious] quest to reduce others to relational objects, we subordinate another person's existence to our own drama, creating an I-It dynamic. In this situation we do not encounter another person but a thing, and this attitude determines the intellectual and emotional developments that emerge from it. Here, the interiority of the Other is all but squeezed out, with only a flat exteriority remaining. Desirous attachment sees the Other as desirable and tries to draw this Other into one's sphere of influence. Aversion sees the other as undesirable and attempts to remove the other. Indifference is an attitude in which the Other does not matter at all. In this way our relationships with Others are limited to the manipulation of a few who impinge on the domain of our personal concern, and the ignoring of all Others.

It is through an existential psychoanalytic process, within a mode and goal of concerned equanimity, that we can see through the superficial veneer projected upon Others by desiring attachment, aversion, and indifference. Under the influence of these attitudes, Others appear to us as though desirability, repugnance, or insignificance were inherent characteristics of their vital essence. For example, desirability seems to come from the very being of a desired person, from each aspect of his or her existence. Yet, when that desire has been satiated, it is interesting to note how quickly this supposedly essential quality disappears, leaving one with an insignificant or even repugnant object-person. The quest for a substantial self, when it involves a motivation to utilize another person as object, is another form of an inauthentic way of being.

This kind of mutability of our inauthentic relationships is based on our subjective projections about what we imagine them to be instead of who they are; unfortunately, these projections are caused by disruptions in our childhood developmental process. Developing equanimity breaks down this disproportionately structured state of interpersonal relations and replaces it with one in which these projections have been stripped away. In this new state of equanimity, we encounter essentially equal humans who had been concealed behind our own projections. In this kind of seeing, no one is desirable, no one is repugnant, and no one is insignificant.

Equanimity can be achieved through a methodological and systematic examination of the current sorts of relations we have with Others. For example we bring to mind a certain person with whom we have a(n) [inauthentic] relationship. We allow the feeling that person evokes to arise; then we step back to a standpoint of detached objectivity. From this detached standpoint, we can disentangle the actual person from the person as he appears to us now. This may require sustained reflection from numerous perspectives, which may include the perspective of Others or the perspective of another time when we knew that person. By engaging in this process with all those we know, equanimity may emerge in which the equal-ness of others comes to the fore and differences become nearly unnoticeable. Equanimity is not an end though. Even though it reduces the tensions and conflicts of desiring attachment and aversion, even though it levels unrealistic distinctions and accepts Others equally, its detachment remains removed from participation. It does prepare one for the next step, which is the task of creating a meaningful pattern of relationships that promotes freedom and integral humanity.

The next step is to realize the essential equality of all human beings. This is a personalization of the earlier process of developing equanimity and requires a similar methodology. In this process, I realize that just as I seek comfort, security, and happiness, and avoid suffering, fear, and pain so do Others. Piece by piece we remove our own self-importance in order to recognize the equal importance of Others. This requires openness to Others in which we recognize the Other as an end and not a means. When we recognize that Others seek happiness and want to avoid pain, we realize that we are the same. This means that I come to the conclusion — at the level of my very being — that I ought to seek the happiness of Others as well as my own and that I ought to protect Others as I protect myself.

As we see, this challenge to our self-concern involves the direct experience of our fundamental mode of being, being-with-Others, which is essential to our very being. In seeing this, we realize that we have moved this seeming center of motivation from its illusory position, exposing that it lacks any ontological foundation. We realize that it has concealed an essential element of our being. This experiential awareness of being-with-Others marks the turning point from inauthentic to authentic being-with-Others. The groundless nature of self-concern is illuminated and the possibility of ontologically grounded authentic relationship opens up. Life is the actualization of possibility and reaches fulfillment only in existence. Here, we realize that being-with-Others is an essential structure that assumes an existential structure as it emerges in the process of actualization, through which we actively participate in the world with Others. When we see that self-concern is a distorted actualization of a fuller set of possibilities for being with Others, the essential passive being-with-Others transforms into an existentially active being-for-Others. In our concrete relations with Others we become concerned for them.

It is authentic concern for Others that pushes against inauthentic self-concern. This conclusion does not come as a result of logical deduction or forced response to any societal norm. Rather, it comes from an immediate and spontaneous awareness (and actualization) of one of the fundamental possibilities of our being. Yet, this awareness does not destroy its opposite, self-concern, so easily. Moving into this new awareness requires methodological practice. It requires cultivation so that it may overcome its dialectical adversary.

This practice involves the exchange of self for Other in which we repeatedly put ourselves in the other's position and try to see things from their position. This is a practice of radical empathy in which we identify the plight of Others as our own. Selfish demands become viewed as obstructions to the fulfillment of our own and of the Other's welfare. As self-concern diminishes, concern for Others becomes stronger through acts of kindness and compassion. Eventually the inalienable rights of self-interest lose their importance.

The meaning of human life is not measured by what we have but by what we are. No matter how much a person has accumulated, he will always be touched by the futility, the emptiness, and the pointlessness of such a life. Well-being does not come from absorption into the world of things, in terms of the illusion that there we are safe. Further, when we decide that the welfare of Others hinges on this same attitude — absorption into the world of things or by the frenzied mode of accumulation — we try to fulfill the Other's welfare by reducing it to matters of material sufficiency, equal opportunity, and adequate education. That is, if I put myself under the spell that I will be fulfilled if I have enough accumulation, then I can neutralize any moral scruples that I may have. Just as I am happy because of what I possess so you must be. Just as I am absorbed into the world of things, so must you be. Then the fulfillment of each Other's welfare becomes reduced to matters of material sufficiency, equal opportunity, and adequate education. Yet, the increasing presence of these things in our society is no guarantee of a more meaningful or fuller life. Their only real value lies in providing a stable basis upon which the inner aim of a human life can be authentically pursued. To subordinate what is human to that which is less than human, such as wealth and knowledge, is defeating, for we end up destroying the very life we set out to save.

The genuine welfare of humanity is found in the optimum actualization of the potentialities of our being. To exist in the fullest possible way in our aloneness and in our relations with others is the fulfillment of the inner aim of a human life. Through the process of actualizing our potentialities we authenticate our existence and reveal this authentication to others in our actions. It is in the very acts of self-authentication and the living presence of a fuller life that one comes to actively participate in the realization of the welfare of Others. By recognizing other's welfare to lie in the fulfillment of what they are rather than what they have allows us the maximum level of authentication of being-with-Others.

Even though there is a conceptual distinction between the two domains, being-alone and being-with, this distinction does not quite match the reality of life; as such, these categories are not so neatly separated in life. This is so because they impinge upon, merge with, and penetrate each other, as the very late Sartre recognizes. The conceptual categories are only an approximation. Yet, life does not mechanically alternate between these two modes; instead, it embraces both in an undivided unity. These two modes are ontological strands that exist together in paradox.

Life constantly actualizes these diverse ontological elements in authentic or inauthentic ways. It becomes inauthentic when full ranges of possibility are overlooked in favor of limited actualization of certain potentials, which allows us to avoid the full responsibility of our existence by restricting our focus to narrowly defined boundaries. In inauthentic being-alone we flee from facing the totality of our existence through absorption in particular entities. In inauthentic being-with we ignore our essential relatedness to others through indulging in self-concerns. We can turn to authentic experience by realizing how we fall into inauthentic patterns, that we are fundamentally alone in our birth and death, but fundamentally with Others in the world. Authentic existence comes about by taking into account our full range of essential possibilities. We seek refuge as we turn away from the things of the world and from self-concern. This allows us a new kind of existential orientation. This may require membership in a supportive community of like-minded individuals. This is the authentic political community that Sartre envisions, and it may involve the ontological inter-penetration of consciousnesses that he acknowledges.

In the case of being-with, even the smallest self-concern will prevent the full realization of the meaning of being-for-Others. Even more so, in order to realize being-with, we must go beyond extinguishing self-concern in order to arrive a state where we actively have concern for Others. As long as concern for others is less than total there will always be some self-concern afoot. Fully authentic being-with requires total and unconditional concern for Others. Further, it is wisdom that develops authentic being-alone and method that develops authentic being-with. But these two elements do not operate independently of each other, nor are they exclusively restricted to their primary domains. They enable each other. Sartre's method of existential psychoanalysis is a promising start toward understanding the relationship between self-deception and moral development. As we said earlier, a deeper project would include a rigorous examination of Sartre's account of consciousness and integral humanity in *CDR*, from the vantage point of existential analysis, as developed in terms of his goal of integral humanity. It would also be fruitful to engage in a more detailed analysis of his very late ethical pronouncements, especially in terms of their similarity to those of Immanuel Levinas. An examination of Sartre's notion of the interpenetration of consciousnesses is a good place to start.

Notes

1. See, Edmund Husserl, *Cartesian Meditations* (New York: Humanities Press, 1960) or *Ideas: General Introduction to Pure Phenomenology*, trans. W. R. Boyce Gibson (New York: Collier, MacMillan, 1962).

2. J.P. Sartre, *Being and Nothingness*, trans. Hazel Barnes (New York: Philosophical Library, Washington Square Press edition), 11.

3. *Ibid.*, 13.

4. *Loc. Cit.*

5. *Ibid.*, 244.

6. *Ibid.*, 139.

7. *Ibid.*, 140.

8. *Loc. Cit.*

9. *Ibid.*, 144.

10. *Ibid.*, 147.

11. *Ibid.*, 76.

12. *Ibid.*, 626.

13. *Ibid.*, 629.

14. *Ibid.*, 654.

15. *Ibid.*, 78.

16. *Ibid.*, 86-116.

17. Jean-Paul Sartre, *Existentialism and Humanism*, "EH," trans. Philip Mairet (Brooklyn: Haskell House, 1977), 51.

18. Jean-Paul Sartre, *The Transcendence of the Ego*, "TE," trans. Forrest Williams and Robert Kirkpatrick (New

York: Farrar, Straus, and Giroux, 1957), 58.

19. *Ibid.*, 81.

20. *Being and Nothingness*, 728.

21. *Ibid.*, 721.

22. *Ibid.*, 728.

23. Jean-Paul Sartre, *Anti-Semite and Jew*, trans. George J. Becker (New York: Schocken Books, 1976), 90.

24. Much of twentieth-century psychology has been influenced by existential philosophy, especially by Sartre. For two examples of this work please see, for example, Rollo May, *Existential Psychology* (New York: Random House, 1969); or see, Viktor E. Frankl, *Man's Search for Meaning* (New York: Simon and Schuster, 1962).

25. *Being and Nothingness*, 72.

26. See Kevin Boileau and David A. Boileau, *The Algebra of History* (New Orleans: Loyola University Press, 2004), 31 et seq, in which I explore this idea.

27. *Being and Nothingness*, 119.

28. *Ibid.*, 33.

29. *Ibid.*, 155.

30. See *Sartre & Psychoanalysis* (Lawrence: University Press of Kansas, 1991). Betty Cannon accomplishes an excellent Sartrean analysis of Western psychoanalysis. She argues that much of the Western psychoanalytic tradition has always assumed that the self was substantial and this meta-belief gave rise to forms of analysis that were misguided; she shows how Sartre's view of the self as non-substantial can give rise to more effective psychoanalytic projects.

31. Hazel Barnes does a great job of summarizing these main usages in her article "Sartre's Concept of the Self," in *Review of Existential Psychology & Psychiatry*, Vol. XVII, No. 1, 1980-81, pp. 41-65).

32. In "The Self and the Circuit of Selfness," *BN*, 155 *et seq.*, Sartre renders an account of a self that is purely ideal, a north star by which we navigate our lives. Pursuit of this self is isomorphic to the project of pure reflection.

33. Barnes, 48.

34. *Loc. Cit.*

35. *Being and Nothingness*, p. 301 *et seq.*

36. See note 30, Betty Cannon, who takes this view in her explication and criticism of Western psychoanalysis. Her excellent ideas have had a significant influence over the genesis of this current project here, in an application of Sartrean ontology to the important problem of moral development.

37. *Being and Nothingness*, 471 *et seq.*

38. Hegel; Nietzsche.

39. Kevin Boileau, *Genuine Reciprocity and Group Authenticity* (Lanham, Maryland: University Press of America, 2000).

40. Ibid., 139.

41. See Kevin Boileau and David A. Boileau, *The Algebra of History*, 199.

42. Jean-Paul Sartre, *Life/Situations*, trans. Paul Auster and Lydia Davis (New York: Pantheon, 1977), 11.

43. Ibid., 12.

44. Jean-Paul Sartre, *Saint Genet*, trans. Bernard Frechtman (New York: New American Library, New Mentor, 1964).

45. Jean-Paul Sartre, TE, 42.

46. *Ibid.*, 31.

47. *Ibid.*, 70.

48. *Ibid.*, 71.

49. *Ibid.*, 100.

50. *Ibid.*, 101.

51. *Ibid.*, 92.

52. *Ibid.*, 64.

53. *Being and Nothingness*, 795.

54. K. Boileau, *Genuine Reciprocity and Group Authenticity*

55. Interview with Benny Levy, "Today's hope: conversations with Sartre," *Telos*, 1980, 155-81.

56. Sartre, *Notebooks for an Ethics*, "NB," (Chicago: University of Chicago Press, 1992), 500.

57. Sartre, *The War Diaries*, "WD," trans. Q. Hoare (New York: Pantheon, 1984), 94-95.

58. Sartre, NB, 9.

59. Trans. In H. Spiegelberg, "Sartre's Last Word on Ethics in Phenomenological Perspective," *Research in Phenomenology*, 11, 1981, pp. 90-107.

60. Kevin C. Boileau, *The Possessory Self: (Modernity's Anthropological Mistake,* which is the next essay (Seattle: EPIS Publishing House, 2012).

61. See my chapters in *Genuine Reciprocity* on this point.

62. Levy, "Today's Hope, 169-70.

63. Sartre's later formulations about the "We" move very close to the ontology that Immanuel Levinas proposes. This is especially true with regard to Sartre's comments about relations that move beyond those that emerge from socio-economic relations of production.

64. Foucault takes up this problem, which I explore in *Genuine Reciprocity and Group Authenticity.*

65. Sartre, *WD*, 72.

66. Sartre, *TE*, 97.

67. *Ibid.*, 86-87.

68. Sartre, *WD*, 53-54.

69. Sartre, *NB*, 418.

70. Sartre, *Sketch for a Theory of the Emotions,* "STE," trans. P. Mairet (London: Methuen, 1962).

71. *Ibid.*, 19.

72. *Ibid.*, 23-24.

73. Sartre, *STE*, 69.

74. See, Sartre, *The Psychology of Imagination,* "PI," (London: Methuen, 1972).

75. *Ibid.*, 52.

76. *Loc. Cit.*

77. *Ibid.*, 63.

78. *Loc. Cit.*

79. *Ibid.*, 81.

80. Sartre, *Nausea*, trans. R. Baldick (Harmondsworth: Penguin, 1965).

81. *Ibid.*, 33.

82. Sartre, *NB*, 479.

83. *Ibid.*, 480.

84. *Ibid.*, 4.

85. Sartre, Existentialism and Humanism, trans. P. Mairet (London: Methuen, 1973).

86. See my work on *CDR* in *Genuine Reciprocity*.

87. Sartre, *The Family Idiot*, trans. C. Cosman (Chicago, Ill.: University of Chicago Press, 1981).

88. Thomas Anderson, *Sartre's Two Ethics* (Chicago: Open Court, 1993), 37.

89. I try to refute this argument in *Genuine Reciprocity and Group Authenticity*.

90. See the *Critique of Dialectical Reason*, Vol. I, trans. A. Sheridan-Smith (London: New Left Board, 1976).

91. *NB*, 491.

92. *Ibid.*, 501.

93. I explore the issue of authenticity relating to group consciousness in *Genuine Reciprocity*.

94. Nietzsche makes this point, too.

95. *TE*, 102.

96. *Ibid.*, 101-3.

97. *NB*, 4.

98. *Ibid.*, 474.

99. See my chapter on Marcel in *Algebra*.

100. *NB*, 448.

101. Sartre, *"What is Literature?" and Other Essays*, "WIL," trans. B. Frechtman (Cambridge: Harvard University Press, 1988), 65; also, see, Schopenhauer on this point).

102. *NB*, 169.

103. *Ibid.*, 9.

104. Sartre, *EH*, 51.

105. Sartre, *WIL*, 108.

106. *NB*, 482.

107. *Ibid.*, 528.

108. Thomas Anderson, *Sartre's Two Ethics*, 61.

109. Sartre, *EH*, 51.

110. See Sartre's theory about groups in *CDR*, in which he shows the plasticity in consciousness, that it can be modified in accord with new goals/values. It is this plasticity that allows the will to change course.

111. Sartre, *NB*, 20.

112. *Ibid.*, 508.

113. Sartre, *EH*, 52.

114. *Ibid.*, 29.

115. *Ibid.*, 45, 51-2.

116. See *Genuine Reciprocity*.

117. Sartre, *EH*, 45.

118. Sartre, *NB*, 16, 25, 11-204, 212-13, 236, 37.

119. See *Genuine Reciprocity*, chapter on Sartre.

120. Sartre, *NB*, 418.

121. *Ibid.*, 414.

122. *Ibid.*, 287.

123. *Ibid.*, 290.

124. *NB*, 288; also see *Genuine Reciprocity*, chapter on *CDR* in which I explore Sartre's theory of groups. Here, he renders an account of a shift in consciousness in certain groups whereby each individual sees each other as the "same," even though this does not imply a super-ontological organism.

125. *Ibid.*, 478.

126. *Ibid.*, 103; also, see, Charles Taylor, *The Ethics of Authenticity* (Cambridge: Harvard University Press, 1991), who argues that the question we need to answer is just what authenticity means. I take him to mean that we must, in the light of our cultural values, determine the specific relation that we want to have toward our freedom.

127. Sartre, *WD*, 111-12.

128. Sartre, *NB*, 475.

129. Sartre, *"Truth and Existence," "T,"* trans. Adrian van den Hoven (Chicago: University of Chicago Press, 1992), 17.

130. *Ibid.*, 18.

131. *NB*, 37.

132. *Ibid.*, 5.

133. *Ibid.*, 486.

134. *Ibid.*, 506.

135. *NB*, 11.

136. Marcel develops this notion of openness or availability, a concept I explore in *The Algebra of History*.

137. Sartre's concrete ethics is based on the ontology of *CDR*.

138. I address Levinas in the next essay in this volume, entitled *The Possessory Self: Modernity's Anthropological Mistake*.

139. One part of the lecture has been translated as "Determinism and Freedom" and published in Volume II of *The Writings of Jean-Paul Sartre*, pp. 241-52. Selections from the French text are published in F. Jeanson, *Sartre* (Paris: Desclee de Brouwer, 1966), pp. 137-38, and B. Levy, *Le nom de l'homme: dialogue avec Sartre* (Lagrasse: Verdier, 1984). See the handwritten manuscript at the Bibliotheque Nationale, Paris, under the title, "Conference a l'Institute Gramsci, Rome, 1964."

140. Sartre, *The Family Idiot*, vols. 1-4, trans. C. Cosman (Chicago: University of Chicago Press, 1981, 1987, 1989, 1991).

141. I carefully examine his work on this shift in consciousness in my *Genuine Reciprocity*.

142. See "The Last Words of Jean-Paul Sartre," published in *Dissent*. Simone de Beauvoir charged that Levy, who was a personal friend of Levinas, extorted these statements from a sick and dying man. Yet there is also evidence that Sartre encouraged the publication of these interviews, which negates this charge. For a review of this controversy, see Busch, *The Power of Consciousness* (Bloomington: Indian University Press, 1990), 96-101, and McBride, *Sartre's Political Theory* (Bloomington: Indiana University Press, 1991), 202-8.

Existential Psychoanalysis: Sartre's Phenomenological Dialectic

Prolegomena to the Possessive Self:
Modernity's Anthropological Mistake

Introduction

This book challenges traditional views about humanism in
which each of us lives in the world in terms of his own mental
categories. In this tradition, we approach Others in terms of
our own subjective interpretation of meaning and analyze
Others relative to what we already know. It is an appetitive
approach in which we consume Others by reducing them
to the same cognitive categories of our own minds and
experience. Because their work is pivotal to the confrontation
with traditional humanism, I will use the ideas of Emmanuel
Levinas and Jacques Derrida as starting points. Emmanuel
Levinas rightly acknowledged that the sort of humanism that
had been constructed in modernity prioritized the subject
over the object. He finds us guilty of an anthropological
mistake and thus spends several years accounting for his
admonition that we shift the source of meaning from the
subject to the object.

My aim is to carefully analyze this anthropological mistake,
explain Levinas's strategy in shifting the source of meaning
to the object, and make a few preliminary comments about
the new kind of humanism he espouses. This is a humanism
of responsibility. Derrida's program of deconstruction can
further help us understand the problem of the Other and

give us some clues about reconstructing a new framework for humanism. In addition, because his position best illustrates modern humanism in which the appetitive "I" is prioritized over the Other, Sartre is unavoidable. Nevertheless, by presenting Sartre's articulation of humanism we can most clearly see the problems with which both Derrida and Levinas were dealing. Finally, Foucault gives us a great deal of historical, psychological, and philosophical perspective about our culture's humanistic tendency toward the objectification of individuals.

My intention, therefore, is to render a descriptive and critical account of the "I" of humanism, i.e., the masterful self that attempts to control and regulate meaning in terms of its own subjective categories. By looking at the received view of humanism, exploring some thoughts on the anti-humanist perspective of Lacan, and discussing the revised views of both Levinas and Derrida, I will prepare the reader for a revised view of an anthropology which is a humanism of responsibility. This is the view that the "I" of humanism should be corrected by a deeper and more accurate anthropological-phenomenological account of the self. Under this new view, the Other is foundational to the self. This creates phenomenological space for an interpretation of oneself that is not primarily motivated by its own appetite but instead is propelled by its absolute responsibility for the Other; it is for each and every Other.

By correcting the anthropological mistake of modernity we can pursue a more accurate phenomenology of humans, especially by focusing on our social dimension. This can provide a foundation for a new ethics as well as provide a direction in value that could guide our social and political theory, science, and philosophy. This necessarily involves the question of how we construct, regard, and treat the Other.

Let me first discuss some of the theoretical commitments and assumptions of modernity in order to fully understand the kind of anthropology that we have to correct. This will help us understand the situation from which the moral consciousness of Levinas emerged.

Modernity

In the early modern period the self was fluid and free to shape itself, although this came at the price of uncertainty. Without allegiance to feudal oaths, one Church, a family history that was embedded in centuries of tradition, and a trusted God, life became uncertain. Moreover, we began anew to ask the questions about what it means to be a human being. We became interested in humanity and progress, especially in terms of quantification and counting, predictability and control. Questioning everything led to a confusion and tentativeness about who we were. It lead to a de-stabilization of the self and a lack of grounding for social cohesion.

Thinkers such as Descartes, Locke, Hume, Montaigne, Rousseau, and Kant were all working within an era of immense scientific learning.[1] They struggled with questions about the kind of knowledge humans can discover, how they attain it, and how they can be certain that it is accurate. They discussed questions about truth and reality, the existence of good and evil, and the nature and place of humans in the cosmos. Further, they asked questions about the relation between mind and body, how it was possible to accurately represent the real world, how ideas were generated, and how a science of psychology was possible. In the realm of values, they started to call traditional beliefs into question, and to discuss truth and morality without direct recourse to God and the Church. By jettisoning "God" as the Unmoved Mover and the origin of value, we left ourselves without a transcendent foundation. This phenomenon, in my opinion, created the seeds for a new kind of uncertainty: ontological anxiety.

During the Renaissance and the early modern period the Church became fragmented and divided over the Reformation; mercantile capitalism became more prominent, and individualism started emerging. These changes influenced the breakup of the religious-military-economic structures at the foundation of feudalism. With increased interest in the study of humans the privilege and authority of the Church was threatened. These new interests also threatened the power of the new nation states that countered with new forms of punishment and control. Thus, the need arose to develop an intellectual justification for the new science of empiricism and to explain why its techniques should be used in moral deliberations instead of those of the Church. Society became less certain about questions concerning morality and value. This further increased anxiety.

People of the early modern period needed new moral guidance and intellectual justification for the overthrow of the relations of power of the Middle Ages. Early modern philosophers came armed with the science of empiricism and ideas about innate rationality, thereby enjoying the success of the physical sciences. In the sixteenth, seventeenth, and the eighteenth centuries, humans had a strong belief that science would solve their confusions about the natural and social worlds, especially about the universal laws of human nature, morality, and value. Locke and Hume, for example, believed that empiricism could discover the truth of human beings whereas Descartes, Leibniz, and Kant argued that it was human rationality that would provide such a foundation. Other thinkers such as Rousseau and Montaigne argued that we ought to use the mirror of nature as our guiding force, instead of the techniques of science. All of them, however, believed in the explanatory capacities of the human mind, the efficacy of reason and nature, and the superiority of observation and logic over tradition and dogmatism.[2] It was at this juncture that we left God as foundation and desperately searched for a new one deep in our own social being.

Both Hume and Kant decided that an empirical science of psychology was impossible. Hume argued that we should not accept explanatory concepts such as causality or the unified self because they cannot be demonstrated empirically. Kant responded by arguing that although humans cannot empirically demonstrate certain concepts, they can perceive them; therefore, the capacity to perceive these concepts must be implanted in the mind. Kant thus invented modern structuralism, an important paradigm in 20th-Century social science. He argued that we naturally possess perceptual structures that allow us to categorize and organize the phenomenal world. In contrast, the noumenal world is beyond our grasp. Because humans can only see through these structures, scientific clarity into the workings of the human mind is not possible.

Even so, philosophers, scientists, and other thinkers began to use the new science of modernity in human affairs and moral guidance. It was a strategy that involved relations of power between Church doctrine and modern science. By getting rid of the old structure of the Church and replacing it with a new one, leaders were able to construct a new *weltanschauung* through the use of new terms and relationships. For example, concepts such as freedom, scientific truth, objectification, and personal responsibility emerged as handrails of the emergence of human individualism. This new framework of power relations carried along with it a program of self-surveillance, self-transformation, self-objectification, disengagement, inwardness, and radical reflexivity.[3] With the valorization of this new worldview, a struggle began over the phenomenological structure of human beings. The modern self was at the very center of this struggle. One can see here how the focus in the creation of value moved from an external source, i.e., God, to the inner source, i.e., each human individual. There was, therefore, an immense amount of pressure placed on each individual to account for his own construction of value. Here, one can see the individual condition that could give rise to a strong motivation to focus the source of meaning directly on oneself.

The changes in the configuration of the self in the shift from the Middle Ages to the Modern era were both reflected in and created by the thinking strategies of the philosophers. Some of the elements of this shift included the removal of God from the material world; the development of an objective stance toward the self, the world, and others; the universalizing of doubt; development of Augustine's idea of interiority; and the valorization of rationality. It was Descartes who best articulated these issues,[4] especially the need for a rationality that could defend a choice in value that was not based on God.

As Charles Taylor asserts, the modern era resituated the order of things from the external world to the internal, intrapsychic world of the mind.[5] Instead of the Jews locating God's law and Plato the realm of the pure forms in the external world, Descartes located the search for truth in the interiorized searching by individual rational agents. By doubting everything, including his own existence, Descartes set about to develop a method for building certain knowledge. By utilizing this logical procedure, human beings could construct a conceptual order of truth about which they could be absolutely certain. Then they could live in accordance with that truth.

Beginning with Descartes, truth building becomes creative within the process of self-discovery. The most important capacity in the world, which is the capacity to order the universe and direct human behavior, is relocated inside each modern individual. In addition, Descartes called attention to his dissatisfaction with the belief of the indwellingness of God in the material world. During the Middle Ages it was believed that the form and order of God's divine realm was reflected in the events and forms contained in the material world on earth. Everything was an unfolding of God's plan. In addition, the Church was the keeper of this divine plan, which meant that to believe in accordance with the medieval worldview was to submit to the authority of the Church.

Descartes removed God from the material world, keeping Him in the realm of the spirit. Although the realms of spirit and materiality interacted with each other they were separate. The material realm takes up space and the spiritual realm does not. According to Descartes, because the material world was disenchanted it must be dealt with on a different basis. He therefore advocated a scientific attitude with an objective stance toward it. This required humans to emotionally (and ontologically?) remove themselves from the world of matter in order to study it mechanistically and understand its functions. This discipline of inwardness and emotionless logic implied that no traditional body of knowledge, including that of the Church, had any prior claim over a scientist or philosopher. This, no doubt, lead to further anxiety over foundations. It is my postulate that these underlying forces must have exerted intense pressure on the self to constitute a world, thereby, assuming itself as the source of meaning and value, departed through rationality.

Universal doubt and logic were of the highest priority. One's body, and that of others, was of the material world and in order to understand it one had to objectify it and remove oneself from any prior body of knowledge about it or the moral laws concerning it. By taking this objective, emotionless stance, the irrational passions could be brought under control. Within this set of techniques, the mind could successfully dominate itself. Through self-surveillance we could come to master ourselves. Thus, for Descartes, we could discover the logical order of the universe by carefully inspecting our innate mental functions, which are also the source of morality. Inwardness thereby took over as the locus for moral authority. Ironically, just as scientists proved that the center of the universe was not the earth, philosophers such as Descartes argued that the center of the moral universe was located within each individual. The Archimedean point thereby shifted in both natural science and social science, including the moral dimension. To me, this furthers conditions of anxiety because by diverging from church foundation, one had no other choice but reason. Yet reason could come to many conclusions and therefore was insecure in its own way. Furthermore, by prematurely accepting one's own rational conclusions, one could cover up the uncertainty in value caused by our transcendent ontological nature. This perhaps created even more pressure to develop a possessive self.

John Locke took some of Descartes' ideas, such as objectification, and thematized them in a way that eventually led to modernist notions of psychology that were based on quantification and categorization.[6] He applied these ideas not only to the material world but to the mind as well, treating it reductively as another manifestation of the natural world. He proposed a methodology of radical disengagement that resulted in the instrumentalization of the natural world, the self, and others. One must disengage from the self in order to remake oneself. On so doing, one becomes an Other to oneself.

This also creates perhaps a new relational dynamic (or at least intensifies this element) that is based on teleology and use instead of deontological regard.

Instead of proceeding in accordance with Church tradition, this new set of power relations valorized the remaking of the self in accordance with scientific discipline. It is important to note that along with Descartes, it was Newton's ideas about bodies and motion that set the stage for this new power dynamic.[7] Scientists and philosophers determined that instrumental control, in terms of early notions of modern mathematics and physics, was the road toward truth. Along these lines, they tested hypotheses for their ability to predict and control human behavior. Thus, there was a link between these new formulations of the self and the need for governments to have control over their populations. Isomorphically if this structure affects individuals it would create a similar relational desire for control.

Locke was a radical empiricist and applied this system to everything, including the human mind. He argued for a kind of radical reflexivity whose goal was to reconstruct the self in a way that was based on sensory experience. This was possible, he thought, because even ideas were of the material world and this was a realm that humans could control. With regard to morality, Locke believed that we must act independently from tradition. Locke's idea of self-responsibility comes from his assumption that we can stand back from ourselves with a critical and objective eye in order to re-make ourselves. This disengagement became one of the hallmarks of modern science because it allowed us to assume control over our representations about the world. Perhaps the most important point here is the extreme egocentrism that arose. By locating power and agency within each individual, wherein the self is the final arbiter of truth and the center of moral motivation, Western individualism arose and developed as a formidable adversary of the Church. It was a hidden question whether this reflexivity was as radical as the culture thought it was.

In contrast to radical empiricists such as Locke, other thinkers such as Rousseau and Montaigne, classified as naturalists, founded their arguments in the transparency of the external world. In contrast to the promotion of disengagement and objectivity, they committed to delving even deeper into the interior of subjectivity. Even though thinkers in this camp did not espouse rational disengagement, they did support the new individualism against the old authority of the Church. Montaigne valorized the uniqueness of each individual.[8] He disagreed with the scientific method of objectification, seeing chaos where others saw order. He added this truth of inner chaos and instability to his arguments against the dogma of Church authority. He asserted that the chaos of the deep interiority of the self disproved the possibility of one universal set of laws of human nature.

For Montaigne, each person is unique, chaotic, and many-sided rather than stable and universal. He believed that external standards of morality were not applicable to humans because these traditional standards did not take individual differences into account; they treated everyone the same, as if we had a universal human nature. Given this assumption, we gain self-knowledge by learning about our uniqueness through introspection. So instead of objective disengagement from the external world we should adopt an even deeper subjective engagement in order to find the truth of our natures. The naturalists, therefore, provided us with a different sense of the concepts of freedom and autonomy, and wove them around the valorization of individuality instead of

universality. The belief in differences between the natures of
men could have further developed a structure that promotes
power instead of virtuous regard. Given that this belief
supports subjectivism, it is easy to see how it contributed to
possessive and controlling interpretations of the self.

Rousseau took up Montaigne's program of introspection
and the understanding of one's limits and perfected it as a
complete antagonism to the Church.[9] For him, we can find
out what we are by listening to our inner voices. This will
guide us as we try to understand how we ought to live.
Whereas Augustine had looked inside and found absence,
which he eventually filled with God, Rousseau looked
inward and found the sole source of unity and goodness
to reside deep inside a fully autonomous, individual self.[10]
Unfortunately, the forces that were holding together this idea
of autonomy were not based on a firm foundation but instead
one that was alienated from the lived and natural experience
of human beings.

Later, Immanuel Kant argued that the laws of morality were
limited by the very nature of reason, which was imbedded in
the innate structure of the human mind.[11] For Kant, morality
did not spring automatically from the objective methodology
of the new empirical science or naturally unfold from the
subjective, inward encounter with the transparent truth of
natural being. In contrast, morality comes from the rational
will and is one of the innate structures of each human being.
He agreed with the naturalists that we must follow what
is generated within our subjectivities. He agreed with the
rationalists that it is only out of universal doubting and the
exercise of reason that humans can figure out how to live.
With Hume, he argued that sense experience alone is unable
to generate foundational concepts and moral laws. One can
see here the attempt to re-fashion God as foundation by

substituting in a "rational" apparatus that is provided by the universe (which is not so far from Church doctrine and content).

Kant argued that moral knowledge is more than pure, natural impulse generated from within. He also argued that it is more than what we can perceive from outside of us, in terms of pleasure and pain. Instead, moral knowledge is produced from the innate structures of rationality and agency. He believed that humans were the only animals that can use the logic of these innate structures to generate moral laws and then to choose them through acts of will. Like Hume and Montaigne, he believed that freedom just is living in accord with what one truly is. Yet he also held that individuals are not limited by an unstable or empirical nature. Instead, he believed that individuals are liberated by their nature because they have been given the structures (by God? by the universe?) and will that could actually lead to the true moral laws.

Kant thought he had saved the epoch from its own contradictions by maintaining freedom from traditional authority, reaffirming autonomy, and upholding personal uniqueness. Like Augustine, he believed that a transformation of the will saves an empty individual. However, in contrast with Augustine, instead of God being the force that fills the internal void and transforms the will, it is the universal structure of rationality that facilitates this transformation. As I mentioned, it is highly questionable whether this move gets us beyond Church doctrine in the formation of value.

Kant's developments took one more step toward the valorization of an isolated, interior, individualist self. This modernist self was powerful and autonomous, but it was removed and isolated from the outer world. Presumably, this meant that it was also isolaed from other humans, caught up

in its own "rational" machinery. It was capable of building
the order of the universe from internal logic and sense
impressions. It had achieved independence from the Church
through radical doubt, observation, and objectification. Here,
spirit was divided from body, which became a disenchanted
world. Further, this self could engage from this divided world
and achieve scientific self-certainty and self-sufficiency.
It was a self that was made of instrumental, independent
consciousness, and it could therefore transform itself. It took
this deep strategic relation and applied it to the natural world
and perhaps most unfortunately, also to the social world. It
was one thing to apply the method of objectification to the
natural world, but when it was applied intersubjectively to
other individuals in the realms of value and morality, we see
the beginning of egocentric social structures.

As we mentioned, it was also the Romantic era of the
eighteenth and nineteenth centuries that asserted a belief
in an autonomous individual who had the capability to
determine its own destiny. Individual uniqueness and the
notion of the mysterious, hidden self became a source of
vitality and self-potential. This notion of interior mysticism
became a source of secular salvation, but when combined
with the rationalist notion of objectification also contributed
to egocentric social relations in which the instrumentalization
of others was foundational.

We are now in a good place to discuss the turn from
modernity to Husserlian phenomenology. This will help us
to understand the intellectual climate from which Levinas's
consciousness emerged. Phenomenologists had to bridge
the gulf between the empiricist and intellectualist traditions
of the past centuries. They believed that neither empiricism
nor intellectualism sufficiently faced the human situation.
By concentrating on either pole of the I-world relation that

is given in consciousness, they distort this relation and fail
to explain human existence in terms of the fact that we are
always with others. Man interrogates the universe but is also
an inherent part of that universe. There are two views that
attempt to understand the nature of this relation. Naturalism
treats man as a being that is determined by physical and
material factors that determine him from the outside. In
contrast, idealist intellectualism views man as having a liberty
in constructing representations of those same causes that act
upon him. The problem arises because man is part of the data
that he tries to understand.

Contemporary naturalism tries to understand the higher,
the spirit, in terms of the lower, which is the subhuman
universe. While the phenomenologists do not directly
attack positive science they do argue against the assertion
that the only truth is scientific truth. Here, scientists assert
something that they take to be an a priori truth, which is by
definition unverifiable. They attempt to reduce the field of
truth to one mode of understanding, and it is this move that
the phenomenologists attack. In contrast, intellectualism
attempts to interpret the lower in terms of the higher, because
it believes that the higher gives the lower its sense. It is
the attempt to reveal the rational structure of the world by
considering its intelligibility independently of any reference to
sense experience, as a sufficient source of knowledge.[12]

Naturalism is a critical empiricism that is either psychologism
or positivism. In the former, all human truth derives from
sense impressions. For the latter, all truth comes from positive
scientific truth. Phenomenologists argue that both forms are
abstractions that are laid upon pre-scientific contact with
the world. This is lived experience. Sense impressions and
scientific "facts" are thereby constructed upon the lived world
of natural perceptual experience. These objects represent only

a portion of the totality of our lived experience, leaving out our primordial experience of the aesthetic, social, and moral domains. For a phenomenologist these objects are not the primary datum. On the other hand, intellectualism mistakenly holds that philosophical reflection is the primary guarantor of truth. Yet there is no idea that does not refer to some perceptual experience from which it has been abstracted. Reflection is always a reference to a prereflective experience that preceded it. Existential phenomenology tries to show that both of these systems are mental constructions and that the better method is to return "to the things themselves."

Another problem of naturalism and intellectualism is that by reducing truth to a single mode they make man's relation to the world unintelligible. Naturalism cannot account for one's temporal experience of oneself within a world of meaning-creating activity. In a naturalist model, meaning comes from a world of pre-determined causal forces and not from an individual who looks to the past or to the future in the domain of possibility. Thus, this approach completely neglects the meaning-giving activity of each us as a free consciousness that can change his or her interpretations of experience. Intellectualism is also a false anthropology because it reduces a person to a bodiless spirit, a disembodied thinking substance. If man is just embodied spirit then he is an alienated interiority without access to the world. Without a link to the world we cannot account for how this interiority manifests itself as exterior, nor could we account for intersubjectivity (except as a self that is possessive and self enclosed).

Descartes' views about consciousness also influenced Husserl's views. For Descartes, human consciousness is always directed toward some object of which it is aware, and that in this awareness, it is also aware of itself perceiving that object. Because consciousness is always consciousness of itself, we have the ability to make a running account of what consciousness is doing at any moment. This precludes the idea of a Freudian unconscious. Descartes based his whole project on the *cogito*, that he could not doubt his own existence as a thinking being. Because he had ideas about others things, including humans, his quest centered on the problem of whether he could ever gain knowledge of the external world. By concentrating on the separation between the mind's ideas and the objects of which they are representations he argued that we must know our own minds better than anything else. It is this point that Husserl and the other phenomenologists seized upon in trying to navigate between the two philosophical traditions with which they disagreed.

In 1874, Franz Brentano published *Psychology from an Empirical Point of View*, in which he argued that all mental activities were directed toward some object. For him, philosophy should be directed toward providing descriptive accounts of the contents of consciousness. Husserl supported Brentano's ideas, arguing that we must analyze the contents of consciousness without utilizing natural laws or knowledge of causes. Phenomenology, therefore, sets aside the normal standpoint, bracketing what we ordinarily think we know about the causes of our experience. It attempts to preclude the involvement of the phenomenologist by reducing experience to the facts themselves. Husserl makes a distinction between the empirical self and the transcendental self. The empirical self is that which is studied by history and psychology. The transcendental self is presupposed by the empirical self and is equivalent to absolute being. Thus, by employing the method in a pure way, an individual could arrive at universal truths about humans. This was Husserl's project of transcendental phenomenology.

French Phenomenology's Interpretation of Modernity

In order to interrogate Levinas's position on one's ethical relationship with the Other, we must first understand how phenomenology broke through Kantian idealism in France (and in Germany, with regard to Husserl). In part, the methodological approach of phenomenology was influenced by the problem of intersubjectivity, which we will discuss in the next four sections of the text.

It can be argued that Husserl was the source of the concept of the "Other."[13] Yet the problem of intersubjectivity remained at the penumbra of his thought in response to the idealistic and transcendental biases of the modernist tradition and therefore to the difficulties of solipsism. Thus it took time for the problem of the Other to emerge in the German epistemological tradition and even longer for the French. For them, the French, the problem was not initially recognized but after the first publication of Levinas's translation of the *Cartesian Meditations* in 1930, it became unavoidable.[14]

Levinas entered a French philosophical tradition that was profoundly Cartesian, interpreted through the twin lenses of Kantianism and scientific positivism. The kind of certainty that Descartes's philosophy provided covered up for some time the solipsism that it implied. It was in the opening of his *Meditations on First Philosophy* that other human beings were lost, along with the rest of the world. Then, in the rest of the *Meditations*, Descartes argued that to the extent human beings reappear they do so only like any other object, as passive fabrications of a cognizing mind rather than active sources of independent agency. It never occurred to him that Others could be rivals to the ego as a means of founding an epistemology or as sources of meaning and value in their own right.

In addition, the version of Kantianism that the French imposed upon their Cartesianism also results in a kind of solipsism. Even though Kant "does think that one must have the concept of other possible individuals endowed with self-consciousness in order to have a grasp of the individuality of one's own self-consciousness . . . Kant does not demand that I actually know that there are other egos in order to ascribe beliefs or desires to myself."[15] The resulting epistemology is hypothetically intersubjective, wherein other points of view are possible but not actual. That is, there is no room for others in their accounts; at best the Other is reduced to a judgment in one's mind. It is certainty not at the level of a phenomenological Other who has an internal relationship to oneself.

Nevertheless, it was Bergson's rejection of both empiricism and rationalism that set the stage for his intuitionism, which was a kind of proto-phenomenology, and an important influence on Levinas.[16] He argued that the method of analysis of the natural sciences restricted itself to partial, finite knowledge about the world. In contrast, intuition was a kind of immediate access that allowed for full and infinite access. It lent itself to an indivisible apprehension and an inexhaustible enumeration of something. Thus, instead of being reductive, which natural science was, it opened an examination that could never be completed because it was hermeutically an open system. Intuition, for Bergson, was a kind of intellectual sympathy by which one placed oneself within an object in order to coincide with what is unique in it and thus inexpressible. In contrast, analysis is the operation that reduces the object to elements already known and common both to it and other objects. One can plainly see that analysis implies the same kind of metaphysical structure as the controlling, possessive, enclosed self. I will later explore

Levinas's concern that analysis reduced the Other to the Same.

Levinas's other main influence came from Husserl, who grounded his initial theory of intentionality in the primacy of the cognizing ego, which unfortunately risked a return to Cartesian solipsism. Nevertheless, by a restoring of objects in his theory of perception he hoped to recover the noumenal world that had been lost by Kant. According to Husserl, the object of perception (the *cogitatum*) is not inaccessible, for it is preserved in the perception (the *cogitatio*) itself. Hence the famous axiom: "To the things themselves." Perhaps most importantly, as we will see later, the relation to the object is not something that inserts itself between consciousness and an object. Rather, the primordial phenomenon is the relation to the object, not a subject and an object that connect to each other. Consciousness is always consciousness of something.

Husserl's new sort of science promised to save world phenomena from the domination of consciousness. He thus extended Bergson by making objects equiprimordial with subjects. Even though we point ourselves intentionally toward objects of the world, we find that in the end they resist us. For example, when I want to know a dog I realize that I can never lose myself in it, that although I can move myself toward it, it is always separate from me. This idea of intentionality undermines the hegemony of the knowing subject and acknowledges the authority of objects in constituting human experience. The doctrine of intentionality embodies thought's relation to its objects without thought digesting these objects. Instead of appetitive philosophies such as idealism and realism, the phenomenological mechanism of intentionality does not digest its objects, instead allowing them, including human objects, their autonomy and alterity. This sets the stage for a later phenomenological criticism of the Cartesian self.

Levinas takes up this notion of intentionality but
specifically applies it to the analysis of human relationships.
He acknowledges that theoretical knowledge always
includes objects, but he uses the distinction between
theoretical knowing and feeling states to make his point.
Phenomenologists disagree with the assertion that feeling is
not a kind of knowing. In contrast, their fundamental idea is
to affirm the relation to the world that feelings bring about.
Feelings are directional and move us places both internally
and externally. Thus, the objective world is not solely in
accord with the model of a theoretical object. Instead, it is
constituted by more complex intentional structures. For a
phenomenologist such as Levinas, reality is richer than the
complexity and texture to which natural science reduces it.
Phenomenology tries to restore to human knowledge all the
richness of our concrete life. This richness comes from our
complex experience of things as beautiful, ugly, frightening,
and so forth, nuances that are not captured by the limited
weltanschauung (and greatly restricted phenomenology) of
natural science.[17]

Further comments about the complex relationship between
Bergson and Husserl are important but need to be treated
in another work. For purposes of our study, I want to
point out that the French downplayed Husserl's Cartesian
idealism. Husserl's thought found an alternative that allowed
the reconciliation of intellectualism and realism. Thus, an
intuition may be ideational without falsifying the meaning
of concrete reality, as Bergson assumed it would. Therefore,
it was Husserl's early realism that followed Bergson that
influenced early French phenomenology.

Nevertheless, after Levinas found Husserl's disciple,
Heidegger, he re-read Husserl in terms of Heidegger, looking
for the seeds of Heidegger's thought in the earlier concerns of

Husserl. Levinas saw in Husserl's phenomenology an implicit ontology, which Heidegger explicitly laid out. According to Levinas, the problem for Husserl's phenomenology was that it favored theory and representation, along with the sovereign, transcendental, autonomous, and spectatorial subject, which Heidegger replaced with his notion of Being-in-the-world. Levinas argued that this move illegitimately elevated theory and representation to the forms of intentionality that are a foundation to all others, denigrating acts of will, emotion, and desire that could also have co-served as foundation.[18] Unfortunately, Husserl privileged spectatorial objectification in a Cartesian way and was therefore unable to move us away from the possessive form of the self.

Heidegger argued that whether our primary stance in the concrete world was not oriented toward a theoretical contemplation of objects. Instead, he argued that our primary attitude toward the world is care, believing that the world is presented as a center of action first and that objects of contemplation are theoretical derivatives. Moreover, Husserl believed in the possibility of an atemporal, suprahistorical perspective about the nature of humanity. Levinas argued in *The Theory of Intuition* that human life could not be viewed from a god's external and eternal vantage point. Thus, historicity and temporality were part of the very fabric of what we are, for Levinas, following Heidegger in this line of thought.

For Levinas, Heidegger shows us the meaning of Husserl's destruction of the noumenal world we inherited from Kant. After Husserl there is no longer a reality hidden behind phenomena. Moreover, Heidegger's ontology shows us that the intentionality of consciousness, like Heidegger's being-in-the-world, makes it possible to construct the theoretical framework of a subject and an object. Thus, even though phenomenology is presented as a theory of knowledge it allows us to pass to a theory of being.

Yet if all this were implicit in Husserl then to be is to emerge into the world through the mechanism of intentionality. By bringing objects out of the noumenal world and into the world where people can access them, Husserl, through Heidegger, restored the richness of the full spectrum of intentional structures. This goes beyond detached theoretical musings and into the realm of passionate involvement in the world, which we see manifested in the life and work of Jean-Paul Sartre. Here, engagement and commitment replace theoretical contemplation.

Yet, the respect the French showed toward the reality of objects did not result in careful attention toward solicitude for other humans or in any kind of distinction between humans and other objects. Sartre shows us that the ego is actually not in consciousness. Instead, it is outside, in the world.[19] Yet, there is still no argument that there is a distinction between relation to other people and relations to other objects. This is obviously a lacuna in Husserl that came to the light with Sartre. Even so, with Sartre we move out of the interiorized realm of pure representations as our intentional structure of consciousness brings us out into the world. We will see that Levinas challenges egological phenomenology, arguing that we need to subordinate it to an intersubjective phenomenology. This move counters the kind of solipsism to which Husserl's egological reduction leads.

Intersubjectivity, Heidegger, and German Idealism

One of Heidegger's main theoretical innovations concerned the primordial relation of one human to another. He based his theory of intersubjectivity on the notion of *Mitsein* — co-being or being with — in the attempt to overcome Husserl's solipsism. In his *Cartesian Meditations*, Husserl founds a transcendental theory of the objective world, but this grounded a theory of intersubjectivity on a solipsistic footing. He needed egological structure to ground his transcendental theory and his intersubjective phenomenology to guarantee objectivity. The problem is in his construction of the ego, which problematizes the experience of the Other by and through an isolated subjectivity. His methodology of experiencing the Other was to proceed by analogy but he never overcame the solipsistic consequences of it.

By the time the *Cartesian Meditations* appeared, Heidegger had already formulated his own reply. He abolished the solipsistic starting point of modern philosophy by attacking Descartes himself, whom Husserl followed. Recall that Descartes' method involves doubting everything that is outside the mind, including other people. With a foundation of certainty we reinstate the world, but the *cogito* is alone from the ground up. Heidegger argues that Descartes' starting point makes it impossible to fathom the Other. In contrast, Heidegger argues that the self is never alone and that it does not come to be except in relation to Others. In contrast to Descartes' solipsism, he believed that solitude, like theoretical distancing from the world, is dependent upon on a relation with other individuals. For Heidegger, the world is foundationally that which I share with Others. Humans, in this view, are ineluctably socially and relationally embedded.

Accordingly, Heidegger rejects Husserl's account of Others as doubles of oneself. Against Husserl, he argued that we do not first constitute isolated subjectivity, then derivatively attain empathy as a function of being-with these Others. Instead, empathy is first possible on the primordial basis of being-with-Others. For Heidegger, because being-with is fundamental, each human is in the world essentially for Others. This is the case because we are inextricably tied to Others at the very base of our humanity and our existence. Further, he makes relations with other humans qualitatively different from relations with other objects. Thus, in our pre-theoretical involvement with the world we disclose objects that we care about. Other humans are necessarily disclosed in the taking care of concern.

Heidegger's purely descriptive account had normative implications but he never worked them out. For example, he delineated some of the ways others concern us, such as "for," "against," or "not-mattering." The last way is one of the modes of deficiency that characterizes everydayness and inauthenticity. Yet, he never explains why these modes are deficient, avoiding the engagement with prescriptivity, believing that his analyses were prior to ethical questions. Yet he avoids a real treatment of the Other, postulating the individualized self in a standoff against the inauthenticity of mass society. Thus, the function of the *Mitsein* (being-with) seems merely a methodological step on the way to his account of the they-world, and its dialectical opposite, authentic existence. This mode of being is not so far away from Cartesian solipsism.

A more substantial lack directly within the concept of *Mitsein* itself is that it implies a neutral social background. The problem with this is that the intersubjective foundations of meaning do not provide normative distinctions that cut across all human experience. Thus, each individual, although obligated to the meanings of his community is not obligated to any particular meanings. For example, Heidegger's doctrine of *Fürsorge* — interpersonal concern — might not be valued in all communities. Further, although the quest for personal authenticity may require the exchange of an old community for a new one, Heidegger never develops the concept of *Mitsein* in a way that leads to a source of potential norms.

The resolution of Heidegger's ambivalence initially followed one of two paths. First, one could take the sociality of selfhood more seriously, thereby saving it from solipsism and from the notion of a suprahistorical norm of relating to Others, implied by authentic concern. This is the communitarian solution attempted by Karl Lowith.[20] As an alternative, one could take the second solution, asserting that the sociality of selfhood does not lead to purely local norms but instead supplies a universalist foundation for a transcendent norm such as Heidegger's notion of concern. The second solution was attempted by Hannah Arendt who tried to overcome the unwarranted step of all communitarianisms, which is to assume that a particular community is the only legitimate interpretation of intersubjectivity. It is therefore, an unwarranted inference to go beyond intersubjectivity to communitarianism.

Lowith based his communitarian response on Feuerbach's dialogical philosophy, dropping Heidegger's notion of *Fürsorge* but keeping his idea that even the most solitary of activities presumes a background of social practices. Recall that for Feuerbach, the Renaissance and the Reformation tried to secure the independence of the individual from both nature and from society. We see that this is true in the valorization of personal autonomy stemming from Descartes's *cogito*, the pure consciousness of Husserl, and the moral autonomy of Kant. The foundation of all these starting points is self-consciousness.

Lowith held an anti-solipsistic position, arguing that the foundation of sociality was an originary co-being in which *Dasein*[21] was concerned about Others as well as itself. A major problem for Heidegger, which Lowith saw, was how Heidegger's notion of mineness (*Jemeinigkeit*) ended in a kind of Kierkegaardian solipsism. Lowith himself argued that individuals are always defined by their social roles. The social context defines who I am, and there is no "I" independent of these relationships. Moreover, I do not create the matrix of relationships that defines who I am; these are created for me through cultural and family history. Thus, for Lowith, Heidegger's use of Kierkegaardian individualism is itself subject to the historical and cultural structure in which it is imbedded.

Nevertheless, Lowith's communitarianism problematically resolves the tension of Heidegger's concept of *Mitsein*. He brought Heidegger's latent ethics to the surface by demonstrating that selfishness and altruism were just different ways of being; there is no normative distinction between them. Interpersonal solicitude is just as much a product of arbitrary norms of a particular community as egocentric selfishness is. This obviously leads to serious moral difficulties. In contrast, let us investigate Hannah Arendt's attempt to resolve Heidegger in the direction of a universalism.

Arendt attacked Heidegger's idea of *Mitsein* for ending in solipsism. For her, Heidegger's construction of *Dasein* was so isolated it was meaningless; in contrast, if it is not isolated but is involved in the everyday "they" world, it would no longer be a self. Heidegger substitutes for the idea of God a conception of the world as the totality of the background of practices and meanings of a culture. Heidegger appropriated this idea from Augustine, as well as his idea of the two kinds of worldliness, which are cupidity and charity (*caritas*). The first kind is solipsistic and the second is not. Arendt uses Augustine's development of radical reflexivity of the self as foundation for understanding Heidegger's *Dasein*; she then utilizes Augustine's two versions of love, above, to provide perspective to the solipsistic position.[22]

The self as foundationally concerned with itself leads in two directions according to Augustine. The first form of introspection attempts to make the self the center of its world, to dominate and possess the things, ideas, and people around it. The other form of introspection discovers the Other at the very bottom and center of the self, and this is the part of Augustine that Heidegger left out, according to Arendt. It is self-involvement that leads to cupidity and a decentering of the self that leads to charity. Further, Arendt saw that Augustine's analysis led to a universalist human phenomenology that was free from any communitarian or religious view. As a note, we can also see how Sartre himself advocated movement away from the God-project, toward constructions of sociality that prioritized the freedom of others as well as one's own.

Solipsistic love is ravenous and attempts to feed the self with everything it perceives. Yet this desire is a desire for oneself, and in this process the self isolates itself from Others. Arendt criticizes Heidegger for only recognizing the solipsistic arm of the tradition and not the other arm, which recognizes intersubjectivity at the very heart of being human. Arendt reads Heidegger as avoiding or neglecting *caritas* in his own understanding of worldliness, as evidenced by his own egological reading of the very tradition he criticizes.

Further, in Arendt's criticism of Heidegger's view of the world as immanently whole, she argued that the world, whether created by God or not, is not whole. Instead, it is given as partial and contingent, populated with conscious humans who are not determined solely by their expectation of death. Instead, we can become aware that the world is not marked by immanence but rather by transcendence; we understand that we come into our earthly life from somewhere else to which we return. The realm of possibility always moves us beyond what has been actualized. Thus, we can interpret love, not as appetitive, but as a longing to transcend our earthly existence. It is up to humans to perfect this lack of wholeness.

Arendt's recognition of Augustine's neglected alternative conception of the world, which he saw as provisional, imperfect, and bounded, radically alters our conception of intersubjective relations. Importantly, the source of meaning and value cannot solely be found in a subjective, egological cupidity. Instead of being located in appetitive epistemologies, we must look in places that extend beyond modernist constructions of reason and knowledge. This means to draw meaning beyond material and earthly elements. It means to locate meaning beyond that which we find in our subjectively-oriented and isolated selves as we exist on earth. Increasing one's ability to live in *caritas* implies letting go of one's individual worldliness. In this new dimension we are the Same.

Even though Arendt does not use Heidegger's concept of *Fürsorge*, she does attempt to construct a new version of selfhood that includes a foundational intersubjective structure built on love as charity. It means to choose the Other over oneself. It means to avoid the appetite for things and instead opt for the infinity found in caring solicitude. Thus, her universalist strategy avoids Heidegger's solipsism and Lowith's communitarianism. Nevertheless, her ideas are not without problems. She had to defuse the implication that man before God is isolated from Others so that a humanity modeled on divinity would have few implications for the social relations of a number of beings. Further, her concept of transcendence devalued rather than moderated the worldliness of humans, a position she later rejected.

Levinas and Heidegger

Lowith's communitarianism is contextualist and thus implies a relativistic morality. Arendt's universalism is bound up with a bounded relation between each man and God, thereby creating a problematic foundation for social relations. Levinas pursued the theological option, detaching *Fursorge* from Heidegger's framework, attempting to state transcendent values in a secular form. As Levinas forayed into a theological approach Arendt left it, considering it a mistake to ground ethics in appeals to a theological source outside of human community. In her later period she argued that morality can not be given externally from obedience to any law that is given from the outside. She then came to argue that only when emancipated from religion was it legitimate to speak of moral philosophy. For her, only when a moral doctrine was secular could it be a moral doctrine at all. It remained to be seen whether Levinas's theological foundation could actually lead to a humanism that was based on secular premises.

A number of ideas could be written about Levinas's interpretation of Heidegger's involvement with Nazism. That serious topic notwithstanding, I need to move forward with a direct discussion of Levinas himself, so we can only make a few comments about it. Levinas saw Nazism as an attack on the modern idealist subject, a detranscendentalizing response to the abstract, disembodied, Cartesian self. Against the position that a human is essentially free of its contexts, including body, family, relationships, culture, and history, Nazism took the opposite view. Western culture had always held an a-historical view about the self, which meant that man was absolutely free in his relations to the world and to his temporal existence. Nazism disagreed.

Both Christianity and modern liberalism purport to set humans free from the material, determined world. Christianity does this through grace and liberalism through transcendence of the material world. Heidegger changes that, showing us that we are bound to history and temporalization. Nazism goes further by making a total break with the culture of transcendental idealism. It makes the self totally immanent, especially the body, without any hope of liberation. In Nazism, the politicization of the body confers legitimacy in terms of consanguinity, validating social forms that come from conquest.[23] Even though Heidegger did not anchor *Dasein* in a physical body, Levinas still connected the rejection of a transcendental subject to corporeal bondage and thus to racism.

Levinas interpreted the brutality of Hitlerism as an inevitable consequence of our attempt to evade the brute truth of being bound to being. Levinas is less concerned with *Dasein* fleeing from itself and more troubled by the attempted escape from being itself.[24] Nevertheless, Levinas recognizes that we cannot escape from being, that it follows us wherever we go. He analyzes different states being such as shame, nausea, and pleasure, as ways that we try to evade being. Yet he holds that these escapist strategies always fail and always involve self-deception.[25] Shame is typically the result. Shame is personal and discloses the fact of being; it is the fact of being fixed to oneself. It always involves the recognition that we cannot successfully flee in order to hide from ourselves. Shame uncovers one's being.[26] This shame may also be an element of the construction of the possessive self, an issue I leave for later study.

According to Levinas, nausea is the need for evasion itself, an experience of pure being, and a refusal to remain in it.[27] In this case, being is more than an obstacle; it is an imprisonment of too much substantiality. It is *de trop*. In contrast, for Sartre, nausea is epiphenomenal to the abyss of nothingness that threatens the self that grasps its own free, subjective autonomy.[28] After 1935, Levinas continued to accept transcendental philosophy's vulnerability to ontological criticism. At the very moment that idealism imagines that it has gone beyond being it is invaded from all sides. Thus, even though Heidegger went beyond Husserl, the move from transcendental phenomenology to existential ontology has a barbaric political result, according to Levinas.[29]

Levinas's Movement Toward Intersubjectivity

It was in the mid-1930s that Levinas started treating the problem of intersubjectivity. This might have occurred because of the demise of transcendental idealism combined with resistance to the world-immanent existentialism of the Heideggerian variety. Transcendental idealism leads to the primacy of the thinking, conceptualizing ego and is incapable of conceiving anything except as knowledge. It therefore reduces bodily phenomena to knowledge of the body. It impoverishes sensibility and results in a kind of understanding that does not seem to be about real people, according to Levinas.[30]

With the Bergsonian and Heideggerian breakthroughs that had inserted humanity back into the world, the new philosophy found itself forced to accept the corporeal reality it had secured. With the feeling that there is being comes the notions that the thinking self is not presuppositionless and that the subject itself is insufficient to understand being. Levinas understands that both Heidegger's ontology and Husserl's egology places humanity in a state of loneliness, an abandoned finitude, a subjectivity that is isolated and alone.

It was in Levinas's review of Louis Lavelle's *La presence totale* that brought him to a place of optimism between the death of transcendental idealism and the horrors of Heideggarian ontology.[31] What Levinas liked in Lavelle, and what influenced him for years, was his attitude toward temporality. Instead of viewing the self as a prisoner of the anticipation of death, he resurrected Descartes' *cogito*, insisting that the self was always in the present. This meant that our fate is always determined in the present, which implies that we have the potential to master our lives by affirming our being, instead of living purely in anxiety toward the future. This optimism spurred him to overcome what he disliked about German existentialism. Next Levinas turned to Rosenzweig as he delved deeply into the problem of the Other.[32]

Levinas understood the considerable influence Soren Kierkegaard had on Franz Rosenzweig. In his *Star of Redemption*, Rozensweig followed Kierkegaard's hostility to the totalizing tendency in Hegel; recall the notion that spirit serves as an all-encompassing forum for every element of human existence. Yet the Hegelian totality that Kierkegaard destroyed in order to individualize existence Rosenzweig reintegrated into a new one. For Rozensweig, subjective protest was impotent against the kind of historical necessity that Hegel advocated. Yet Rozensweig remained Hegelian to the extent that he wanted a substitute for the Kierkegaardian protest against imprisonment in a historical system.

Levinas adopted the Kierkegaardian opposition to Hegel
while attempting to avoid the subjectivist result. Keep in mind
that subjectivism taken to the extreme, in its attempt to avoid
losing itself in the universal, rejects all form. Some of the
challenges for Levinas in the 1930s involved the avoidance
of radical subjectivism and the secularization of Rozensweig.
Levinas duly followed Rozensweig's communitarianism
and historicism, and he also tried to secularize the account
of revelation in *The Star of Redemption* as an alternative to
Heideggerian ontology.

Kierkegaard believed that in the service of human abstraction,
the methods of philosophy and science preclude consideration
of the absurdity of life. That is, the theoretical rules could
never apply to actual life situations. As such, Kierkegaard
turned to the absurd and faith instead of to reason and
morality. Further, speaking of the story of Abraham and Isaac,
he argued that the ethical way of viewing life needed to be
suspended for the sake of faith. Levinas was keenly aware
that the world war had destroyed the confidence of humans
in the value of reason, thereby opening the door to the more
irrational and savage elements in human nature.

Levinas pointed us to Kierkegaard's priority of the individual
construction of meaning over the construction of meaning by
universal reason. Yet, he acknowledged Kierkegaard's affinity
for Socrates, the greatest of all rationalists. This, Levinas
knew, separated him from flat-flooted irrationalism. This step
allowed him to turn the suspension of the ethical into the very
foundation of ethics.

Levinas was also highly influenced by Jean Wahl's revolt
against finished systems of thought. Wahl, a longtime
Sorbonne professor, followed Kierkegaard's attack on
Hegelianism, and famously problematized the dialectic

between theology and philosophy.[33] Wahl naturalizes Kierkegaard's insistence on the qualitative difference between God and man, as well as his sense of its philosophical relevance for understanding the self. In his "The Concept of Anxiety," Wahl argues that humans are primarily driven by their search for the Other. If I interiorize my anxiety about Others and direct this anxiety to what is Other in myself, then this anxiety could become the absolutely Other.[34] The development of selfhood thus requires a dialectical process with the Other in oneself in a way that overcomes anxiety. Further, the role of existential therapy is to make a place for that Other. Although the route to solicitude for the Other may be derailed by narcissism, the ultimate destination is never the solitary self.

If Kierkegaard is a solipsist only so far as human Others are concerned then Kierkegaard could be appropriated simply for human relations if a secular philosophy of intersubjectivity were the goal. Yet Wahl did not only identify a kind of theological template for Levinas's doctrine in Kierkegaard's work. Wahl himself meant to translate Kierkegaard into French thought in a philosophical and not simply a theological way. Both Wahl and Levinas tried to detach the transcendence of the Other from background theological conceptions. This, however, still lands humanity into the position of ontological anxiety (and apparent fear of the Other).

The central philosophical debate in France in the 1930s concerned the prospects for a secular theory of transcendence. On December 4, 1937, Wahl staged an international event in which he gave his famous lecture, "Subjectivity and Transcendence," on the topic of transcendence.[35] It was to be Levinas's first major public expression of the concept "the Other," and represents a turning point in 20th-Century intellectual history. It is clear that Levinas drew much from

Wahl's ideas presented in this book.

The central question that Wahl raised in his essay was whether Kierkegaard's idea of transcendence allows for a secular translation. He saw this as a problem in the light of Kierkegaard's existential focus on God as the single Other even though he never completely denied human Others. There is a difference between the notion of transcendence and the notion that there is an absolute reality beyond normal human affairs. Transcendence is a subjective, existential experience, very different from the reality of God. Levinas posed Kierkegaard's transcendence of the Other as the fundamental alternative to Heidegger's immanent philosophy of being-in-the-world.

In wondering whether Kierkegaard's Other could be secularized, Wahl had missed the fact that for Heidegger the discovery of the Other is not a goal. For Levinas, Wahl's formulation of the problem as that of translating Kierkegaard's other into secular terms understated the radicalism of Heidegger's attempt to abolish the problem of transcendence, to substitute "ontological difference" for the intersubjective Other. Levinas argued that Heidegger attempted not to secularize but to overcome the concept of transcendence, sharply distancing existential philosophy from theology. The discourse of the encountered Other, for Heidegger, refers to the ontic realm; this is the transcendence between two beings. Levinas rightly undersands that for Heidegger the important point is that at the base of our ontic experience there is something more than a relation of one existent with another. There is the comprehension of Being itself on a more fundamental level. Thus, human existence only interests Heidegger because it allows penetration into ontology, into the question of Being.

For Heidegger, human existence, along with religious
or interpersonal transcendence, is not of independent
significance except as a means of addressing the question
of Being. In other words, transcendence for Heidegger is
not about a relation between beings; instead, it is a relation
between an existing being toward Being itself. It is in his
distinction between the ontic and the ontological that he
breaks with theology. Levinas constructs the problem as a
choice in the very meaning of transcendence. Either it means
transcendence between beings or transcendence from a being
to Being itself. Thus we see how Heidegger marginalized
Kierkegaard, whose position Wahl himself wanted to
secularize. Levinas came to share Wahl's position, which
bankrupts all philosophies of immanence, putting humans
directly into contact with one another. It is a clear preference
for Kierkegaard's interpretation of transcendence over
Heidegger's ontological definition.

Even though Levinas shifted Kierkegard's focus from the
existential drama of the self to the solicitude toward all
Others, Kierkegaard's notion of human alterity remained. By
severing the individual from the inclusiveness of the historical
process so that the self could search for God, Kierkegaard
anticipated Levinas' opposition to a fully historical and
world-immanent picture of human existence. In the 1930s,
Levinas interpreted transcendence as a divine category
and pitted monotheism against paganism. He argued that
it was paganism that led to Hitlerism, and that it was the
philosophy of transcendence that led to a way out of this,
through Judaism. He argued that as a form of paganism,
Hitlerism constrained all humans to a world of immanence;
as anti-paganism, Judaism operated as a trans-historical ideal
for all humans. Levinas saw paganism as a powerlessness to
leave the world; Judaism was a religion of transcendence that
insisted on limits to the world, which included a Heideggerian

metaphysically-closed world. Thus, for Levinas, it was the Jews who recognized God's exteriority to the historical process. Levinas thus starts with an appeal to God, who is the original transcendent Other. He then spends the rest of his life giving humans the same transcendent value in which ethics becomes first philosophy.

Levinas's Choice of the Ethical

Immediately after the war, Wahl published his *Petite histoire de l'existentialism*, which traced the history and development of existentialism from Kierkegaard through Jaspers and Heidegger to Sartre, including a piece on Levinas.[36] Wahl explains Kierkegaard's solution to enter into a relation with the absolute, infinite Other, who is an absolutely heteregenous Other to an individual human. As for Heidegger, Wahl explains how his definition of transcendence ends in the sort of immanentism resulting in Nazism. In short, Heidegger's notion of resoluteness is so formal that it is not an ethics at all. Levinas acknowledged that Kierkegaard profoundly influenced and popularized Heidegger.

Levinas acknowledges Heidegger's use of the term "ontological difference" in his existential account of transcendence in which existents presuppose existence.[37] He, like Wahl, explains how the quest for ontology had ended in paganism/Hitlerism and goes on to explain being as an unavoidable presence, that we are bound to it.[38] In describing existence, he appealed to Durkheim's theory of religion, arguing that Durkheim had not transcended the point of view of a subject facing an object. This is very different from, Levinas argued, Levy-Bruhl's notion in *Primitive Mentality* of participation, which identified the essence of primitive religion as a living experience that occurs prior to the distinction between self and world. Thus, Levinas says

that "existence deprived of each term [subject and object] .
. . returns to an indistinct source" and this creates a horror-
stricken world of existence to which Heidegger wanted
to guide philosophy. It was thought to be pagan because
it reverted to a world without subject and object and thus
existence all by itself.[39]

By making the move from abstract existence to concrete,
particular existents, Levinas created the possibility of escape
founded on a transcendence internalized to the asymmetrical
relationship to the other person. Levinas here turned
moral philosophy into something quite new by locating
transcendence in asymmetrical intersubjectivity. Through
concrete relations with specific Others, a self can preserve
itself through its possibility of not returning to itself, but
at the same time break through the grasp of the ego. This
structure clearly reflects Kierkegaard's own in the relation
between the self and the divine; it also prioritizes existents
over existence, pushing even farther away from Heidegger's
program of immanence.

After the war, Levinas used Sartre's work on the Jewish
question to fashion a new sense of Jewish identity.[40] Sartre's
work had been commonly criticized for defining Jewish
identity solely as an effect of anti-Semitism but even so, put
the issue squarely in the public eye. Even though he thought
Sartre mistakenly attributed Judaism's historical being for its
metaphysical essence, he praised him for his new, existential
analysis. In the past, Jews had to insist on the rights of all
men universally in order to protect their rights specifically,
which had forced them into a sacrifice of the intellect,
which Sartre recognized. Out of the need to defend human
dignity, intellectual Jews had been compelled to ground
their claims in the outdated and inaccurate claims of the
Enlightenment, which presented human beings as atomized

rather than socialized, emphasizing their cognitive rather than their existential traits. This is the main point of the present essay: to expose the deficient anthropology of the self of the European Enlightenment.

The Jewish emancipation had to link a universal conception of human dignity to and within the *weltanschauung* available to them. This was the analytic conception of man constructed by Descartes and Newton that viewed a human being as independent of his circumstances and his social condition. Thus, in order to defend themselves against anti-Semitism, Jews had to argue from a foundation as autonomous choosers free from all historical facts, including their own Jewish identity. Sartre changed this by offering a basis for rights that did not emerge from the anthropological mistake of the Enlightenment. Instead, he chose to develop a theory that included specific features of a historical condition.[41]

Sartre examined humanity not as abstract mind but rather as concrete and situational. This allowed Jewish intellectuals to re-situate their appeal away from Cartesian modernity toward a new philosophical anthropology. Levinas accepts Heidegger's destruction of the abstract, theoretical subject as an extension of Husserl's intentionalistic immersion of mind in an object world. He found Sartre's strategy useful because it, like Heidegger's, eroded the premises of universalism and egalitarianism while separating itself from the nefarious political undercurrent of immanence and Nazism. By insisting in his descriptive analysis of anti-Semitism on the inseparability between the essential self from its social and historical identities that the Enlightenment argued were accidental, Levinas believed that Sartre allowed for a new understanding of Judaism that was based on situation rather than choice.

Levinas did not agree with Sartre's claim that the identity of the Jew was formed from reaction to anti-Semitism. Levinas responded by developing a position about authentic and essentialist Judaism. Levinas did, however, argue that Sartre's position helped pave the way to a new humanist position. Basically it was that we could never separate out an essential self from social, historical, and religious identities that the Enlightenment thought were accidental. Judaism thus became a situation not a choice. Levinas further developed his position about authentic Judaism, that the Jew had a special perspective and knowledge within his historical situation to understand the conditions under which we all live. This move allowed Levinas to pull out a secular account of ethics that is free from theological considerations.

Levinas's work after *From Existence to Existents*, entitled *Time and the Other*, shows that the focus on solitude in Heidegger's work had mistakenly shown the need for an account of why primitive participation broke down into modern individuation and solitude, an account that Heidegger never provided.[42] According to Levinas, Heidegger had obscured the relationship between sociality and solitude by failing to think through his concept of the ontological difference. Levinas faulted Heidegger for not considering the existence he discovered apart from the individual existents that had access to ontology. For Levinas, if existence were considered the starting point, separately, with solitude and sociality following, it would be possible to preserve the ontological difference and to rearticulate the relation of solitude and sociality on this basis.

Existence, for Levinas, was not really social at all except in the primitive relationship with everything else. It follows that *Mitsein* is not a social doctrine at all but one that suggests that selfhood and sociality emerge from a more primordial domain. This level is prior to the separation and recognition of self and others, like Levy-Bruhl's notion of participatory existence in which primitive man just is the Other. This sort of access does not really count as a doctrine of sociality because intersubjectivity requires subjects. Levinas thus suggests that Heidegger's account of solitude, which was absent in the primitive world and present only in the modern world, explained why collectivist fusion is not satisfactory as a description of primitive sociality or could serve as a vision for modern sociality.

Fusion presumes prior solitude, which primitive men did not possess. Yet, fusion could not overcome prior solitude of modern man. Participation itself could not deliver us from solitude. Levinas says that solitude "does not appear as a privation of a previously given relation to the other." It emerges out of anonymity not out of sociality.[43] Levinas saw solitude as the premise of sociality because for an individual existent to be social it first had to be individual. He says, "Solitude is the very unity of the existent, the fact that there is something in existing starting from which existence occurs. The subject is alone because it is one."[44]

Levinas's starting point seems even more solipsistic than Heidegger's, but he reverses the relation between solitude and sociality in order to render a dyadic rather than communal conception of sociality. Even though Levinas retained Heidegger's ontology, he thought that the concomitant account of sociality needed to be clarified. Levinas thought that all of Heidegger's existential analyses were worked out in terms of the impersonality of everyday life or in terms of a solitary *Dasein*.[45] Heidegger's account of sociality was only to show the collective preconditions of individual existence or the polarized standoff between the collective and an individual. Levinas broke with Heidegger in order to redefine sociality as an achievement that presupposes solitude.

Levinas also analyzes Heidegger's concept of anxiety.
For Heidegger, anxiety is the being toward death and the
experience of nothingness. For Levinas, death is always in the
future, and we can never experience nothingness. It is always
an event in abeyance, is ungraspable, and reverses one's
activity into passivity. More importantly, we can understand
that we are in relation to something that is absolutely Other
that we cannot assimilate. Solitude is thereby broken through
death. Instead of sociality being a sort of communion, the
Other is always more than unknown. It is unknowable. Later,
Levinas extends this analysis to the alterity of other people.

Levinas also argues that Eros is as strong as death. It is not
fusion, struggle, or knowledge but is an insurmountable
duality. It is a relationship with what always slips away as a
mystery, a point that Nietzsche cogently made in the 1880s.
It never becomes us or ours but its alterity is preserved in the
relation. For Levinas, sociality is thus founded on a dyadic
relationship, transformed from a theological to a secular
ethics. This relational alterity, which is dyadic in character,
became the bedrock of Levinas's later, more mature ethical
thought. What is more, it is phenomenological in method, as
we will continue to see, as we explore his developed account
of ethics.

One of the main problems Levinas was dealing with was
the dialectical tension between the neo-Kierkegaardians
and the neo-Hegelians. The Kierkegaardians reacted to the
totalizing tendencies and the use of historical reason of the
Hegelians, arguing that existence remained individual rather
than collective. For the Kierkegaardians life has to be lived
morally in the present and not in some speculative future. For
the Hegelians, culture must go through several evolutions of

development that, for the Kierkegaardians, is unacceptable because even Hitlerian atrocities can be justified on this view. The totalitarianism of neo-Marxism, structuralism, and Hegelianism in the 1940s and 1950s in Europe pushed a number of French intellectuals such as Levinas directly into the moral arena. They waged war against this totalitarianism but in so doing created an alienation from history. Yet it is precisely this alienation from history that may have prevented (and could continue to prevent) us from gaining a close enough view to understand it.

Levinas was influenced by the ideas of Gabriel Marcel, which I discuss at length in a previous work.[46] Marcel, a Christian existentialist, wrote extensively on the subject of intersubjective morality using a phenomenological analysis of everyday experience. Marcel criticized Sartre because his work failed to render an account of love and charity. Marcel argued vehemently against egocentrism, in which a person remains shut up in his own mind and fails to connect with another person. Nevertheless, one can overcome the prison of oneself by becoming available to another. It involves the capacity to open oneself to another. Levinas focused on face-to-face intimacy, and saw morality as an active engagement with the Other. He re-presented Judaism as an active morality leading to a relationship between people. It was his version of moral realism.

Levinas, like Sartre, saw that this active sort of morality requires engagement. New thought is always discomfiting, according to Levinas, but life must be lived in accordance with its dangerous aspect. Levinas pushed his agenda forward by trying to distill an ethics right from Judaism but in a way that reversed Rosenzweig. Note that for Rosenzweig, human ethics were derivative of divine encounter, neither identical to nor analogous with it. Thus, for Rosenzweig one must first surrender to God; it is only then that one could see how to properly love another human. In contrast, in the early 1950s, Levinas internalized the Other to the human realm, humanizing what Rosenzweig had divinitized. More radically, Levinas severed the connection man potentially had to God, making human ethics the only intermediary to the divine.

Levinas's position was that ethics was not a corollary of a revelatory vision of God. The transcendent divine that Kierkegaard had extolled and that Rosenzweig had hoped to recover for theology was now internalized to the human realm in the form of the human Other. As the 1950s led into the 1960s, Levinas began to distinguish ethics from history and politics. For him, moral problems are eternal and not historical. They are interpersonal and not political; for him, this put moral responsibility squarely on the individual and not on any collective. He argued that the Jew spoke for all, universally. Debates broke out, with some arguing that politics is not the opposite of morality but is rather the true forum of moral opportunity. Further, it was argued that he took the Kierkegaardian principle of transcendence too far, in a way that avoided the vagaries and moments of present history. We now turn to Levinas's fully blown transhistorical theory of intersubjectivity, which he presents in *Totality and Infinity*.[47] The problem required finding the balance between the extreme of complete a-historical morality and a morality that was completely informed by its political context.

Levinas's *Totality and Infinity*

Levinas directs us toward the divine but only through the appeal of the face of the Other. This is a reversal of Heidegger's prioritization of existence over existents, and squarely locates his method as phenomenological. In *Time and the Other*, Levinas clears a path for selfhood to emerge from anonymity into dyadic intersubjectivity. But this work left ontology fundamental, anonymous rather than social, a horrific presence out of which sociality and selfhood had to arise. With *Totality and Infinity* (*TI*), the path to disclosure of the Other occurs as a matter of subjective discovery. This disclosure breaks the illusion of solipsism and reveals a prior and more fundamental dependence. Levinas makes it clear that ethical bondage is constitutive of the self rather than an achievement of a pre-existing self. This conceptual move is a radical departure from the philosophical anthropology of the self of modern humanism.

By replacing the primacy of existence with the primacy of the interrelationship of human existents, Levinas reaches back to the phenomenological method of Husserl, and especially Husserl's reading of Descartes. Levinas re-approached the solipsistic quandary that Descartes had left us with, in the light of Rosenzweig's transformation from metaethical solitude to revelatory intersubjectivity, as we saw earlier. Levinas focuses on the recovery of God in the Third Meditation through the use of Descartes' ontological argument. This argument deduces the Other from the idea of infinity, which could only have been planted in a finite being by an infinite one. Levinas makes it clear that solipsism did not have the status of a reality but instead of a necessary methodological/experiential illusion in the discovery of the dependence on a higher Other that had never genuinely disappeared. The priority of the Other in the methodological order requires a discovery of this priority, which in turn mandates the priority of the ego in the order of the discovery. For Descartes, the Other is divine whereas for Levinas the Other is human.

TI is structured around an opposition between solipsistic or separated self and the encounter with the Other, or between interiority and exteriority, an opposition that Levinas later associated with the distinction between appetitive enjoyment and solicitous desire. Levinas argues that exteriority is dependent upon interiority, which is a prior separation of the self. *TI* begins by giving an exhaustive account of the existential dignity of individuality prior to consideration of how this egocentricity is to be moderated.[48] Levinas believes that the self eventually realizes that it depends on another prior to it.[49] Initially the self sees itself as independent through constituting everything that there is. According to Levinas, this immature, less-developed, illusory state is necessary.

Levinas contrasts one's consciousness of separation with the kind of totalization that occurs within history. Interiority institutes an order different from historical time in which totality is constituted, an order where everything is pending. In interiority, an individual cannot be reduced to historical explanation of the whole. Thus, historical explanation sacrifices interiority, which makes up a secret and essential part of what is real.[50]

At this stage, Levinas attacks Husserl's use of intellectual/cognitive representation as the model for intentionality. For Husserl the exteriority of the world to the self leaves no residue when it is represented. It is converted to the Same which is why he fastens on representation as the right interpretation of intentionality for his program of transcendental phenomenology. Yet, Levinas argues that Husserl's theory of knowledge misses a deeper continuum of intentionalities involved in a self's enjoyment of the world. He says "the strictly intellectualist thesis subordinates life to representation."[51] In contrast, like Heidegger, Levinas argues that there is much more to life than representational thinking; he asserts that pragmatic and utilitarian attitudes are prior to theoretical activity. An account of the pragmatic world, which

Levinas connects to the notion of enjoyment, reveals the
limits of the Husserlian approach. Representation is not the
model for activity generally within Levinas's objection.

Even though Levinas thought that intentionality restored
a connection to the world that idealism had severed, he
also thought that it was flawed because it only allowed
for resistance instead of acknowledgment from the Other.
Thus, it was still mired in the alimentary orientation of the
solipsistic understanding of the self. Unlike representation,
other forms of enjoyment consist "in holding on to the
exteriority which the transcendental method involved in
representation suspends."[52] For Levinas, when one intervenes
in the world instead of simply watching it, the world resists
and fights back. The representational bias is put on shaky
ground by the experience of the body, which converts the
world from something to be observed into something to
consume. The "indigency" of the body requires more active
forms of intentionality in interacting with a world that resists.
"To overcome an obstacle, or to do away with an enemy: to
doubt, to labor, to destroy, to kill—these negating acts assume
objective exteriority rather than constitute it. To assume
exteriority is to enter into a relation with it such that the same
determines the other while being determined by it."[53]

These nonrepresentational forms of intentionality reveal the
self to be a part of the world that even when interiorized
begins outside of itself. It is how Levinas overcomes Husserl's
(and modernity's) optical bias. Thus, for Levinas, the self
is pragmatic before it is theoretical. Interiority is the life
of enjoyment in which needs are met through pleasurable
interaction with the world. The characteristic attitude of
the solipsist is appropriative, which leads to satiation or
enjoyment. Nourishment transmutes the Other into the
Same. The other's energy becomes my energy and therefore,

enjoyment is "alimentation."[54] For Levinas, this process of nourishment is at the root of all states of the psyche and is the very pulse of the self. "Subjectivity originates in the independence and sovereignty of enjoyment."[55]

Levinas stresses that natural participation in the cycle of work that fulfills need is actually enjoyable. He emphasizes the enjoyment that comes from the fulfillment of need. As he says, "life is not the naked will to be. . . . Life is love of life, a relation with contents that are not my being but more dear than my being: thinking, eating, sleeping, reading, working, warming myself in the sun. . . the reality of life is already on the level of happiness."[56] Yet, enjoyment is morally tainted when it takes the form of representation. The activity of representation takes to the limit the reduction of the Other to the Same. Reduction and appropriation persist even when the self is forced to acknowledge the resistance of the exteriorized world. Even though this resistance is forced on the self the response of the self is to overcome it. The result is the reduction of the Other to the Same. Levinas uses Plato's *Gyges Myth* to explain the negative potential of interiority. He says the "Gyges' ring symbolizes separation. . . . Gyges is the very condition of man, the possibility of injustice and radical egoism, the possibility of accepting the rules of the game, but cheating."[57]

He develops his position by attacking Heidegger's notion of being-in-the-world. According to Heidegger, the world of use-objects is originally ready to hand (*Zuhande*) and becomes present at hand (*vorhande*) when a tool fails to work and the activities of theory and abstraction are required to make repairs.[58] The self for Heidegger is originally pragmatic rather than theoretical. For example, an artisan uses a hammer mindlessly, without contemplation, until it breaks. But Levinas argues against Heidegger that our primary attitude toward objects is not merely utilitarian but instead, results in enjoyment.[59] That is, I make use of a hammer ultimately out of neediness and the impulse toward satiation. Thus, even though I use an instrument for utilitarian reasons, these are part of a deeper motivation of enjoyment.[60]

Heidegger's use of the concept *Sorge* is value neutral, and it is this proposition with which Levinas takes issue. For Levinas, we utilize implements of the world for our enjoyment; thus *Sorge* is already always normative in content. The enjoyment of *Dasein* that Heidegger described as neutral is also intended by Levinas to disconfirm Heidegger's picture of existence as being thrown into a world one did not choose so that one feels at home only by living in an inauthentic and everyday state of consciousness. In contrast, Levinas argues that man is not thrown into an absurd world that limits his freedom. Instead, he enjoys an abundant world that can gratify him. Thus, "the love of life does not resemble the care for Being. . . . The love of life does not love Being but loves the happiness of being."[61] He goes even further by saying that "insecurity cannot suppress the fundamental agreeableness of life."[62] Particularly, it is Levinas's notion of the dwelling that allows the self to feel at home, that contradicts Heidegger's analysis in *BT*. Levinas asserts that in *BT*, "the home does not appear apart from the system of implements."[63] The restoration of this element of life to being-in-the-world provides a much richer texture of human experience than Heidegger's portrait of a self who feels anxious about his impending death.

Levinas also argues that Heidegger himself did not see what was negative about interiority, for the possessive attitude of separation is morally tainted, even though enjoyable. It is not immoral to have a predatory attitude toward food and land, according to Levinas, except insofar as it implies extending this attitude toward other humans. Yet, the enjoyment of interiority is a necessary step to Levinas's doctrine of intersubjectivity. One simply cannot think about intersubjectivity without subjects. All the articulations of separation, including egoism and enjoyment, are necessary in order for the idea of infinity, which is a relation with the Other that opens first from a separated and finite being

For Levinas, the human Other is qualitatively different from finite, everyday objects. The Other's nature is infinite, which opposes the finitude of the self. It is transcendent and opposed to the immanent. This allows a separated being who is fixed in its identity to contain within itself that which it cannot contain nor receive solely by virtue of its own identity.[64] In contrast to objects whose nature is finite and that are there to be appetitively enjoyed, other subjects whose nature is infinite can only be desired with unfulfillable longing. For Levinas, the distinctive character of desire, as opposed to enjoyment, is that it is not to be satisfied through possession. It is a desire that cannot be satisfied.[65]

For Levinas the Other is infinitely transcendent and infinite in his being; he cannot be perceived, and across this void is absolute difference. Although Levinas never repudiated his Kierkegaardian-influenced position regarding transcendence, he also argued that the relation between self and Other is "not enacted outside the world."[66] Thus even though a self is uprooted from history when it truly approaches the other, this encounter is reflected within the totality, within history.[67]

Further, staying true to the phenomenological method, Levinas concretizes the infinite in the face of the Other, which also includes any part of the body that expresses.[68] We must, however, pay close attention to his special use of the term. He denies that the face is an image. He says: "The face is not resplendent as a form clothing a content, as an image, but as the nudity of the principle, behind which there is nothing further."[69] For Levinas, the face is something above and beyond the phenomenal form. It is a presentation that is irreducible to manifestation, a face-to-face encounter without the intermediary of any image.[70] Thus the face is not an image; instead it is an expression.[71] Thus, even though the face is concretized provisionally, as immanence, this provides access to the transcendent.

In order to further clarify the face, Levinas writes that "the face of the other at each moment destroys and overflows the plastic image it leaves me, the idea existing to my own measure and to the measure of its ideatum—the adequate idea."[72] The face is no ordinary datum and thus "the eyes break through the mask."[73] It, the face, is present "in its refusal to be contained."[74] Even so it is still a "thing among things," revealing continued tensions between transcendence and immanence.[75]

Of great historical importance is Levinas's break with Kant's identification of man's godliness as the capacity for freedom, from which duties to Others flow. In contrast, Levinas humanized the divine directly through the human Other so that the self moves to its higher realm only in recognition of its intersubjective relations. Recall that Heidegger solved Husserl's solipsism by adverting to a sociality prior to the centralizing ego. Levinas agreed that this was an important advance over the intersubjective doctrine of Husserl's *Cartesian Meditations* by saying that "in Heidegger coexistence is, to be sure, taken as a relationship with the Other irreducible to objective cognition."[76] Yet, even though he seemed to overcome Husserl's quandary with his promising account of *Fürsorge* (licensing his moralizing contrast of authentic versus inauthentic existence), Heidegger unfortunately retreated from his promising step. According to

Levinas, Heidegger's initial mistake involved the presumption that once the autonomous self has been overruled as the source of norms, whether of cognition or action, the fused community is revealed as the true source. For Heidegger, intersubjectivity is a We prior to an I and the Other; it is a neutral intersubjectivity.[77] Yet, it does not follow that just because the self is not autonomous, it is a product of community.

Levinas takes the intermediate position, that the intersubjective dyad, which is neither the autonomous self nor the entire community, is originary. This, for Levinas, is the fundamental structure of intersubjectivity in all social contexts. Further, it is the very source of meaningfulness. Thus, before a self is a member of a community, it is a member of an originary dyad.[78] This, Levinas believed proved that existents were prior to existence, against Heidegger's attempt at a fundamental ontology.[79] As he continues, "This revelation of infinity does not lead to the acceptance of any dogmatic content," because the ethical claim is not exhausted by any finite list of obligations, but also to stress that the face's revelation is a secular revelation.[80] The supersession of totality by infinity, the self through the other, is for Levinas the "most profound teaching."[81] He went on to say that this ethic does not require a particular religious faith, but is "known by knowledge."[82]

Thus, we see Levinas completely break with Rosenzweig's theology, although one could argue that he recasts divine revelation as a purely human phenomenon. In contrast to Rosenzweig, if God is to be found at all in Levinas's theory of the Other it is only as a possible result of relations with other people instead of as their precondition. Thus the norms governing human conduct do not have a divine origin even though Levinas borrows the idea of infinite qualitative difference from theology. On the other hand, one could argue

that Levinas merely internalizes external, divine authority
and ultimately does not really break from theology. We
are now at an appropriate place to discuss the influence
Levinas had on Derrida, whose ideas we can also utilize to
develop our account of the deficiency of the anthropology of
traditional humanism.

Derrida

Derrida takes the Western philosophical tradition to task
through his approach of deconstruction. By presenting and
interrogating his account, we will be able to understand
Levinas from a more contemporary position. Moreover,
we will be able to gain a more critical perspective about
the moral implications of the "I" of humanism. According
to the 1989 Oxford English Dictionary, deconstruction
involves "exposing unquestioned metaphysical assumptions
and internal contradictions in philosophical and literary
language." According to Royle, it is "not what you think: the
experience of the impossible: what remains to be thought:
a logic of destabilization always already on the move in
'things themselves': what makes every identity at once itself
and different from itself. . . ."[85] Perhaps most importantly,
deconstruction involves the decentering of the logos and a
human being, especially the ego *cogito*.

Deconstruction is not a method but rather it is something that
happens in the middle voice. It is not the result of a master
interpreter; rather it happens within texts. It is not merely
negative; in contrast it is a double movement and results
in a re-building. Thus, in the undoing, decomposing, and
de-sedimenting of structures, it also involves a reconstitution
of them in terms of different foundational values. At bottom,
within this radical questioning, it involves itself with the
Other. It is a positive response to an alterity that motivates

it. It is a response to a call by the Other and is therefore a political project.[84]

Deconstruction is a response to the Other. It is especially concerned with the Other of language. It is vigilance for the Other. A community of language users creates objects that are fixed by the language. It can go as far as pinning individuals through rigid descriptive categories. As we will see, however, the process of deconstruction can release individuals from being pinned. This movement is a kind of infinitization, a release from descriptive categories. What is at stake here involves the dynamics of human intersubjectivity. Derrida focuses directly on Husserl's vision of selfhood and identity in his transcendental phenomenology, which follows Descartes. Husserl portrays an isolated and private self, which triggers the ethical domain from the bottom up. In contrast, Derrida's position is that being human is essentially relational, that there is an "irreducible nonpresence as having a constituting value."[85] The insularity of a self-present ego is haunted at the very foundation by a non-present and even transcendent Other. Further, the phenomenological ego is even constituted by this non-presence.

Speech and Phenomena (*"SP"*) is Derrida's Levinasian meditation on the originary relation to the Other that constitutes a subject as a subject. We are always already constituted by Others and thus responsible to them. For Derrida, Husserl's theory of signs (*Logical Investigations*) is symptomatic of the metaphysics of presence.[86] In Levinas's critique of Western ontology, philosophy has privileged the "Same," which is the sphere of the knowing subject that assimilates all that is Other. Thus, in order for something or someone to be known, a phenomenon must submit itself and conform to the conditions of the knowing subject. As a result, what is known, the Other, must lose its alterity and otherness

in order to appear within the sphere of the Same. In the
Western tradition we have privileged that which can be made
present within the sphere of the Same, within the categories
of thought that we have created. Anything that fails to appear
within these categories cannot be made present and as such
is absent. Yet, what is absent is what is Other. By privileging
presence the ontological tradition privileges the Same and
thereby marginalizes that which is Other and that which
cannot appear. The metaphysics of presence is a way to talk
about the ontological xenophobia of the West.

Husserl's theory of signs falls into this metaphysics of
presence. For him, meaning can only be linked to presence.
He believes that we can carve out a region of expression that
is purified of the taint of absent Others, deep within interior
mental life. This region of pure self-presence just is the sphere
of the Same, but it is isolated and alienated, shut out from
Others. In order to reach pure expression, Husserl had to
bracket all that was Other, analogous to the later reduction
to the "sphere of ownness" in the *Cartesian Meditations*.[87] This
has far-reaching implications for intersubjectivity, community,
and ethics, for Derrida.

Derrida suggests that Husserl inscribes a form of
ethical solipsism into the very heart of phenomenology,
unsuccessfully retreating from a relation to an absent,
transcendent Other. In the *Logical Investigations*, Husserl
brackets all that is linked to communication and all that is
linked to community, to intersubjective relationships. Husserl
knew that as soon as speech is communicative it involves
another. Insofar as it involves another it is confronted by
an essential absence.[88] If there is an aversion to absence in
Husserl, it is an aversion to alterity. We see this exemplified in
Husserl's exclusion of any communicative expression in order
to secure a pure self-presence.

For Husserl, communication represents a loss of pure presence. The intersubjectivity of communication demands a mediation that constitutes a loss of full presence. This privileging of pure self-presence results in seeing the Other as a threat. This position comes perilously close to Sartre's notion that contamination comes from other people. For Derrida it is not just that pure self-presence is a retreat from intersubjectivity and from responsibility. Rather, the very notion of pure self-presence cannot be maintained. Husserl grants that one speaks even in soliloquy.[89] This opens the door to the Other, for speech as a mode of language is a cultural and public phenomenon.

If the ego's solitary consciousness operates on a kind of speech then language is the condition of consciousness. Derrida argues that thought requires language, in opposition to Husserl's belief that there is prelinguistic, pure consciousness. Insofar as language is communal, the ego depends upon Others for thinking. He says that the "other is in me before me: the ego . . . implies alterity as its own condition. There is no "I" that ethically makes room for the other, but rather an "I" that is structured by the alterity within it, an "I" that is itself in a state of self-deconstruction, of dislocation."[90] Thus, we are always conditioned by intersubjectivity even in our solitude.

The interruption of self-presence by the Other also has a temporal dimension. In Chapter 5 of *Speech and Phenomena*, Derrida shows us that perception depends upon what is temporally absent, i.e., the past and the future. In this way the self is constituted by what is absent, different, which is alterity. Memory and expectation condition possibilities in the present.[91] This alterity is the condition for presence, presentation, and thus for *Vorstellung* [representation] in general.[92] The goal for Derrida, therefore, is to make room for the Other. Alterity is the condition for self-consciousness. Transcendence is the condition for immanence. The sphere of the Same is constructed by the original interruption of the Other.

On a political level, in *Of Grammatology*, Derrida shows how the metaphysics of presence infects the work of thinkers from Sartre to Heidegger.[93] Using Rousseau and Levi-Strauss as examples, he shows how logocentrism is really underwritten by an ethnocentrism.[94] Logocentrism, which we see in Husserl, privileges the voice as a site of pure presence that effects the transmission of thought without it being tainted by cultural contingencies. Spoken words are taken to be a mirror of reality because they have an immediate relationship to the mind.[95] In contrast, writing is seen as a kind of corruption involving mediation, interpretation, and a dangerous labyrinth of signification. This view of writing as both violence and contamination contains within it an idea of the Other as violating a self's privacy and enclosure. It is an anti-communal account of intersubjectivity.

Levi-Strauss's example concerned the Nambikwara tribe, whose members were not allowed to use proper names. The episode concerned a wrong done by one tribal child against another, and both children whispered the name of the other to Levi-Strauss.[96] Strauss figured out, as Derrida recounts, that the introduction of the proper name into the public domain of language corrupts the purity of an absolute idiom, just as writing corrupts the purity of speech. This violence of naming is analogous to the violence of writing, exterior to the purity of speech.

If writing is linked to mediation and interpretation through violence, "there is, as the space of its possibility, the violence of the arche-writing, the violence of difference, of

classification, and of the system of appellations."[97] To be
in community with Others is to already be implicated in
structures of violence. The violence of naming is inscribed
into the very nature of language and therefore into the
very core of consciousness. In contrast, arche-writing is
to think the unique within a system.[98] Derrida calls into
question the politics of the ethnocentrism that underwrites
logocentrism. He calls into question liberal notions of an
autonomous individual who is later inserted into threatening
intersubjective relationships. He depicts an essential and
original interrelationality whose relations are always already
violent, thus implying some remnants of liberal autonomy.

As foundation for Derrida, even Rousseau argued that
there is a classical distinction between a pure nature and
the interruption of a violent culture, linking writing to
the later imposition of culture onto natural speech. Even
though writing is seen as a necessary supplement to a nature
that is lacking, it is also viewed as a necessary addition.
"When Nature, as self-proximity, comes to be forbidden or
interrupted, when speech fails to protect presence, writing
becomes necessary."[99] Therefore mediation goes all the way
down which, in reverse, means that the self is always already
communal, situated in relationships to Others to whom we
are responsible.

As Derrida reveals, the Western tradition has privileged
speech over writing, as the site of immediacy and self-
presence. Yet, Derrida goes further and shows that mediation
of this immediacy affects not only writing but all language
in general. Arche-writing is a synonym for what Derrida
also calls "difference."[100] As the condition of possibility for
language, arche-writing "cannot, as the condition of all
linguistic systems, form a part of the linguistic system itself
and be situated as an object in its field."[101] Difference, then, is

neither a word nor a concept. It is the condition of possibility for words and concepts.[102] It marks the distinction between words or concepts, as well as interposing a delay, a temporal spacing that puts off until later what is presently denied.[103] It indicates both nonidentity and Sameness, since they share a common root. This sameness that is not identical is difference. The difference that marks the space between signs is that which makes signification possible. Thus, that which is present is always related to something that is not.

Derrida, therefore, explains difference/spacing in terms of alterity, his account of writing parallel to the critique of Husserl. As he says, one could suggest that "the absolute alterity of writing might nevertheless affect living speech, from the outside, within its inside" just as the alterity of the Other constitutes the conscious ego.[104] Within this construct, there is no aspect of our experience, either in life or in writing that escapes the play of signifiers or the conditioning of difference. Humans mediate their experience by signs. Therefore, there is no access to the world or to ourselves that is not subject to difference. This implies that the world and consciousness are never fully present. For Derrida, each subject human is a function of language. He speaks only by conforming his speech to the system of differences in which he lives.[105] Even a subject's self-consciousness is constituted by a relation to an outside, to a community of Others with an established language. The subject is therefore constituted by the Other.

What is at issue here for Derrida is the nature of intersubjective relations that operate as the primary condition of ethics. He says "there is no ethics without the presence of the other but also, and consequently, without absence, dissimulation, detour, difference, writing. The arche-writing is the origin of morality as immorality. The nonethical opening of ethics. A violent opening. . . the ethical instance of violence must be rigorously suspended in order to repeat the genealogy of morals."[106] This is so because arch-writing — the deconstructive process — names the fundamental relationality that constitutes human beings; this includes being in relation to Others and being obligated to Others. For Derrida, in place of the metaphysics of presence there is a quasi-ontology of the trace, i.e., presence-in-absence. Instead of an isolated, self-conscious subject fully present to itself in the interiority of a pure consciousness, Derrida portrays a subject who is constituted by a relation to an exteriority, the alterity of the Other in the communal networks of signification.

In the *Margins of Philosophy*, Derrida gives an excellent account of how literature is a site of alterity and Otherness, precisely because it embodies singularity. It calls into question the linguistic ideal of immediacy and one univocal language. If the ethics of deconstruction is an ethics of obligation to the Other, this is not because the Other is not merely an individual but a singularity, unique. Derrida is here borrowing from Kierkegaard, against Levinas, as a proponent of subjective existence. Let me properly define what I mean, lest I create more confusion. I am talking about a dynamic in which one person respects the Other as subject and not as object; as a singularity and not as a placeholder within a system of structural positions. In this way the first person, who regards the Other as subject, does so not from his own subjective position but from a new position of objectivity. It is an attempt to move away from seeing someone in terms of one's own mental categories; we earlier called this "Sameness."

Derrida later continues this link with literature in *Gift of Death* by arguing that "every other is wholly other" precisely because every other is "singular" and "secret."[107] For Derrida, what interests him about literature is what is autobiographical—memoirs—because it is directly linked to the secrets of subjectivity. He says that the "autobiographical is the locus of the secret."[108] Derrida links the secret not only with subjectivity but also with marginalized political spaces that have been excluded. He is wary on both the social and individual levels of a public space that demands that one give up all secrets to enter for to do so would be to let go of one's own singularity and alterity.[109] Literature thus takes to task univocal languages by clearing a space for the Other but also guarding the Other's secret.

Derrida also interrogates the idea of metaphor to further delineate what deconstruction is and how it liberates the Other. Philosophy strives for univocity; in contrast, literature valorizes metaphor, in which there is an explosion of meanings that allow marginalized voices to be seen and heard. By exposing philosophy to the otherness of literature, Derrida shows us that metaphor goes all the way down. We never get through play and slippage of metaphoricity to arrive at the one, univocal sense. Yet this does not lead to interpretative anarchy nor destroy reference. Neither does it destroy an interrogation of the limits of context, which is perhaps the core of deconstruction. For Derrida, a context can never be fixed, nor can humans master a given context, especially because it is never complete. Nevertheless, he does hold that communities of users who fix meaning often attempt to determine interpretive context.

For Levinas, the relation to the Other is a question of justice. Furthermore, the call that emanates from this relation is hospitality, which means that we make room for the Other. We receive the Other as wholly Other. Interestingly, for Derrida as well, ethics is hospitality.[110] Here, he shows us that hospitality is not one kind of ethical thing to do; it is, rather, the condition of possibility for ethics. He says "insofar as it has to do with the ethos, that is, the residence, one's home, the familiar place of dwelling, inasmuch as it is a manner of being there, the manner in which we relate to ourselves and to others, to others as our own or as foreigners, ethics is hospitality."[111] In a way, because deconstruction makes room for the Other, deconstruction is ethics.

Derrida's cases of welcome give us great insight into his philosophical anthropology, an account of intersubjectivity whose core involves a fundamental relation to the Other. It is not an isolationist design. Instead, it is an account of relationality that is asymmetrical and non-reciprocal. I am originally obligated to the Other, an obligation I did not choose. Insofar as the Other is absolute, infinite, and unconditioned, I relate to him by way of absolute and infinite welcome. To establish conditions on this welcome would be to reassert a kind of egoism in which a sovereign "I" sets rules of engagement, where the "I" governs the conditions for relationship.

If deconstruction supports alterity then we ought to expect a link between religion and Derrida. Religion is another sort of arche-writing or deconstructive language to a univocal philosophy. Religion is an inbreaking of transcendence and alterity which is at the same time a call to be responsible for the Other. The revelation of the wholly Other commands a consideration of every other wholly Other, which implies the link between human Others and the divine Other. It is precisely in those moments that we refuse being philosophical that we have some presentiment of the Other, which carries us away from ourselves into the unknown, and is usually attended by fear, anguish, or ecstasy. Thus we see here Derrida's flirtations with religious views of alterity, especially through the influence of Kierkegaard and Levinas.

Levinas's concern for the Other is at the very crustacean bed
of deconstruction. It is also deep into the heart of Derrida's
program. It is Levinas's notion of the trace that Derrida
picks up to think about "the enigma of absolute alterity, that
is, the Other," for it is the notion of the trace that permits
the possibility of thinking beyond the binary opposition of
presence and absence.[112] Levinas orients the discourse of
OG through this role of the trace in the deconstruction of
presence.[113] Yet Levinas is also present in the ethical domain
of Derrida's early work. Thus, at the core of *OG*, Derrida
suggests that his investigation is concerned with the very
possibility of ethics.[114] This brings us also to the link between
ethics and politics for both Levinas and Derrida.

Levinas's ethics of hospitality presents a double problem
when we consider the addition of the "third." If I am infinitely
responsible to the Other then I can never measure up to the
call of the face that confronts me. But when another Other
comes upon the scene, the "third," then I am faced with the
additional problem of adjudicating infinite claims. With the
third comes the advent of politics. Derrida deftly makes
the claim that "a sharp distinction must remain between the
ethical subject and the civic one."[115] Derrida argues that our
obligations to the third actually protect us from our infinite
obligation to the Other; thus, betrayal is at the very heart of
justice. To be just and law-abiding implies a failure of one's
infinite obligation to the Other. It is "necessary," according to
Derrida.[116] Further exploration of justice, and its demarcation
from ethics, must be left for a further work. For now, let us
continue to focus on the notion of ethical responsibility.

Derrida's reading of Levinas has always been filtered through
Kierkegaard. When Derrida reflects on Kierkegaard in
The Gift of Death, he extends the Levinasian account of a
fundamental, infinite obligation to the Other. What he finds

highlighted in Kierkegaard is what Derrida defines as the essential aporia of responsibility. It is a situation without a way out; a double bind where one must decide but one does not know what to do. Derrida takes a look at this aporia of responsibility in the "Force of Law."[117]

Derrida contrasts responsibility with the Kantian notion of giving oneself the law, and it requires that a decision be made without the application of a precedent or rule. He says, "for a decision to be just and responsible, it must, in its proper moment if there is one, be both regulated and without regulation: it must conserve the law and also destroy it or suspend it enough to have to reinvent it in each case."[118] If a judge simply applies a rule he is a calculating machine and therefore not just; but neither is he just for withholding application of the law. Thus we are in a double bind with our decision, in the present. It is a paradox.

The second paradox of responsibility is the problem of undecidability. The condition for ethical responsibility is the dual state of not knowing what to do but at the same time being obliged to decide. The undecidable does not involve a choice between two decisions. It is, rather, that which is foreign to the order of the calculable and the rule, and is still obliged.[119] There is always a gap between knowledge and justice. There is a gap between calculable, rational knowledge and the risky, non-rational order of ethics. Thus, because we always lack full knowledge, there is "no moment in which a decision can be called presently and fully just."[120]

A third double bind or paradox regarding responsibility involves temporality. There is always urgency to justice that cannot wait for the filling in of incomplete information. "A just decision is always required immediately, 'right away.' "[121] The very finititude of the moment precludes the possibility of

having the requisite knowledge to calculate what is ethical.
This lack of knowledge and urgency is the very root of
responsibility.

These aporias, for Derrida, are the very beginning of ethics.
Together, they are the conditions of responsibility. Thus, there
is no moral way that can be guaranteed or calculated. This
lack of a way is the very condition of ethics. My responsibility
starts when I do not know what to do. For if I merely apply
a rule I am not taking responsibility; if I invent a new rule
I am. Thus, an ethics with guarantees is not an ethics at all.
This position does not imply paralysis. Rather, it highlights
our ethical situation that we must act without complete
knowledge. We must act in spite of our lack of knowledge.
It is this lack of knowledge that makes our situation ethical.
Ethics starts with undecidability.

To decide in a situation of blindness is a kind of madness, a
responsibility that is heterogeneous to knowledge. Yet it is
a responsible madness that Derrida finds in Kierkegaard.
Abraham is the paradigm case of the aporetic and paradoxical
nature of responsibility.[122] He is commanded by the wholly
Other—God—to sacrifice his only son, Isaac, a clear
transgression of all moral rules he knows. Because the call
is singular, Abraham cannot appeal to any rule or law that
would justify his actions. The universality of ethics is, in this
case, a temptation. According to Derrida, if Abraham were
to act in accord with knowledge of ethical rules, this would
be the height of irresponsibility.[123] From the perspective
of the ethical law, acting on this call is madness; yet, from
Abraham's point of view it is faith.

Much of what passes for ethics, including deontological
and utilitarian systems is representative of irresponsibility,
according to Derrida.[124] Rules and formulas of justification

only undo our responsibility for they attempt to reduce
the situation of decision to one of knowledge. According
to Kierkegaard we overcome our anxiety by trading this
madness for rationality.[125] The activating of responsibility
always takes place before and beyond theoretical or
thematic determination, independently from knowledge.[126]
This formulation of Abraham's situation allows Derrida to
translate Kierkegaard into Levinasian terms. If responsibility
means to respond to the wholly Other, then once we
understand that every Other is wholly Other we can see that
this situation of infinite responsibility under conditions of
undecidability is everyone's situation. Every decision holds
infinite responsibility.

Deconstruction attempts to reconstruct the form and purpose
of reason. It promotes a kind of reason with a sense of
obligation that begins with the Other. This is a reason that
no longer operates in terms of calculation. Contrary to the
modernists, rationality is more than calculation and operates
in terms of the incalculable. For example, the role that
dignity plays in Kant's *Groundwork for the Metaphysics of Morals*
belongs to the order of the incalculable. In the kingdom of
ends it is opposed to what has a price on the market and
so can give rise to calculable equivalences. In our world,
which is governed by the logic and calculability of global
capitalism, the rational is identified with market values; here,
deconstruction lurks, opening a space for a rationality that
is directed by the incalculable, which cannot be reduced to
a commodity or a dollar amount. Such a radicalized reason
is deeply opposed to the confident and certain teleology of a
calculative reason.

This new interpretation of reason is open to the Other, to
hospitality. This will require a disassociation of reason and
knowledge from its link to power.[127] Deconstruction ought to

unsettle the type of rationality that has been operative within the structures of power, including institutions, government, and so forth that have been predominant in the modern era. This would involve the universalization of singularities within a culture that could create a new kingdom of ends. We need to open reason to its Other. Derrida says that "it is a matter of thinking reason, of thinking the coming of its future, of its to-come, and of its becoming, as the experience of what and who comes, of what happens or who arrives – obviously as other, as the exception or absolute singularity of an alterity that is not reappropriable by the *ipseity* of a sovereign power and a calculable knowledge."[128] It will require a universality that is opposed to the corporate brands of globalization, relativism, culturalism, ethnocentrism, and nationalism, a breaking-in on the present by the Other. Let us now turn to the radically anti-humanist view of the psychoanalyst, Jacques Lacan, in order to further clarify the humanist perspective.

The Psychoanalytic View of the Other: Lacan

In a discourse parallel to that of existential phenomenology, psychoanalysis has constructed its own view of the Other. In my attempt to further illuminate the assumptions of modern humanism, I must now turn to the trans-humanism of Freud and the anti-humanism (or what I call "hyper-humanism") of his interlocutor, Lacan. In my view, Lacan goes too far because it is unclear whether his position leaves any room for moral agency and freedom. By taking a critical look at this radical position, from a Sartrean perspective, we will be better equipped to understand the social and moral implications of Levinas's thought. I utilize Sartre because he has the strongest voluntarist view, and even though he does not extricate himself from the Cartesian anthropology, his presentation is very clear. It is so strongly and well written that it clearly shows us the nature of the traditional humanist view. While we can use it to attack Lacan, we can also use it to help us understand the advantages of Levinas's alternative anthropology.

Lacan bases his theory of the unconscious on language and transforms Freud's pronouncements about the family and the body into assertions about culture. For him, psychoanalytic theory becomes a study of the construction of the subject in language.[129] Repressed unconscious desire becomes the search for meaning in language and the symbolic father of the Oedipal struggle becomes the power relations imbedded within language.

Lacan believes that the unconscious can only be accessed though speech and writing. He is interested in Freud's dream analysis and techniques of free association, and he argues that the unconscious is structured like a language. In his quest, Lacan appropriates Saussure's linguistic theories in order to conceptualize the unconscious as part of an endless chain of unconscious meanings that we can find only in language in the spaces between conscious meanings. He modifies Saussure's structural model of meaning by arguing that there is an endless signifying chain from the conscious construction of meaning down to the unconscious, which constantly reveals itself in language. A sign is a physical object that has meaning just like a word, and it has two parts. The first part is the signifier, which is the physical, tangible part of the sign, such as characters on paper or an object of some sort. The signified is the meaning that is attached to the signifier.

According to Lacan, subjectivity emerges from these strings of interconnecting meanings and structures in language. Personal identity arises from the way personal narratives are created within these meanings. This Lacanian subject is always inhabited by the Other, which is comprised of all Others and other significations within the overall linguistic structure. The subject, or self, always carries around the Other with it and has no inherent substance, personality, or traits of its own; it is dependent upon the intersubjectivity of language for its very existence. Signifying processes are seen as a series of events, and the construction of personal identity takes place through these events. Further, our view of the world is always constrained by the pre-determined meanings that exist. The complete linguistic structure in which one lives is the universe from which one's self can emerge; the danger is that we can never step outside these pre-determined meanings. They act as Kantian filters and mediate our experience of the world, Others, and ourselves from our very foundation in being. Thus, we can only interpret reality in terms of the language that we use, the language that speaks us. Further, it is through our use of language in our search for knowledge that we live our repressed desires.

Lacan asserts that our identifications only lead to a sense of identity, not an actual identity, but that it is always based on misrecognition. In addition to the Real, Lacan divides his structural theory into two other parts, including the Imaginary and the Symbolic. It is within the Imaginary and the Symbolic realms that we create ourselves. Using Freud's idea of primary narcissism, Lacan asserts that when we are infants we initially exist in an undifferentiated ego mass with the mother. Eventually, within this morass of emotion, sensations, and drives, we begin to sense that we have a distinct self with definable boundaries. This is the realm of the Imaginary. Yet this identity is always based on an image of oneself that is reflected back from someone else, much like the reflection from a mirror. He calls this the mirror stage.[130] The person we usually identify with at first is our mother, but although this sense of identity appears real to us it is not because it depends on something external. This early sense of identity comes when we feel, unconsciously, a coherent sense of self through the eyes of the Other, even though otherwise our self is dissipated and dispersed. In this state, our self or ego is never our own because it depends solely on our identifications, including people, things, and ideas.

Lacan also argues that we establish a subjective kind of identity, what he calls subjectivity (in translation). We acquire this new kind of identity in the Symbolic realm as we acquire language. Here, we think that the apparently fixed meanings in language give us a much more stable sense of identity, and we look for the truth of who we are in language. By believing that these relatively stable meanings can give us some coherence to our identity, we attach ourselves to the way we define ourselves linguistically. Yet, even in the realm of the Symbolic we do not gain the stable sense of identity that we want, for the unconscious reappears in the spaces between words.

Our belief that there are stabilized meanings always runs the risk of being de-stabilized by unconscious desire and early loss. There is always a gap between the conscious "I" that we construct and a deeper, unconscious sense of who we are. Lacan seizes upon this assumption and argues that our conscious identity, which we formulate through the use of the regular and conventional categories of language, is always false. The identity we create through language, in the Symbolic realm of consciousness and culture, is only another reflected identity without substance. For him, it is no different than the imaginary one we created in the mirror stage, in the Imaginary realm. So, there are two identities. There is the pre-verbal, bodily one that gets constructed in the mirror stage in the Imaginary realm; there is also the one that gets constructed in the social, cultural Symbolic realm.[131]

Lacan's argument is that we psychologically invest in false images of ourselves in both the Imaginary and Symbolic

324

realms. He believes that there is a fictional element in the construction of our identities from the ground up, and utilizes Freud's theory of narcissism and stress on language as a form of the mastery of early loss. Yet, a major distinction between the two concerns how they view the status of the ego. For Freud, the ego really is a substantial self that can develop from a primitive state of narcissism. In contrast, for Lacan the ego is always false because it is based on reflections in the Imaginary realm.

Lacan replaces Freud's structural model of identity that includes the Id, the Ego, and the Superego with his own system that represents, not parts of one self-identity, but rather various intersubjective, structural orders. We can use these structural orders to analyze the construction of identity. Lacan replaces Freud's concept of biological drive (instinct) with the process of searching for meaning and identity through language, a constant appeal to the Other through language in the hopes of locating the final truth about ourselves. We lose access to the mother's body during the Oedipal crisis, which propels us into a constant search for this lost unity and self-completion in the Imaginary realm. We use linguistic substitutes in the Symbolic realm in the attempt to fill the emptiness caused by this lost unity, but it is an impossible search. Both Freud and Lacan believe that the fulfillment of our desires is an impossible task. For Lacan, symbolic castration by the father, which is represented by the constraints language puts on reality, sets limits to our desires that are created in the Imaginary by coercing us into culturally acceptable meanings and behavior.

In language we find our subjectivity, but we will never find the ultimate meaning about who or what we are because language cuts us off from the object of our desire, which is the mother from whom we lost unity. This object of our desire, the lost mother, exists in the realm of the Real, which is everything that lies beyond the symbolic process. This realm exists in both the mental and physical worlds and includes the ineffable, pre-Imaginary plenitude that we seek out with futility. This plenitude, the all, the lost unity, always lies out of reach of the Imaginary realm and the kind of subjectivity language seems to offer us in the Symbolic realm. The Real includes not only this impossible plenitude but the materiality of objects, psychosis (where all of the symbolic order is rejected), and death, which is where the Real triumphs over subjectivity and meaning. Yet, even though language cuts us off from the objects of our desire (mother and mother substitutes) it returns desire to us. It provides us with a new sense of identity as we move from one meaning to the next in a constant pursuit of correspondence between our constructed subjectivity and the lost plenitude. Language becomes the transformative site for the Oedipal crisis, standing in for the actual father. In fact, language becomes the Other and places itself between us and the objects of our desire, constantly de-stabilizing and moving these objects so that we never reach them. Desire for Lacan is futile. So, even though it is language that hollows the being of the Imaginary realm, it is also through language, through the pursuit of meaning, that we can articulate the fullness of the imaginary and the imagined plenitude.

At the same time a child is subjected to the laws of language it also recognizes its gender, through sexual difference, by noticing the phallus.[132] The symbolic father signifies this sexual difference through his association with the phallus, which is a sign of power and not the actual physical penis. This symbolizes sexual difference (the recognition of which blooms during the Oedipal phase) as well as the underlying difference between those that have and those that do not. The unconscious becomes a container for the loss of the mother,

and the associated desire is incited by the recognition that
the child (of either sex) cannot have the phallus the mother
wants. The girl lacks the penis; the boy fears castration.
Thus, the phallus symbolizes both desire and loss. Further, it
signals to the child that having a viable identity can only come
at the price of the loss of the mother and that being human
can only come about as the consequence of the division into
consciousness and the unconscious.

Thus, the child recognizes that identities that are not fused
with the mother in the Imaginary realm come into being
through language, the Symbolic realm, as a result of the
perception of sexual difference, which is represented by the
phallus. The metaphor of the father, which is symbolized by
the phallus, mandates that the child must take its place within
a family that is defined by sexual difference. This allows the
child to understand the concepts of same and difference.
This difference that is represented by the phallus also teaches
the child the concept of exclusion, because it cannot be its
parents' lover, as well as the concept of absence, because of
the loss of the mother. The child thereby forms its identity
based on an unconscious recognition of difference, exclusion,
and absence. Lacan links the sexual world symbolized by the
phallus with the symbolic world of language. As the child
discovers sexual difference it also starts to acquire language.
In its discovery of language the child unconsciously learns
that the units of language only have meaning because they are
different from other units and that signifiers, like the phallus,
can represent things that are absent. Words stand in for
objects and operate as metaphors. As the child unconsciously
learns about the meaning of sexuality in the discovery of
exclusion and difference it also learns about meanings based
on difference and exclusion in language. Thus, it moves
isomorphically from the bodily, pre-verbal realm into the
cultural, linguistic realm of culture. Recognition of the

metaphor of the father in the sexual realm prefigures the recognition of the linguistic and symbolic law.

When the metaphor of the father—the phallus—invades the child's Imaginary relation with the mother, it creates the underlying logic and law of how we perceive the world within language and culture. This third term, i.e., the father, alienates the child from the mother simultaneously as it plants itself as pre-established meaning and law. As we have said, this process operates through the concept of difference, and sets limits to our search for meaning through the rules of logic and grammar. These limits create symbolic castration by cutting us off from what we desire while allowing us to enter into culture and to become subjects. Here, we can see Lacan's linking of the psychosexual dimension with the dimension of culture. We unconsciously recognize the phallus as a sign that is a precursor to all signs in language. Language is comprised of empty chains of meanings that have arbitrary assignments so that we can live together in community. By entering into language from the foundation of the phallus, we become members of society with particular subjectivities.

Yet, Lacan recognizes that the power of the phallus is arbitrary and that there is always misrecognition of its perceived power (where females always signify a lack and boys have the chance to achieve the paternal metaphor). The meaning of the phallus is, therefore, spurious. Given that it is the first signifier on which all other symbolic meanings are based, what follows also involves misrecognition of the identity within language that we create in order to cover up our pain because of the loss of the mother. As a boy begins to recognize his sexual difference he also realizes, unconsciously, castration by the father. He experiences powerlessness. Likewise, as a girl recognizes her sexual identity, she must also accept that she, too, lacks what her mother wants, which includes cultural power and social identity. She constitutes herself negatively, as a lack, because she does not possess the phallus, and this is in addition to her losing the union with her mother's body. Effects for both genders are repressed into their unconscious, according to Lacan.

Lacan asserts that at an unconscious level we understand the illusory nature of the construction of identity that is based on the spuriousness of the phallus. He bases this on Freud's belief that the unconscious constantly subverts the intended meanings of language. Language forces us to abandon the Imaginary realm, but it is also the best source of identification that we have. Through the entry into language we achieve some kind of mastery over our original desire and loss of the loved object. We do this within the rational, objective, and coherent construction of meaning through that language even though this domain never quite satisfies our deep craving for unity. The seduction comes from the apparent stability of meaning within language. For Lacan, the strategy of attempting to ground the meaning of who we are through language, through the foundational metaphor of the phallus is futile, and engages us in an endless search for the meaning of who we are, for our completion. This metaphor functions as a pivotal structural concept that ostensibly regulates all other meanings. Yet, for Lacan, the phallus has no status in reality and our unconscious is aware of this more or less.

In Lacan's conception of the unconscious, there is a constant concealment and distortion of meaning. In free association there is a constant dissolving and evaporation of meaning, as he says, "an incessant sliding of the signified under the signifier."[133] That is, veiled unconscious meanings may be different from the conscious meanings lying at the surface. In terms of our identifications with various discourses of truth about who we are, we think that we achieve a coherent and

unified identity. Recall that for Lacan this occurs at the level
of the Imaginary ego. Thus, when we believe in any stability
and truth in language and knowledge, in actuality we make
an imaginary identification with an image of ourselves that
is reflected back to us from words whose meanings are as
illusory as the identities we build on the basis of them.[134]
There is, therefore, a split in our identity between what we
are and what we take ourselves to be. For example, when
we make an assertion of the kind "I am going to do x," the
"I" that is the subject of the sentence is different from the "I"
that is doing the enunciating. The "I" of the sentence covers
up the "I" that is doing the speaking. We think that both are
unified into one self, but they are not, for this conclusion is
only in the Imaginary realm. There is no sign that can sum
up my entire being and therefore it is impossible to represent.
In fact, most of what I am can never be represented through
language. For him, the subject is always constructed through
the transforming of the Imaginary into the Symbolic, in which
we transfer the experience of our senses into the world of the
signifer, the world of which we speak.

Let us explore Lacan's metapsychology of the subject more
carefully. Lacan attacks the idea of an essentialist subject that
is transparent to itself and fully representable in theoretical
discourse. It is this Cartesian subject which is also the subject
of the humanist tradition that Lacan calls into question,
just as Freud did. For Lacan, "it is nonetheless true that the
philosophical *cogito* is at the centre of the mirage that renders
modern man so sure of himself even in his uncertainties
about himself."[135] Yet, this essentialist illusion, which reduces
subjectivity to the conscious ego, reveals itself as a "myth
of the unity of the personality, the myth of synthesis . . . all
these types of organisation of the objective field constantly
reveal cracks, tears and rents, negation of the facts and
misrecognition of the most immediate experience."[136] As

Lacan says it in the "Freudian Thing," as a result of Freud's discovery of the unconscious, the "very centre of the human being is no longer to be found at the place assigned to it by the humanist tradition."[137] Further, Lacan also opposes any project that asserts the autonomy of the essentialist subject, saying that "the discourse of freedom . . . [is] fundamentally biased and incomplete, inexpressible, fragmentary, differentiated, and profoundly delusional."[138] In fact, it is the very subversion of the subject as *cogito* that makes psychoanalysis possible.[139]

For Lacan, the essence of man is not to be found in his conscious representation of himself.[140] In fact, the subject is not a psychological substratum that can be reduced to its own representation. If, indeed, there is an essence in the Lacanian subject it is as a lack of essence.[141] Nevertheless, his subject is different from the traditional metaphysical notion of the subject that is at the heart of the *cogito*. He takes Freud's idea of Spaltung, or splitting, in reference to fetishism and psychosis and generalizes it as constitutive of all humans. Thus, the self is radically ex-centric to itself, heteronomous rather than autonomous, and more attached to the other than to itself.[142] For Lacan, the ego is different from the subject. The ego is a kind of sedimentation of idealized images that are internalized during the mirror stage, which we explained above. Yet, there is always a gap between the imaginary ego and the lived experience of one's body, beginning in infancy. This gap implies that the ego is always an alien alter ego "whereby the desiring human subject is constructed around a center that is the other insofar as he gives the subject his unity."[143]

Any imaginary unity based on the mirror stage is founded on an irreducible gap: "the human being has a special relation with its own image – a relation of gap, of alienating tension."[144] Unity in the Imaginary is a result of captivation,

of a power relation between the infant and its image. This
captivation, which anticipates unity and synthesis, does not
eliminate the alienating character of its own foundation.
Thus, we attempt to identify with anything outside ourselves
in order to recover the lost unity. Yet, what seems to be ours
always contains an element of difference and alienation. As
Yannis Stavrakakis says, "this alienating dimension of the
ego, the constitutive dependence of every imaginary identity
on the alienating exteriority of a never fully internalised
mirror image, subverts the whole idea of a stable reconciled
subjectivity based on a conception of an autonomous ego."[145]

It is because the imaginary image of ourselves does not give
us a stable identity that we seek it out in the symbolic register,
through language. We are not speaking chronologically here,
but logically, in that the symbolic always presupposed the
imaginary and even pre-exists as a network of anticipated
meanings even before birth. Thus, Lacan says "while the
image equally plays a capital role in our domain . . . this role
is completely taken up and caught up within, remoulded
and reanimated by, the symbolic order. The image is always
more or less integrated into this order."[146] Whereas the
ego is formed in the Imaginary, the subject emerges in the
Symbolic. In fact, the subject takes its very structure from
the signifier, which is constitutive for it. The subject of the
signifier is the subject of lack, which carries power with it
at its very foundation, i.e., the loss of certain possibilities, as
well as its acceptance of the Symbolic realm. As it enters into
the Symbolic it is constituted through power; it is, therefore,
subordinated to those to which it is attached.

The signifier is the very epicenter of the power that forms the
subject and is based on the recognition of difference as well
as a certain order. It is psychoanalysis that is the science of
the signifier, as applied to the formation of subjectivity. Lacan

argues that the symbolic function of psychoanalysis situates it in the "heart of the movement that is now establishing a new order of the sciences, with a new putting in question of anthropology."[147] Further, he believes "this new order signifies nothing more than a return to a conception of true science whose claims have been inscribed in a tradition beginning with Plato's *Theaetetus*. This conception has become degraded, as we know, in the positivist reversal which, by making the human sciences the crowning glory of the experimental sciences, in actual fact made them subordinate to experimental sciences."[148] Lacan continues his criticism of our modern conception of science by saying that "our physics is simply a mental fabrication whose instrument is the mathematical symbol [and that] experimental science is not so much defined by the quantity to which it is in fact applied, as by the measurement it introduces into the real."[149] Lacan, indeed, was wrestling with scientific methodology, and believed that linguistics could be the foundation for a new scientific order.

Lacan's advice was to "read Saussure."[150] Furthermore, it was Freud himself who saw language as the foundation for his discourse of the unconscious. Lacan recognized this when he asserted that Freud's goal had always been to explore an elaboration of the linguistic structure of dreams, that Freud had already recognized the primary status of language.[151] Thus, Lacan's goal was to reconstruct Freud in terms of modern linguistics. Even so, we must keep firmly in mind that Freud's failure to develop beyond the paradigm of nineteenth century materialist science contributed to the failure of contemporary psychoanalytic theorists to get beyond the illusion of substance as they attempted to describe the development of the ego or self. Let us now take a look at Lacan from a Sartrean point of view.

Lacan and Sartre

Lacan agrees with Sartre that the ego is an object, not a subject, of experience, and that therapeutic attempts to develop ego structure are misguided. In contrast to Sartre's belief that humans can transform their behavior and attitudes into more authentic experience, Lacan believes the best we can do is accept that we are determined by the linguistic unconscious. For Sartre, we discover ourselves as objects of Others, but because of the pre-reflective aspect of consciousness we can overcome this. In contrast, for Lacan we literally take the other for ourselves and we can never overcome this fundamental alienation. Further, Lacan is a structuralist and believes that language speaks the person. Thus, he is also a reductionist who is searching for a scientific explanation for psychic phenomena that is experience distant and not experience near. In contrast to Freud, who discovers this in our biology, Lacan finds this in structural linguistics. Sartre objects to Lacan's determinism because it prevents the possibility of free and authentic action of individuals. Here we can see Sartre's prioritization of consciousness over Lacan's idea of the structural unconscious.

But there is some agreement between the two. Sartre would agree with Lacan's belief that the ego is an object that is more often an object of misunderstanding than of understanding. Lacan echoes Sartre when he compares the subject to a paralytic who has been hypnotized by his image in a mirror—the ego. Sartre had similarly described the ego as a false representation of itself with which consciousness has hypnotized itself.[152] Sartre's subject is stultified by the image of a substantial self whereas Lacan's subject is hypnotized by the substitution for a self of its own mirror image, and both agree that the rigidity of the ego must be questioned.

334

Derivatively, both thinkers criticize psychoanalytic attempts to build ego structure, given that the ego is illusory for them.

Even so, for Sartre, the therapeutic enterprise would involve building a new reflective relationship with the ego; for Lacan, the ego is a fundamental alienation that can be acknowledged but not overcome. According to Lacan, even though human conflicts may appear on the horizon of the experience of the gaze, their actual origin is not the desire to co-opt the Other as a mirror for me as an object. Instead, their origin comes from the desire to mimic the other and gain a self. Thus, Lacan rejects Sartre's fundamental ontology.[153] For Lacan, both the self and the Other are objects, never subjects, which prevents the kind of positive social transformation that is possible within Sartre's ontology, in terms of viewing both the self and Others as subjects that are deserving of respect. In Lacan's metapsychology, we all are objects merely trying to capture an image of wholeness by means of which the Other originally captured what might have been a self. In fact, the Lacanian ego is Otherness absolutely and completely, and this means that there is no transcendent consciousness that can reflectively alter or develop the ego. In contrast, for Sartre, we can purify the ego by understanding that we are never trapped or determined by it. Here, we give up the false hope of attaining a substantialization of the self by understanding that the ego is only an effect and not a cause. In this process, we would understand that the ego is just a story that we tell about ourselves and that this story can be changed as we re-interpret our memories of the past. There are two parts to the ego for Sartre. There are the judgments of Others and a reflective *ipseity* that allows us to accept or reject those judgments of Others. This reflective capacity could allow for a radical conversion to a philosophy of freedom that promotes authentic relations with Others.

As a structuralist, Lacan tries to reduce psychic phenomena to unconscious linguistic structures by removing human intentionality and meaning. By reducing the conscious subject to an "effect of the signifier," Lacan precludes meaningful transformation.[154] His structuralism, as a new positivism, has moved from a determinism based on historical causation to a determinism based on unconscious structural causation. Both forms of determinism are manifestations of an analytical reductionism that misses out on the power of Sartre's idea of intentional *praxis*. For Lacan, we are just playthings of the linguistic unconscious, which prevents us from using language as *praxis*. On this point, see Ragland-Sullivan, who notes that Lacan was "generally pessimistic about the possibilities of altering the Symbolic order."[155] This is consonant with his position that there is no transcendent subject who could possibly effect such change.

Even though Sartre also believes that language inscribes the Other into the heart of each person's being, he thinks that we have freedom in how we live that Otherness. Such Otherness is unconscious in the sense that it is not usually examined, but it is not unconscious in the sense of being beyond consciousness. There is a continuum of sorts between living ourselves in language as *hexis* or as *praxis*. Lacan's position — what Sartre would call *hexis* — is that language speaks us; as such, we are inert objects that are pure otherness and there is no chance for transcendence. As an inert repository of past *praxes*, language is always an invitation to *hexis*. Using language inserts us into a cultural order and, as a result, Otherness inscribes itself into our own intentional projects. Sartre's position, on the other hand, is that we can live language as *praxis*, which means to use it creatively and intentionally. It is the creative aspect of language that Lacan avoids. By neglecting intentionality and denigrating consciousness, Lacan's position becomes very close to the

one Sartre ascribes to Flaubert.[156] By placing the source
of Otherness inside the linguistic unconsciousness, Lacan
considers normal the kind of alienation Sartre describes in his
concept of *hexis*.

Lacanian alienation is unsurpassable because it is solely this
Otherness that has created each of us as a speaking subject.
For Lacan we always enter into a world that is filled with
symbols, and we can never return to a place that is outside the
cultural-linguistic order. Thus, as Ragland-Sullivan asserts,
Lacan does not include an intentional element in his idea of
consciousness. "Instead, consciousness has become a mode
of perception which negotiates Desire via substitutions."[157]
It is in the dimension of the Other, the unconsciousness,
that "the recognition of desire is bound up with the desire
for recognition."[158] Thus, it is there in the repressed primal
relationship with the mother and in the linguistic laws that
have been placed there after the encounter with the primal
signifier that the various substitutions one uses make sense.
For Lacan, the most one can do is to understand that we
are the playthings of the linguistic unconscious, that one is a
signified rather than a signifer, an object pretending to be a
subject. In contrast, Sartre thinks that we can use language in
a way that transcends the Lacanian position.

We are trying to uncover some phenomenological aspect
of the contemporary self that has the tendency to avoid
a humanistic ethics of the Same. This is, perhaps, not
equivalent to Sartre's idea of transcendence, but it may enjoy
similar consequences. Lacanian analysis is not ego analysis,
but is discourse analysis, in which we try to understand how
conscious discourse emerges from its unconscious source.
Recall that Lacan absolutely rejects the attempt by ego
psychologists and object relations theorists to reconstruct
the development of the ego. For him, these approaches are

an unproductive rendering of Freud in that they are directed by the false ideal of "normal" development, a concept that Foucault attacks and which we will explore shortly. Lacanian analysis focuses on understanding the illusory nature of the ego in the interest of a fuller experience of subjectivity that subsists beyond the phallic signifier. Thus, Lacan argues that attempts to shore up or reconstruct the ego result in a "reinforced alienation,"[159] primarily because these theorists do not understand that the ego is an illusion.[160] Instead of being a force for reality organization, the ego "represents the center of all the resistances to the treatment of symptoms."[161] This occurs because the ego is organized around the specular images that give the individual a sense of imaginary coherence based on identification. Therefore, ego analysis takes place in the Imaginary register and, in opposition, Lacan believes that effective analysis occurs "on the frontier between the symbolic and the imaginary."[162]

Instead of restructuring the ego, Lacan advocates the reconstruction of the signifying chain by which a person has been constructed. The goal is "full" or "true" speech that occurs without the disrupting intervention of ego identifications. Full speech differs from "empty speech" in that it "realizes the truth of the subject," that subjectivity is an illusion. In empty speech the subject "loses himself in the machinations of the system of language," implying that this loss entails entanglement in "the labyrinth of referential systems made available to him by the state of cultural affairs to which he is a more or less interested party."[163] Thus, for Lacan, movement toward the unconscious is theoretically preferable to movement toward the social order. In order to understand oneself as a product of the "discourse of the Other," one must understand that one is integrated into its circuit. Thus, when we identify ourselves in language, we lose ourselves in it like objects where our future is already

determined by the chain of signifiers into which we are
inserted. Thus, the best we can do is to understand that
"subjectivity" is merely an illusion and to understand our
destiny within discourse.

Lacan is advocating a kind of synchronic determinism in
which humans are caught in signifying chains. Since we
always exist within a linguistic system, we can never step
outside of it. We can never transcend it so as to gain subjective
perspective. The best one can do is to understand that one is
decentered, that one is caught within the "gears" of language
and therefore "isn't master in his own house."[164] The problem
for him, though, is that no genuine praxis is possible in a
system where the conscious subject is merely an effect of the
unconscious signifiers. As Antoine Vergote says, for Lacan,
"the subject is but the locus of the combinative production
of autonomized signifiers. The clinician might even wonder
if this is not the nonsubject of schizophrenia, the one who is
the stake of the word but who is no longer playing the game
of language."[165] Yet it is clear that the truth of the human
"subject," for Lacan, is in the inhuman interrelation among
signifiers, and he inverts Descartes's dictum, saying that "I
think where I am not, therefore I am where I do not think."[166]

In contrast with Lacan, for Sartre, proactive living would
involve not movement toward the linguistic unconscious,
but rather a transformation of hexis into praxis in which one
would develop an intersubjective world of intentionality.
This does not mean that Sartre believes we have absolute
control over the meaning of our words, for this would be a
distortion opposite to Lacan's belief that we are products
of the symbolic order. For Sartre, we can actually use the
symbolic order to change the phenomenal and intentional
order. This is possible because of prereflective consciousness,
which can always purify the ego. In this light, Sartre asserts

that the "necessary attitude for comprehending a person is empathy."[167] This means that we must go beyond an analytical evaluation which leaves out an understanding of future directed intentionality and its meaning. Further, even though we can attempt to reduce human action to its component parts, including determinist chains of causation, we will never understand humans if we do not attempt to understand our creative abilities to make new meaning out of old structure.[168] That is, even though our facticity suggests lines of *praxis*, this does not mean that it creates subjects out of whole cloth, for Sartre. Language for him includes both possibilities for praxis as well as *hexis*. Further, in contrast to Lacan, an individual is both constituted and constituting, and we have the freedom to reconstitute ourselves in such a way that we transcend the objectifying elements of the gaze of Others. We will see how Foucault's analysis of the constituted self can shed further light on the relation between Lacan's structuralism and Sartre's phenomenology.

According to Sartre, we can never completely rid the ego of the Other, because we can never step outside of our culture, our history, and our concrete situation. Yet, we can reflect on our identifications to the extent that they are based on unreflected appraisals of Others. This means to use language proactively and creatively in order to transcend one's way of living as *hexis*. Psychological practice for Sartre would always include the clarification of the relation between one's freedom and the established world of necessity. More importantly, it would promote the transformation of passivity into authentic action, thereby increasing free choice. Now that we have seen the opposition between the purely voluntarist position of Sartre and the radically anti-humanist views of Lacan, let's discuss some of the ideas of Michel Foucault. He is careful to mediate between radical existentialism and structuralism, showing us that we do have a realm of moral freedom, but that we are not trapped by the isolating qualities of the Cartesian self. By attacking the masterful self of the Enlightenment with its subject-object dualism, Foucault opens theoretical possibilities with which we can entertain the Levinasian anthropology. We should also be clear that some of Sartre's middle and later ideas about the plasticity of consciousness also help us move toward, and construct, a Levinasian position.

Foucault

Recall that for Lacan, we cannot escape our objectifications, which is a view directly in conflict with Sartre's belief that we can. Foucault's work is interesting because, while he believes that the self is constituted discursively through relations of power/knowledge, he also believes there is a realm of freedom that is resistant to this tendency toward the kind of objectifications in which our culture engages. Foucault is neither a structuralist nor a phenomenologist.

In his later work, Foucault concerns himself with the processes within which humans are made into subjects. He replaces Sartre's notion of a transcendent, constituting subject with a version of the self that is constituted by relations of power. In Foucault's conception there is a docile aspect of the self that is created by the effects of power. There is also an antagonistic aspect that can resist power by avoiding the will to truth and, instead, create new forms of subjectivity. In *Discipline and Punish*, Foucault offers a genealogy of the modern individual as a docile and mute body by presenting the interplay of disciplinary technology and social sciences with their standards of normativity.[169] Here, he argues that individuals are socially constructed, based on categories produced by the relations of power in the human sciences. In *Discipline*, he gives an account of the modern history of power from the seventeenth century to the present, showing how power has evolved from being primarily repressive to mostly productive. By the nineteenth century, power emanates from all levels of society, producing various effects along with the repressing of behavior, a structure that he calls "bio-power."[170]

As modern states promote the growth of their populations, interest in human sexuality and economic production grows. Scientific knowledge of the processes of the human body explodes as the state forms a disciplinary technology of these bodies for the purpose of manipulating them as objects. By the nineteenth century, the exercise of power had shifted from imprinting itself on bodies through torture to processes of self-surveillance in which subjects are formed through the repressive effects of language. In *Discipline*, Foucault traces this historical development of the modern individual as a docile and mute body by showing the evolution of disciplinary technology within the penal system, but keep in mind that he is also concerned about the docile body in other domains. Most importantly, it is through techniques of self-surveillance and normativity that individuals are constituted as subjects. In *Birth of the Clinic*,[171] Foucault gives us his history of the body, showing how the clinical gaze focuses on the bodies of the dead through autopsy, creates categories of disease, and thereby reveals truth. In this way, the body is fractured into a complex of diseased organs that are responsible for death. Moreover, in *Madness and Civilization*, Foucault demonstrates that madness is also constituted in the domination of individual bodies.[172] Here, the category of madness arises from the practice of separating those with sane minds and productive bodies from those with insane minds and unproductive bodies, confining the insane and unproductive to asylums. Madness, laziness, and poverty are thereby associated in a complex of moral perception that results in the judgment that madness must be isolated and treated by medical experts.

In these historical studies Foucault shows the isomorphism between power exerted on a person's body and the power relations of the society in which he lives. In this schema, the body politic is "a set of material elements and techniques that serve as weapons, relays, communication routes and supports for the power and knowledge relations that invest human bodies and subjugate them by turning them into objects of knowledge."[173] As we have alluded to, the two main strategies used in the new disciplinary technology are surveillance and normalizing judgment.[174] Normalizing judgment places each individual into an objective category and evaluates him by how far he deviates from the norm in any particular way. These strategies force individuals into certain roles in society and account for each person's place in the disciplinary grid. Deviations from the norm are punished so as to correct for improper behavior. Most individuals accept these roles and live by them, although others engage in strategies of resistance.[175]

Foucault believes that in our current era of bio-power, influenced by Newton and Descartes, we primarily view the human body as a resource or a machine. Knowledge of the body causes its dispersion into a complex myriad of political strategies and techniques. In contrast to Aristotelian man who was self-grounded, Foucault sees modern man as "as an animal whose politics places his existence as a living being in question," as social creations who are not their own ground.[176] As Foucault develops in his work on sexuality and subjectivity, bio-power, in part, views bodies as sexual and operates on them through strategies of law, biology, and psychoanalysis. Sex is driven by knowledge of sexuality that uses various scientific discourses to normalize sexual behavior of the body. Each body is evaluated against the norm, thereby creating a tension within each person. Spontaneity is necessarily opposed to the norm created by a science that is driven by capitalism. Thus, the body becomes divided against itself as it is fractured into various discourses of truth. In order to understand this production of truth, I must discuss Foucault's notions about power.

Both the phenomenologists and the structuralists influenced Foucault. It is his beliefs about power that tie these influences together and synthesize competing claims about explanation in the social sciences, thus we need to say a bit about what he means. For most of the twentieth century, the debate in the social sciences has been between those who see power as exercised by individuals and those who see power as the result of structural factors within systems. Voluntarist theories view power as being exercised by individuals. Structuralist theories view power as the result of the structures within systems.[177] Foucault attempts to synthesize these contrasting positions by showing that there are two levels or perspectives of power, and that both agency and structural factors have an explanatory role. He presents us with the intriguing statement that "power relations are both intentional and nonsubjective."[178] Foucault's objective is to study the effects of power, and he does this by focusing on how power is exercised rather than how it is possessed and by whom. In contrast to Marxist theories of power, which hold that power is a substance that can be held, Foucault adopts the Nietzschean position and is nominalistic about it. Power, for Foucault, is not a thing and cannot be possessed.[179] Instead, it is the name we attribute to a complex strategic situation in a particular society.[180]

At any point in time a society is structured by a set of rituals of power that create asymmetrical relationships between humans. Foucault analyzes this web of unequal relationships by focusing on how people relate to each Other on the

most local and interpersonal of levels. Relations of power
are thus immanent in all kinds of relationships. Further,
power does not come from the top and trickle downward;
instead, it emanates from all directions and, as we have
said, is productive.[181] Because he believes that power
relations are intentional and non-subjective means that
they can be explained from two perspectives. He believes
that these relations are always imbued with calculation,
aims, and objectives.[182] Yet, this does not mean that power
is necessarily exercised through the choice of an individual
subject.[183] At the local and tactical level of political activity
there is conscious decision-making; intentionality is present.
Here, individuals are aware of what they do and every act
is planned and deliberated. In contrast, at the structural
level, which is the underlying matrix of power relations,
there is no subject. Exercises of power are not the result of
anyone's direct, conscious planning. Thus, relations are non-
subjective. This means that even though agents are aware
of their decisions, the broader consequences of local actions
are not planned or coordinated.[184] There are results that are
beyond the intentions of any one agent. Yet, these patterns,
which emerge historically, have a logical form. They are the
result of the underlying strategic interplay of all the unequal
relations of domination. The direction of these local practices
is influenced by the underlying technologies of power that
instantiate a particular society at a particular time. Foucault's
intention is to analyze these tactical practices.

Foucault argues that there is a government of power relations
that limits individual actions in various relationships. It
is, as he says, "a total structure of actions brought to bear
upon possible actions."[185] This structure provides a context
within which possible actions can occur and "consists in
guiding the possibility of conduct and putting in order the
possible outcome."[186] That is, the underlying structural

level governs a field of possible actions at the tactical level in any kind of relationship of power.[187] Rational agents have a range of choices delimited and made possible by the underlying power structure. This structure changes through history, sometimes as a result of successful resistance or by the transgression of previously established limits. Foucault links power relationships and their inherent potential for reversal by arguing that they are unstable states and can easily rupture into the other. These relationships of power are reciprocally relationships of struggle. They limit each other and each is always the possibility for the other. It is the region of struggle that can be explained by the purposeful actions of a subject. When struggle reaches its limit, though, and becomes a relationship of power, actions are better explained by structure, not by subjects. In a power relationship, the nature of that particular relationship determines the limits of behavioral choices each individual has. These individuals are not, according to Foucault, traditional subjects who are their own ground of choice. Instead, the structure of the relationship determines the choices. Thus, even though the behavior of the individuals involved is intentional within the power relationship, this intentionality is grounded within the matrix of power operating within society at that time, and further refined by the specific relation of power involved.

According to Foucault, in the eighteenth century, the Modern state reorganized the pastoral power that individualizes humans.[188] He believes that the individualizing power of the modern state was, and is, concerned with the health and welfare of both individuals and the populations as a whole instead of the healing of souls. State power forms a type of individuality with which individuals identify. This power questions the status of and governs individuals by forcing them to scrutinize themselves and see where they fit within patterns of normalization.[189] It forces individuals to seek the truth about who they are and, for Foucault, these phenomena emerge most clearly in the domain of sexuality.[190] Foucault saw the practice of a politically effective ethics as a means of disabusing ourselves of the notion that our desires speak the truth about who we are, which is the type of individuality that has been constructed for us in the modern period. This hermeneutics of desire involves a relation to oneself whereby we attempt to discover the true nature of what we are by attaching ourselves to various human knowledges through our personal identity.

Foucault's historical construction of humans as desiring people is not new. Socrates, Plato, and Aristotle were aware of this facet of our humanity and discussed it a great deal. Even Augustine and other Medieval Christian thinkers were interested in this problem. Yet, Foucault's version sets this problem within a different historical context. In it, he implies that there is a direct relationship between what one does and what one is. By desiring things, values, people, and ideas, we move toward them, and we attach ourselves to them as we frame our personal identities. But in this, he adds a hermeneutics of truth to desire, for how we act on our desires speaks the truth about who we are. Most importantly, this truth is always embedded in relations of power. Experts, who make claims to knowledge, tell us who we are through the strategies of individuating power. Recall that individuating power categorizes humans of a society according to the claims of the human sciences, culture, and religion. The recognition of where persons are located in relation to the universe of human data makes individuals into subjects and each person recognizes himself as an individual with a personal identity. Please note that there are two facets of this recognition: one by Others and one by oneself, along with degrees of resistance and transgression.

One's personal identity has a relation to truth that carries with it substantial political implications. Foucault shows us that what passes for ultimate truth is dependent upon our historical circumstance and the power relations underlying them. Thus, we have regimes of truth that vary with historical time and place.[191] More importantly, these regimes force us to believe that the truth is at stake in whatever we do. This causes us to discover where we are located in relation to truth, playing real-life "games of truth."[192] Humans are led to believe that by attaining the knowledge about who we are we will be better equipped to transform ourselves. Foucault traces the histories of these truth games and how they are used as a basis for self-identity and behavior toward others. His inquiry ultimately leads him toward ethics, and thus he says that his "problem is to know how men govern (themselves and others) by means of the production of truth. . ."[193]

It is the production of truth that constitutes who we are. For example, we can try to locate ourselves within the categories of psychopathology, relying on various measurement tools and practices such as the *DSM*.[194] Foucault argues that we are subjected to these games of truth by the power that individuates human beings. For him, "subject to" means that one is "subject to someone else by control and dependence," or "tied to his own identity by a conscience or self-knowledge." Both meanings suggest a form of power that subjugates humans to scientific knowledge.[195] Individuals are forced into a connection with knowledge, and power makes certain that we are dependent on that knowledge for our identity. My subjectivity arises from the recognition of myself. Foucault shows us that in the modern era, humans see themselves primarily as sexual (desiring) beings. Therefore, we subject ourselves to the games of truth associated with our sexuality, thereby constituting our subjectivities through that sexuality. Recall that power creates docile subjects that are manipulated by these truth games. Yet, each of us can influence the way these games affect us. Thus each person, for Foucault, is divided into two components, a subject and an object. The objectivized self appears both socially and personally and is one part of the split subject that emerges from the dividing practices of the relations of power. It is these dividing practices, both on the social level and on the individual level, that objectify us and subject us to the process of normativity.[196]

There are two levels of dividing practices. There is the social level where individuals are divided from others at points where they deviate from the norm. There is also the individual level where individuals divide themselves into subjects and objects, in which the objectified realm emerges from the attachments of personal identity. Various discourses on knowledge arise because of the power formations in society. Those who espouse the truth of various claims to knowledge gain power over those who are subjected to that knowledge. Thus, when mental health professionals assert various truths they often alter the behavior of individuals who become subjected to the knowledge employed. A psychotherapist subjects his clients to a system of truth to which he or she is aligned. Yet, if one changes therapists one is subjected to a different brand of the truth, for instance, Gestalt therapy instead of Rogerian therapy, or self psychology instead of Freudian analysis. A different truth is raised by each new relationship to knowledge that a person creates for himself.

My criticism is directed toward the dualist, spectator philosophy, in which the subject-object dichotomy objectifies humans, framing perceptual data about them in terms of a reductionistic theory. Foucault helps us understand the underlying political foundation of this tendency from a historical perspective. Foucault believes that Sartre's theory speaks from the assumption of a self that can transcend its historical constitution and that Sartre is trying to define self-constitution for all humanity and for all time. Nevertheless, with Foucault's formulations about power, the traditional masterful subject is gone. Because power traverses everything, the categories of subject and object collapse as well.[197] Although Foucault's work ends in a self that cannot transcend the relations of power within its own history, it does open up possibilities for new forms of subjectivity.

Like Sartre, who presents freedom as our very ontological essence and a practical possibility, Foucault speaks of freedom as resistance to disciplinary forms of objectification, saying "at the very heart of the power relationship, and constantly provoking it, are the recalcitrance of the will and the intransigence of freedom."[198] This resistance to power is resistance to the Other's look and involves an individual's struggle to unfold his own image in the world. Whereas for Sartre, the very structure of consciousness implies the possibility of a radical freedom from objectification, for Foucault we cannot escape it. The best we can do is to release ourselves from the will to truth and, instead, creatively search for new forms of subjectivity by living in the aesthetic mode through our creativity. For Foucault, individual freedom is limited by the field of power relations, which are intentional and nonsubjective. The subject that he tries to destroy is the traditional, masterful self who controls the "objective" world around him. This is the subject whose consciousness remains on the interior, separate and apart from the body, and who encounters an outside world. But, for Foucault, this is the subject that is the result of biopower, the force that creates subjects who define themselves in terms of the positive sciences. By collapsing the oppositions of internal and external, and subject and object, Foucault argues against a sovereign subject who is radically free and whose consciousness is independent from the world.

In the light of Foucault's notions about power, we must reinterpret the Sartrean-Husserlian notion of intentionality in terms of the discussion above. For Foucault, there is no such thing as radical freedom, and individuals are not the center of their own movement within culture. In contrast, the autonomous self is decentered by relations of power that pervade it. This means that we are not radically separate and independent from the external world or from other individuals, and therefore, all intentionality is historically, culturally, and socially conditioned. Furthermore, because Foucault's analysis of power shows that there cannot be such a thing as a masterful subject, it must also be the case that there is no mastery of the "objective" as a totality. This implies that an individual can never objectively interpret the world because no one can ever step outside the network of power. Each individual is always a part of that which is to be interpreted, and each interpretation can be re-interpreted by Others, *ad infinitum*, in order to come to a final and objective interpretation. But this is impossible, for there is no place to stop this process of re-interpretation. Thus, any science or body of knowledge that purports to explain a facet of human nature is always incomplete. We are always more than the sum of what science, culture, religion, and society claim that we are, a point to which Levinas is deeply committed.

This does not render Sartre's notion of the pre-reflective self without force, for there are serious questions about who or what is doing the resisting in Foucault's conceptualization. After Foucault, we may not end up with a self that transcends an external world, yet he suggests we can "get free of ourselves" and believes that we can analyze our subjectivities in terms of the relations of power that bind us. This leaves us with more than the objectifications of the relational theorists

and more than the kind of objectification Lacan espouses.
Perhaps these new kinds of subjectivities are best left for
individuals as a kind of mystery. Let us say a bit about Lacan
now, from a Foucauldian perspective.

The relation between Lacan and Foucault is a complex one
that has been written about by a number of theorists.[199] Let us
first keep in mind that Lacan was a structuralist and was very
opposed to the phenomenological notion of intentionality,
even as modified by Foucault's pronouncements about
power. In contrast, Lacan tries to reduce psychic phenomena
to unconscious linguistic structures by removing human
intentionality and meaning. By reducing the conscious subject
to an effect of the signifier, Lacan precludes meaningful
transformation. For Lacan, we are just playthings of the
linguistic unconscious, which prevents us from using
language as *praxis*. This is consonant with his position that
there is no transcendent subject, in the Sartrean sense, who
could possibly cause such change. Presumably, this also
means that there is no Foucauldean subject who could cause
changes either.

Lacan's position is that language speaks us. As such, we are
inert objects that are pure Otherness and there is no chance
for transcendence. As an inert repository of past *praxes*,
language is always an invitation to *hexis*. Using language
inserts us into a cultural order and, as a result, Otherness
inscribes itself into our own intentional projects. Foucault's
position (and Sartre's) is that we can use language creatively
and intentionally, subject to contextual factors that emerge
from relations of power and knowledge. It is the creative
aspect of language that Lacan avoids. Thus, Lacanian
alienation is unsurpassable because it is this Otherness that
has created me as a speaking subject. For Lacan, we always
enter into a world that is filled with symbols and we can never

return to a place that is outside the cultural-linguistic order. For Lacan, the most one can do is to understand that one is a signified rather than a signifer, an object pretending to be a subject. Thus, for Lacan, the signifier represents only a subject, but not a referent nor a signifier. He thereby defines the subject in terms of representation, as a discourse of the Other, in which each subject has himself represented by a signifier to another signifier. Further, each subject, though speaking himself amongst signifying chains, concomitantly absents himself from them, in the mode of being other than his identifying signifiers.

For Foucault, in the modern era, these signifying chains largely revolve around discourses of sexuality in which subjects recognize the truth of themselves as subjects of desire. Subjects of desire are located, for him, in terms of relationships to desire in which we form ourselves by distancing ourselves from that desire. As Charles Scott says, "desiring, then, is at a distance from the subject of desire, and this distance is structured by relations of power."[200] Each of us exercises these relations of power in our relation to desire, which gives each of us a certain relation to the truth of who we are. Thus, desire, truth, and power are fragmented into various discourses in the human and social sciences. As Scott rightly notices, Foucault's genealogy exposes a kind of surface freedom that accompanies the fragmentations that run through our constituted selves.[201] Within this line of reasoning, we cannot say what selves are, but we can talk about the kind of self that has formed within a certain lineage of subjection. That is, we stay outside of the metaphysical question about what we are and, instead, focus our inquiry on the line of subjections that define the range of selves we can become. We are fragmented across discourses and we are both subjected to, and resist, the confining forces of the relations of power to which we belong and identify.

Freedom is, for Foucault, a freedom of fragmentation that comes from not being essentially anyone, a "freedom that accompanies the differences that constitute a lineage of loose alliances, relations of resistance and mastery and confederations of fluid interests, . . ."[202] One position to take is that Foucault's idea of freedom does involve subjects at some level of intentionality, a position we write about in a previous work. Even though this resisting element may not rise to the level of a Sartrean transcending self, it is arguable that subjects have some locus of power to effect transformation in their subjectivities.[203] Even so, it is also arguable, and perhaps with more force, that freedom does not belong to subjects and that, instead, it means the kind of fragmentation and malleability that occurs within structure. This allows the Dionysian element to always have a play, in which selves are always in question and always problematized, and in which we come to ourselves by fleeing. As I argued in *Group Authenticity*, this play in structure allows selves to creatively re-arrange the elements that comprise their subjectivities. With regard to Lacanian structuralism, this is where Foucault parts company, for in Foucault's system, subjects have some power to influence the cluster of power relations that make up their personal identities. It is not so clear for Lacan that we can do anything beyond accepting our fate in strategies of "full speech."

Concluding Remarks about the "I" of Humanism

People typically think of Sartre as a philosopher of alienation. Yet, it can be shown that Sartre, more or less, overcomes this charge. No one disputes that his early philosophy is a fierce argument that social life is nothing more than a conflict of gazes in which each person attempts to master a present situation. His famous quotes such as "hell is other people" or that "the other is a gun pointed at me" demonstrate his absolute commitment to dualist ontology and an alienating dynamic. In order for there to be a masterful subject there must also be an objective world, including other people, which can be mastered. He has an unquestioning belief in a foundational subject-object dichotomy. He assumes that a human can objectify anything that one is but can always make oneself other than what is objectified. Consciousness itself is just this fundamental alienation that manifests itself individually. Moreover, in his analysis of the "Look," Sartre shows how this subject-object dichotomy plays out in the social realm. Narcissistic love, Sartre argues, is an attempt to overcome our fundamental alienation, but this pursuit fails because is it impossible to overcome the subject-object duality in our being.

Nevertheless, even Sartre seems to overcome much of the alienation his Cartesian-styled theories imply. For example, with regard to individual alienation, the very idea of the pre-reflective self, when brought to the forefront of human experience through pure reflection, seems to transcend the antagonism and alienation wrought by the Other's gaze. Giving up the God-project in which we try to become the foundation of our own freedom through narcissistic attachments to Others, and replacing this by the project of radical freedom, promotes an authentic self relationship, as well as authentic political community. Further, at the social level, though Sartre never explicitly gave up his dualistic ontology, he makes great strides toward the overcoming of alienation with his cogent theories about the transformations of group consciousness in the *Critique*. Hazel Barnes does a fine job of explaining that positive reciprocity, through the Look-as-Exchange, is possible even given Sartre's early ontology. Additionally, in a late interview, even Sartre recognizes the possibility of positive reciprocity in love, through the appeal of the Other, saying that "I wrote Saint

Genet to try to present a love that goes beyond the sadism in which Genet is steeped and the masochism that he suffered."[204] Finally, in *Being and Nothingness*, Sartre suggests that empathy ought to be the primary tool in existential psychoanalysis; in *Search for a Method* and in the *Critique of Dialectical Reason*, the proper method is comprehension, which implies an ability to understand the Other.[205] Thus, even though he fiercely clung to his dualistic ontology, we can see Sartre stretching it to the limits as he attempts to overcome the inevitable alienation his theories imply, moving closer and closer to a Levinasian social position.

With regard to Lacan's alienating structuralism, he believes the best we can do is to accept that we are determined by the linguistic unconscious. For Lacan we literally take the Other for ourselves and we can never overcome this fundamental alienation. For him, both the self and the Other are objects, never subjects, which prevents any kind of positive social transformation. In fact, the Lacanian ego is Otherness absolutely and completely, and this means that there is neither transcendent consciousness nor Foucauldean intentionality that can reflectively alter or develop the ego. By placing the source of Otherness inside the linguistic unconsciousness, Lacan considers normal the kind of alienation Sartre describes in his concept of hexis. For Lacan, the best one can do is to understand that we are the playthings of the linguistic unconscious and that one is only an object pretending to be a subject. It is the Cartesian subject that is also the subject of the humanist tradition that Lacan calls into question. He believes that the philosophical *cogito* is an essentialist illusion and argues that the centre of the human being is no longer to be found in subjective experience. Recall that Lacan advocates the reconstruction of the signifying chain by which a person has been constructed. The goal is full speech that occurs without the disrupting intervention of ego identifications. It

differs from empty speech because it realizes that subjectivity
is an illusion. In order to understand oneself as a product
of the discourse of the Other, one must understand that
one is integrated into its circuit, lost in it like objects, where
our future is already determined by the chain of signifiers
into which we are inserted. The best we can do within this
condition is to understand our destiny within discourse.

The problem for Lacan is that no genuine praxis is possible
in a system where the conscious subject is merely an effect
of unconscious signifiers and there is no possibility for
resistance. His tenacious grip on the Cartesian dictum, even
though reversed, implies an absolute attachment to the will
to truth — and to objectification, and perhaps this is where
Levinas would respond first. By attacking subjectivity as
an illusion, Lacan confirms it as one part of the dialectical
tension in any kind of dualistic distinction between mind
and body. Recall that Descartes's starting point implies an
isolated, thinking individual in which there is a dualism
between the thinking subject and the objective, material
world, which includes the human body. The existentialist
tradition quarreled with this dualism by arguing that
philosophy must begin with the concrete individual who
is fully engaged in the world and thoroughly involved in
relationships with others. A concrete philosophy begins not
with the certainty of thinking but with the experience of
immediate existence. This is one major place where Levinas
parts company with Lacan. Furthermore, instead of turning
toward the aesthetic realm like Foucault does, Levinas turns
to the phenomenology of the encounter with the unknowable
Other. By letting go of the will to (scientific) truth, in terms
of dualist ontology, Levinas avoids the kind of objectification
into which Lacan lands.

Levinas rejects the consequences of mind-body dualism — a

humanism of the Same—in favor of a philosophy that
prioritizes the Other as an unknowable face. He believes
that only through incarnation do we recognize ourselves to
be subjects in the world and not through abstract minds who
process ideas. For him, we come to know the world through
the body, and the way we relate to our body is the way we
relate to the world. Yet, as incarnate beings, we do not adopt
the materialist position that we are merely the chemical
and material components of our bodies. Idealism is wrong
because humans are not just minds accidentally residing in
bodies. Materialism is wrong because humans are not bodies
accidentally housing minds. In contrast, to be incarnate
means that the only way we can think about the world is
through a trans-rational interdependence with the Other. This
necessarily involves our co-incarnate encounters with Others
in dimensions that transcend Cartesian rationalism.

Recall Derrida's position that the Other is necessarily
involved in our very thinking, and that each of us is
responsible for all Others from the ground up. Moreover,
he shows us how the ontological tradition has privileged
a metaphysics of presence over absence—a xenophobia—
that degrades anything that is Other. Thus, in order for
something to be known, a phenomenon must submit itself to
the categories of the knowing subject. In turn, what is Other
must lose its alterity in being known. This xenophobia stems
from Cartesian dualism and, as the early Sartre convincingly
shows us, results in a conflict of gazes in which each attempts
to master the Other.

Sartre shows us most clearly the consequences of the "I" of
humanism, in which ego structures carve out a world solely
in terms of their own subjectivity. Here, there is no room for
an Other that presences itself. Instead, it remains suppressed,
as Derrida shows. Yet, as I have shown, there is something

in Sartre's more mature position that suggests the seeds of destruction of the Cartesian self. This is the plasticity in consciousness that can lead us toward a non-conflictual gaze that is reciprocal, positive, and constructive. Furthermore, his work in *Saint Genet* leads the way toward a theoretical framework that overcomes the sado-masochistic dynamics he so carefully accounts for in *Being and Nothingness*. Finally, in his most late ideas, he realizes the importance of the appeal of the Other, in relation to (virtue of) empathy, which strikes very close—at least in spirit—to Levinas. It is somewhat ironic to suggest this, but it is the very same Sartre who guards so carefully the Cartesian Weltanschauung who is also the bridge to the Levinasian position. Foucault's own criticism of Sartre only confirms that deeper phenomenological inquiry, the kind that Levinas engages in, produces a descriptive account of the contemporary self that is not at all isolated and humanistically irresponsible.

In traditional humanism, each of us lives in terms of his own mental categories, approaches Others in terms of his own subjective interpretation of meaning, and analyzes Others relative to what he the subject already knows. Levinas finds that this sort of humanism that had been constructed in modernity prioritizes the subject over the object, and has resulted in horrendous behavioral errors. He, therefore, finds us guilty of an anthropological mistake and attempts to shift the source of meaning from the subject to the object. My goal has been to present an account of this anthropological mistake so that the reader fully understands what has been, and is, at stake in the challenge Levinas set out for himself. My hope is that I have adequately prepared the reader for future exploration and analysis of a new anthropology and a modified "I" of humanism that engenders new prospects for social relations.

Notes

1. For a nice introduction to the writings and thoughts of these thinkers and others, the reader might consult a history of philosophy, for example, *The Routledge History of Philosophy* (New York: Routledge, 2003). Also, see Stumpf, *Philosophy: History & Problems* (New York: McGraw-Hill, 1994).

2. This is sometimes called the "Great Experiment."

3. See my *Genuine Reciprocity and Group Authenticity* (Boston: University Press, 1999), for a detailed discussion of the ideas of Michel Foucault on these issues.

4. See Routledge, *History*, Vol. 4 ; also see Descartes, *Meditations on First Philosophy*, trans. Laurence Lafleur (Indianapolis: Bobbs-Merrill, 1978) for a clear statement of Descartes's basic position.

5. Charles Taylor, *Sources of the Self* (Cambridge: Harvard, 2000), 144.

6. See John Locke, *Essay Concerning Human Understanding*, Ed. Alexander Campbell Fraser (New York: Barnes and Noble, 2004).

7. Newton, *Principia*, trans. Cohen and Whitman (Berkeley: University of California, 1999).

8. Montaigne, *The Complete Works*, trans. Donald Frame (Stanford: Stanford University Press, 1957); also, compare Nietzsche's position which seems quite similar to Montaigne's thoughts on this issue.

9. Rousseau, *The Social Contract* (New York: Washington Square Press, 1964); also see, *Confessions*,

10. Augustine, *Basic Writings*, ed. Whitney Oates (New York: Random House, 1948).

11. Kant, *Groundwork of the Metaphysics of Morals*, trans. H.J. Paton (New York: Harper & Row, 1964).

12. See Descartes's notion of "clear and distinct" ideas in his *Meditations*.

13. I'll use caps for the thematized use of the term and lower case for regular usage. Also see, Samuel Moyn, *Origins of the Other* (Ithaca and London: Cornell University Press, 2005), whose historical exegesis I follow in these sections, regarding Levinas and intersubjectivity.

14. Edmund Husserl, *Cartesian Meditations*, trans, Dorion Cairns (The Hague: Martinus Nijhoff, 1973).

15. Pierre Keller, *Kant and the Demands of Self-Consciousness* (Cambridge: Cambridge University Press, 2001), 243, note 5.

16. Henri Bergson *An Introduction to Metaphysics*, trans. T.E. Hulme (Indianapolis: Bobbs-Merrill, 1978).

17. See Wilhelm Dilthey, *Selected Works, Vol. 1, Introduction to the Human Sciences*, eds. Rudolf Makkreel and Frithjof Rodi (Princeton: Princeton University Press, 1989) for an excellent, edited selection of Dilthey's work showing the limits of natural science interpretations of human life.

18. Emmanuel Levinas, *The Theory of Intuition in Husserl's Phenomenology*, trans. A. Orianne (Evanston: Northwestern University Press, 1973).

19. Jean-Paul Sartre, *The Transcendence of the Ego* (New York: Farrar, Straus and Giroux, 1957).

20. Karl Lowith, *Habilitationsschrift, The Individual in the Role of Fellow Man* (First published in German, 1928, as *San Individuum in der Rolle des Mitmenschen: Ein Beitrag zur anthropologischen Grundlegung der ethischen Probleme*, Munich: Drei Masken Verlag).

21. This is Heidegger's name for the self.

22. Hannah Arendt, *Love and Saint Augustine*, ed. Joanna Scott and Judith Stark (Chicago: University of Chicago Press, 1996). Also, see her *The Origins of Totalitarianism* (New York: Harcourt, Brace, 1958) and *On Revolution*, rev. ed. (New York: Viking Press, 1965).

23. See Michel Foucault's *Discipline and Punish*, trans. Alan Sheridan (New York: Vintage, 1979) for a trenchant historical analysis of the relations of power that are imprinted upon the body. I have written about this in my *Genuine Reciprocity and Group Authenticity*.

24. Levinas, "De l'evasion," *Recherches philosophiques* 5 (1935-36): 381.

25. *Ibid.*, 383.

26. *Ibid.*, 385.

27. *Ibid.*, 386, 375.

28. This is an interesting contrast that requires extensive exploration.

29. Levinas, "De l'evasion," 391.

30. Levinas, *Recherches philosophiques* 6, 1936-37: 388-90).1

31. Levinas, *La presence totale*, Paris: Ferdinand Aubier, 1934, reviewed in *Recherches philosophiques*, 4, 1934035: 392-95, at 392-93).

32. Franz Rosenzweig, *The Star of Redemption* (Madison: University of Wisconsin Press, 2005).

33. See Wahl's works on Descartes, Kierkegaard, Heidegger, Bergson, and Hegel.

34. Jean Wahl, *Etudes kierkegaardiennes*, chap. 7, *Par l'angoisse vers la hauteur,"* 251.

35. See *Bulletin de la Societe francaise de philosophie* 37, no. 5, October-December 1937: 161-63, 166-211. Also see Wahl's book form of the debate, entitled *Existence humaine et transcendence*, Neuchatel: Editions de la Baconniere, 1944.

36. Published in English as *A Short History of Existentialism*, trans. Forrest Williams and Stanley Maron (New York: Philosophical Library, 1949).

37. Levinas, *De l'existence a l'existant*, Paris, 1947. Published in English as *From Existence to Existents*, trans. A. Lingus (The Hague: Martinus Nijhoff, 1978).

38. *Ibid.*, 94, 96.

39. Levinas, *De l'existence*, 99.

40. Jean-Paul Sartre, Anti-Semite and Jew, trans. George Becker (New York: Schocken, 1976).

41. See Sartre, *The Critique of Dialectical Reason* (London: NLB, 1976) which I treat at length in my *Genuine Reciprocity*.

42. Levinas, *Time and the Other*, trans. R. Cohen (Pittsburgh: Duquesne University Press, 1987).

43. Levinas, "Le Temps et l'autre," in Jean Wahl, *Le Choix, le monde, l'existence, Cahiers du College philosophique 1*, (Grenoble: B. Arthaud, 1947), 131.

44. *Ibid.*, 144.

45. Levinas, *Time and the Other*.

46. Kevin Boileau and David A. Boileau, *The Algebra of History* (New Orleans: Loyola University Press, 2004).

47. Levinas, *Totalite et infini* (The Hague: Martinus Nijhoff, 1961); trans. as *Totality and Infinity*, trans. Alphonso Lingus (Pittsburgh: Duquesne University Press, 1998). Regarding references to *TI*, I put the French version first and the English second.

48. See Marcel on this same point in Marcel, *The Existential Background of Human Dignity*, Cambridge: Harvard University Press, 1963, esp. 130.).

49. See Sartre's work on groups in *CDR*, which I carefully analyze in *Group Authenticity*.

50. Levinas, *Totality and Infinity*, 25-26/55.

51. *Ibid.*, 143/168.

52. *Ibid.*, 100/127.

53. *Ibid.*, 100-101/128.

54. *Ibid.*, 83/111.

55. *Ibid.*, 85-86/113-114.

56. *Ibid.*, 84/112.

57. *Ibid.*, 148/173.

58. Martin Heidegger, *Sein und Zeit*, (1927; Tubingen: Max Niemyer, 1953); *Being and Time*, trans. Macquarrie & Robinson (New York: Harper & Row, 1962). Hereinafter, *BT*.

59. Levinas, *Totality and Infinity*, 82/110.

60. *Ibid.*, 106/133.

61. *Ibid.*, 118/145.

62. *Ibid.*, 123/150.

63. *Ibid.*, 144/170.

64. *Ibid.*, xv/26 *et seq.*

65. *Ibid.*, 3/33-34; also see Lacan on this point, as well as Fryer, *The Intervention of the Other* (New York: Other Press, 2004), for an excellent study comparing Lacan with Levinas on the nature of the self.

66. *Ibid.*, 147/172.

67. *Ibid.*, 23, xi/52,23).

68. *Ibid.*, 239-40/262.

69. *Ibid.*, 239-240/262.

70. *Ibid.*, 174/200.

71. *Ibid.*, 273-74/297-98.

72. *Ibid.*, 21/50-51.

73. *Ibid.*, 38/66

74. *Ibid.*, 168/194.

75. *Ibid.*, 172/198.

76. *Ibid.*, 39/67.

77. *Ibid.*, 39/68.

78. *Loc. Cit.*

79. *Ibid.*, 15-16/45.

80. *Ibid.*, xiii/25.

81. *Ibid.*, 76/102-3.

82. *Ibid.*, xii/24.

83. Royle, "What is Deconstruction?" in *Deconstructions: A User's Guide*, Ed. Nicholas Royle et al. (New York: Palgrave, 2000), 1-13.

84. Derrida, "Deconstruction and the Other," Interview with Richard Kearney, in Kearney, *Dialogues with Contemporary Continental Thinkers*, Manchester: Manchester University Press, 1984, 105-26).

85. Derrida, *Speech and Phenomena*, trans. David Allison (Evanston: Northwestern University Press, 1973), 6.

86. *Ibid.*, 26. Also see, Derrida, *Of Grammatology*, trans. Gayatri Chakravorty Spivak (Baltimore: Johns Hopkins University Press, 1976), 49.

87. *Ibid.*, 41.

88. *Ibid.*, 37.

89. Derrida, *Limited Inc*, G. Graff (Ed.), trans. Samuel Weber (Evanston, Illinois: Northwestern University Press, 1988) 279.

90. Derrida, *A Taste for the Secret*, Giocomo Donis and David Webb (Eds.), trans. Giocomo Donis (Cambridge: Polity, 2001).

91. Derrida, *Speech and Phenomena*, 64.

92. *Ibid.*, 65.

93. Derrida, *Of Grammatology* (1974, 1976, 1997 [corrected version].

94. *Ibid.*, 3.

95. *Ibid.*, 11.

96. *Ibid.*, 110-11.

97. *Ibid.*, 110.

98. *Ibid.*, 112.

99. *Ibid.*, 144.

100. Derrida, *Speech and Phenomena*, 129-160.

101. Derrida, *Of Grammatology*, 60.

102. Derrida, *Speech and Phenomena*, 130.

103. *Ibid.*, 129.

104. Derrida, *Of Grammatology*, 314.

105. Derrida, *Speech and Phenomena*. 145-6. Derrida, *Of Grammatology*, 140.

106. Derrida, *The Gift of Death* trans. David Wills (Chicago: University of Chicago Press, 1995), 100-01, 109.

107. Derrida, *Taste*, Giocomo Donis and David Webb, (Eds.), trans. Giocomo Donis (Cambridge: Polity, 2001), 57.

108. For comparison, see Marcel's notion of "mystery," which I write about extensively in *The Algebra of History*.

109. Derrida, *On Cosmopolitanism and Forgiveness*, trans. Mark Dooley (London: Routledge, 2001), 17.

110. *Ibid.*, 16-17.

111. Derrida, *Speech and Phenomena*, 152.

112. Derrida, *Of Grammatology*, 47, 70.

113. *Ibid.*, 139-40.

114. Derrida, *Adieu to Emmanuel Levinas*, trans. Pascale-Anne Brault and Michael Naas (Standford: Stanford University Press, 1999), 32.

115. *Ibid.*, 35.

116. Derrida, "Force of Law: The Mystical Foundation of Authority," *Cardozo Law Review*, reprinted in *Deconstruction and the Possibility of Justice*, Drucilla Cornell, Michael Rosenfeld, and David Gray Carlson (Eds.), New York: Routledge, 1992.

117. Derrida, "Force of Law," 23.

118. *Ibid.*, 24.

119. *Loc. Cit.*

120. *Ibid.*, 26.

121. *Gen.* 22.

122. Derrida, *The Gift of Death*, 24.

123. *Ibid*, 25-6.

124. *Ibid.* 63.

125. *Ibid.*, 26.

126. See my *Genuine Reciprocity*, especially with regard to Foucault's power analytics and the link to governmentality.

127. Derrida, "The 'World' of the Enlightenment to Come (Exception, Calculation, Sovereignty)," trans. Pascale-Anne Brault and Michael Naas (*Research in Phenomenology* 33, 2003), 39.

128. Jacques Lacan, *Ecrits: A Selection* (New York: Norton & Company, 1977); *The Four Fundamental Concepts of Psycho-Analysis* (New York: Norton & Company, 1981).

129. Lacan, *The Four Fundamental Concepts*, 227, 257, 279; also see *Ecrits*, Ch. 1.

130. Our very concept of authenticity emerges from the symbolic realm, but Lacan argues that it is illusory.

131. Lacan, *Ecrits*, "The Signification of the Phallus," Ch. 8.

132. *Ibid.*, 154.

133. *Ibid.*, 70.

134. *Ibid.*, 165.

135. Lacan, *The Seminar of Jacques Lacan, Book III, The Psychoses*, 1955-6, Jacques-Alain Miller (Ed.), trans. Russell Grigg (New York: Norton, 1997).

136. Lacan, *Ecrits*, "The Freudian Thing," Chapter 4, 114.

137. Lacan, *Seminar, Book III*, 145.

138. Lacan, *Ecrits*, "The Subversion of the Subject," Chapter 9.

139. Lacan, *Seminar, Book I, Freud's Papers on Technique, 1953-1954*, Jacques-Alain Miller (Ed.), trans. Russel Grigg (New York: Norton, 1991), 68.

140. G Chaitlin, *Rhetoric and Culture in Lacan* (Cambridge: Cambridge University Press, 1996).

141. Lacan, *Ecrits*, "Agency of the Letter in the Unconscious," Chapter 5, 171.

142. Lacan, *Seminar, Book III*, 39.

143. Lacan, *Seminar, Book II, The Ego in Freud's Theory and in the Technique of Psychoanalysis, 1954-1955*, Jacques-Alain Miller (Ed.), trans. Sylvana Tomaselli (New York: Norton, 1991), 323.

144. Yannis Stavrakakis, *Lacan & the Political* (New York: Routledge, 1999), 18.

145. Lacan, *Seminar, Book III*, 9.

146. Lacan, *Ecrits*, 72.

147. Lacan, *Ecrits*, 72.

148. Lacan, *Ecrits*, 74.

149. Lacan, *Ecrits*, 125.

150. Lacan, *Ecrits*, 259.

151. Lacan, *Seminar, Book II*, 50. Also, see, Sartre, *Transcendence of the Ego* (New York: Farrar, Straus and Giroux, 1957), 101.

152. Sartre, *Being and Nothingness and Transcendence of the Ego*, or Kevin C. Boileau, *Genuine Reciprocity*, for a detailed examination.

153. Lacan, *The Four Fundamental Concepts*, 207.

154. Ellie Ragland-Sullivan, *Jacques Lacan and the Philosophy of Psychoanalysis* (Urbana and Chicago: University of Illinois Press, 1986), 303.

155. Sartre, *The Family Idiot, Volume 1*, trans. Carol Cosman (Chicago: University of Chicago Press, 1981).

156. Ragland-Sullivan, *Jacques Lacan and the Philosophy of Psychoanalysis*, 91.

157. Lacan, *Ecrits*, 172..

158. Lacan, *Ecrits*, 272.

159. Lacan, *Seminar, Book I*, 53.

160. Lacan, *Ecrits*, 23.

161. Lacan, *Seminar, Book II*, 254-55.

162. Lacan, *Seminar, Book I*, 50.

163. Lacan, *Seminar, Book II*, 307.

164. Joseph Smith and William Kerrigan (Eds.), (*Interpreting Lacan* (New Haven, Conn. And London: Yale University Press, 1983), 202.

165. Lacan, *Ecrits*, 166.

166. Quoted by Hazel Barnes, *Sartre and Flaubert* (Chicago: University of Chicago, 1981), 9.

167. For an examination of Sartre's ideas about structuralism, see: *The Critique of Dialectical Reason* (London: NLB, 1976).

168. Michel Foucault, *Discipline and Punish: The Birth of the Prison*, trans. Alan Sheridan (New York: Vintage, 1979).

169. Hubert Dreyfus and Paul Rabinow, *Michel Foucault: Beyond Structuralism and Hermeneutics* (Chicago: University of Chicago Press, 1983), 7.

170. M. Foucault, *The Birth of the Clinic (An Archaeology of Medical Perception)*, trans. A.M. Sheridan Smith (New York; Pantheon, 1973).

171. Foucault, *Madness and Civilization*, trans. Richard Howard (New York: Vintage, 1988).

172. Foucault, *Discipline and Punish: The Birth of the Prison*, 28.

173. Foucault, *The History of Sexuality: An Introduction, Volume I*, trans. Robert Hurley (New York: Vintage, 1980), for an advanced discussion.

174. See Kevin Boileau, *Genuine Reciprocity*, 27.

175. Michel Foucault, *History of Sexuality, Volume I*, 143. *this is in one of the references from endnote 169 on. It is probably in History of Sexuality, Volume I.

176. David Couzens Hoy, "Power, Repression, Progress: Foucault, Lukes, and the Frankfurt School," in *Foucault, A Critical Reader* (New York: B. Blackwell, 1986), 123-147.

177. Foucault, *History of Sexuality, Volume I*, 94.

178. Foucault, *History of Sexuality, Volume I*, 94.

179. Foucault, *History of Sexuality, Volume I*, 93.

180. Foucault, *History of Sexuality, Volume I*, 94.

181. Foucault, *History of Sexuality, Volume I*, 95.

182. Foucault, *History of Sexuality, Volume I*, 95.

183. Foucault, *History of Sexuality, Volume I*, 95.

184. Foucault, "The Subject and Power," in *Michel Foucault: Beyond Structuralism and Hermeneutics*, 220.

185. Foucault, "The Subject and Power," 221.

186. Foucault, "The Subject and Power," 221.

187. See K. Boileau, Chapter 3, *Genuine Reciprocity*, for discussion about the Christian influence on this pastoral, individualizing power.

188. Foucault, "The Subject and Power," 21.

189. Foucault, "Sexuality and Solitude," in David Rieff (Ed.) *Humanities in Review I* (New York: Cambridge University Press, 1982), 10.

190. See, Thomas Kuhn, *The Structure of Scientific Revolutions* (Chicago: The University of Chicago Press, 1962).

191. Foucault, "The Ethic of Care for the Self as a Practice of Freedom," in James Bernauer and David Rasmussen (Eds.), *The Final Foucault* (Cambridge: MIT Press, 1988), 1.

192. Foucault, *"L'Impossible Prison*, Michelle Perrot, Ed. (Paris: Editions du Seuil, 1980), 47.

193. *Diagnostic and Statistical Manual of Mental Disorders*, 4th (Washington, D.C., American Psychiatric Association, 1994).

194. Foucault, "The Subject and Power," 212.

195. Foucault, "The Subject and Power," 208.

196. The collapse of these categories is part of the postmodern movement. Nietzsche masterfully portrays this view in *Thus Spoke Zarathustra* (Baltimore: Penguin, 1975). It is difficult to view these radical separations in other ways, i.e., where we could view two subjectivities belonging to two different individuals as not so radically separate. Our continued need to see in terms of this distinctive dualism stems from the radical individualist element that accompanied the Enlightenment project. Foucault and Nietzsche both demand that we try to see how historically embedded and contingent these radical oppositions are.

197. Foucault, "The Subject and Power," 221-222.

198. With regard to the relation between Foucault and Lacan, see: John Forrester, *The Seductions of Psychoanalysis* (New York: Cambridge University Press, 1999); also, see, John Rajchman, *Truth and Eros: Foucault, Lacan, and the Question of Ethics* (New York: Routledge, 1991).

199. Charles Scott, "The Pleasure of Therapy," in Sonu Shamdasani and Michael Mumchow, (Eds.), *Speculations After Freud: Psychoanalysis, Philosophy and Culture* (New York: Routledge, 1994), 211.

200. Charles Scott, "The Pleasure of Therapy," 212.

201. Charles Scott, "The Pleasure of Therapy," 212.

202. K. Boileau, *Genuine Reciprocity*. Since the publication of that work, I have retreated from that position and am willing to entertain the notion that freedom may come indirectly from malleability in structure. To some extent this obviates the need for a voluntarist position.

203. Sartre, "An Interview with Jean-Paul Sartre," in Paul Arthur Schilpp, (Ed.) *The Philosophy of Jean-Paul Sartre, The Library of Living Philosophers*, Vol. 16 (La Salle, Illinois: Open Court, 1981), 13. Also, see, Sartre, *Saint Genet*, trans. Bernard Frechtmann (New York: George Braziller, 1963), 327-328. I engage in a critical study of Sartre's notion of "circuit of selfness," along with the discussion of sado-masochistic interpersonal dynamics in the preceding 2nd Essay in this volume, entitled *Existential Psychoanalysis*. Please read for a book-length discussion of this issue, especially in relation to Sartre's notion of pure reflection.

204. See earlier references to *BN* and to *CDR*. Also, see, Sartre, *Search for a Method*, trans. Hazel Barnes (New York: Vintage, 1968).

Index

Abraham 287, 319, 320

abstract ethics 215, 227, 232

abstraction 120, 121, 123, 125, 129, 287, 303

Abstract morality 201

abstract thought 120, 129

accessory reflection 181, 184, 202

acorn theory 179

aesthetic 114, 122, 136, 187, 192, 194, 195, 204, 269, 350, 358

agent 37, 64, 65, 108, 166, 167, 179, 180, 230, 345

alienate 207, 215, 217, 221

alienated 40, 119, 121, 188, 198, 205, 228-231, 265, 269, 309

alienated moralities 228, 229, 231

alienating 84, 93, 134, 135, 165, 226, 332, 355, 356

alienation 84, 86, 87, 89, 90, 116, 120, 133-135, 154, 187, 212, 217, 219-222, 226, 297, 332, 334, 335, 337, 338, 353, 355, 356

Allport, Gordon 6, 42

alterity 273, 290, 296, 308-311, 313-317, 321, 359

ambiguity 155, 216, 221, 225

ambiguous 17, 216, 235

Anderson, Thomas 196, 248, 249

anguish 151, 153, 162, 198, 216, 223, 317

annihilating 176, 199

anthropological 2, 39, 187, 193, 196, 246, 251, 253, 255, 256, 293, 360

anthropology 2, 8, 25, 37, 39, 47, 85, 118, 186, 256, 257, 269, 293, 299, 307, 316, 322, 333, 341, 360

anti-Cartesian 127, 190

anxiety 8, 43, 59, 60, 71, 96, 130, 169, 184, 234, 235, 258, 261, 262, 286, 288, 296, 320

Apollinian 138

a posteriori 67, 181

appetitive 255, 256, 273, 282, 300

a priori 51, 60, 65, 149, 179, 181, 268

Arendt 279-283, 363

Aristotelian 42, 63, 65, 106, 343

306, 309, 335, 355, 356, 358

operationalism 12

oppression 197, 212, 213

optical 302

original 28, 81, 122, 132, 149-153, 156, 166, 167, 171, 175, 183, 188, 195, 196, 204, 220, 227, 291, 311, 312, 329

other 3, 4, 6, 9, 12, 14, 16, 21, 29, 30, 32-34, 38-40, 48, 49, 52, 53, 55, 57, 62, 63, 65, 67, 73, 75, 77-81, 83, 84, 86-89, 91, 93, 101, 103, 105, 108-110, 114, 116, 121-123, 126-132, 134-136, 148, 149, 152, 154, 155, 159, 160, 164, 165, 167, 170-180, 182, 184, 185, 191, 195, 197, 199, 200, 203, 207-220, 223, 226, 230-233, 235, 236, 238-241, 249, 250, 255, 256, 258, 259, 261, 262, 264, 266, 267, 269-273, 276-278, 281, 282, 286, 288-292, 294-302, 304-311, 313-321, 323-326, 328, 329, 331, 332, 334-337, 339, 340, 342, 345-347, 351, 353, 355-359, 362, 364-367, 374

otherness 87-89, 93, 116, 122, 135, 215, 309, 314, 315, 335-337, 352, 353, 356

others 16, 18, 21, 25, 48-53, 56, 58-61, 67, 68, 70, 73, 74, 86-88, 92, 93, 106, 111, 112,

114, 122, 125-127, 130-132, 134, 136, 138, 142, 148, 152, 154, 161, 168, 174, 175, 177-179, 183, 185, 192, 194, 195, 198, 199, 206-214, 216, 217, 220-222, 226, 230, 231, 235-241, 255, 260-262, 264, 267, 268, 270-272, 275, 277-281, 283, 288-290, 292, 295, 305, 309, 310, 312-314, 316, 317, 323, 334-336, 340, 343, 348, 349, 351, 355, 357-359, 361

paganism 290, 291

paradigm 2, 3, 6, 8, 10, 13, 15-18, 20, 25, 27, 29, 31, 39, 40, 58, 73, 86, 103, 104, 132, 259, 319, 334

passivity 93, 175, 190, 196, 296, 341

pastoral 109, 141, 346, 373

pastoral power 109, 346

person 11, 19, 23, 25, 40, 51, 57, 58, 63, 67, 75, 86, 91, 92, 107, 110, 112, 120, 121, 127-130, 133, 135, 154, 156, 160-162, 170, 191, 192, 194, 196, 199-205, 207-209, 211, 213, 217, 220-222, 226, 230, 233, 235-237, 239, 264, 269, 292, 297, 314, 324, 334, 338, 340, 344, 348, 349, 355, 357

personal identity 50, 73, 74, 110-112, 185, 323, 347-349

transcendent 67, 87, 88, 104, 116, 135, 158, 163, 164, 174, 176, 181, 188, 189, 194, 197, 203, 217, 226, 258, 262, 279, 283, 291, 298, 304, 305, 308, 310, 335, 336, 341, 352, 356

transcendental 21, 23, 158, 188, 201, 270, 271, 275, 277, 284-286, 301, 308

transcendental ego 158, 188

transcending 63, 117, 130, 162, 219, 354

translucence 180

translucid 66, 67, 71, 159, 180, 184

transparency 157, 178, 188, 264

true self 55, 65, 182

truth 14, 20, 21, 23, 39, 40, 74, 75, 77, 78, 82, 91, 92, 97, 104, 105, 107, 110-112, 114, 116, 117, 125, 129, 136, 142, 154, 182, 225, 230, 250, 257-261, 263-265, 268, 269, 284, 324, 325, 330, 338, 339, 342, 344, 347-350, 353, 357, 358, 374

unconscious 5, 20, 26-28, 30, 35-38, 45, 46, 71-74, 76, 79, 81-83, 85, 86, 88-92, 96, 99, 103, 115, 116, 135, 136, 158, 159, 190, 236, 270, 322, 324, 327, 329-331, 333, 334, 336-339, 352, 356, 357, 370

understanding 2, 5, 6, 12, 14, 25, 31-33, 40, 56, 74, 87, 88, 90, 92, 102, 123, 125, 133, 158, 165, 179, 184, 191, 196-198, 200, 210, 231, 242, 265, 268, 281, 285, 288, 294, 301, 334, 335, 338, 340, 361

universalism 280, 283, 293

universal values 231

Unmoved Mover 163, 169, 257

unreflective 152, 155

unsubstantial 203

utilitarian 233, 301, 303, 320

valuations 152, 156

value , 5, 8, 26, 27, 62, 64, 68, 69, 71, 119, 120, 125, 133, 148, 150, 151, 157, 160, 161, 165, 168, 169, 174, 179-184, 191, 192, 195, 196, 198, 201, 202, 204-209, 211, 213, 220, 221, 223, 226, 227, 229, 231, 233-235, 240, 256, 258, 260-262, 266, 267, 272, 282, 287, 291, 303, 308

values 110, 119, 148, 151-153, 155-157, 163, 187, 195, 197, 198, 203, 205, 208, 220, 221, 224-226, 230, 231, 249, 250, 257, 283, 308, 320, 347

vertigo 175

violence 311, 312, 314

virtuous 138, 177, 265

voluntarism 164

About EPIS Publishing Co.

We established EPIS Publishing Co. in the objective of publishing new work in the following areas of inquiry:

1) existential psychoanalysis & phenomenology;

2) traditional & contemporary psychoanalysis theoretical and clinical;

3) critical philosophy as it pertains to psychoanalysis, culture, phenomenology, and philosophy of mind;

4) new literature in phenomenology and psychoanalysis;

5) any related work as it bears on these issues, including neuropsychology and psychoanalysis.

For more information go to
www.episeattle.com
or write us at
Epispublishing1@gmail.com

Notes